Listening Awry

Listening Awry

Music and Alterity in German Culture

David Schwarz

University of Minnesota Press
Minneapolis • London

English translations of five songs by Franz Schubert ("Die liebe Farbe," "Der Wegweiser," "Ihr Bild," "Die Stadt," and "Der Doppelgänger") are by George Bird and Richard Stokes and reprinted from *The Fischer-Dieskau Book of Lieder* (New York: Alfred A. Knopf, 1977).

For audio components and other features related to the text, visit http://www.upress.umn.edu/Books/S/schwarz_listening.html

Every effort has been made to obtain permission to reprint copyrighted material in this book. If any acknowledgment has not been made, we encourage copyright holders to notify the publisher.

Published by the University of Minnesota Press
111 Third Avenue South, Suite 290
Minneapolis, MN 55401-2520
http://www.upress.umn.edu

Library of Congress Cataloging-in-Publication Data

Schwarz, David, 1952–
   Listening awry : music and alterity in German culture / David Schwarz.
     p.   cm.
   Includes bibliographical references and index.
   ISBN-13: 978-0-8166-4449-0 (hc : alk. paper)
   ISBN-10: 0-8166-4449-7 (hc : alk. paper)
   ISBN-13: 978-0-8166-4450-6 (pb : alk. paper)
   ISBN-10: 0-8166-4450-0 (pb : alk. paper)
   1. Music—Psychological aspects. 2. Music—Germany—History and criticism. 3. Other (Philosophy). 4. Music—Philosophy and aesthetics. I. Title.
   ML3830.S278   2006
   781'.110943—dc22
                                                2006010714

To the Schwarz, Stolow, Ganzburg, and Sklarinsky family members lost in the Holocaust

Contents

Preface

This book began with simple auditory experiences that have been re-peated and varied in countless ways throughout my life: (1) hearing the whistle of a passing train (how odd that you can hear a sound bend as a train passes while the conductor on the train hears the "same" sound as a steady, sustained tone or interval); (2) feeling a sudden sense of fright at a loud noise (sounds penetrate the body all at once at various sur-faces of skin); (3) turning at the sound of a call not meant for you (the call meant for the other embarrasses); (4) listening to the sounds of a language you do not understand (like all objects that circulate in social spaces, words are projections that are language, culture, and context specific); (5) thinking about the discrepancy between seeing the source of a sound and hearing the sound later as it strikes the ear (we "see" a sound as a carpenter hits a distant roof with a hammer; between that moment of sight and the delayed sound striking our ear, we hear silence).

Such experiences have caused me to wonder how sounds affect the body and the psyche, how music as representation of structured sounds affects the body and psyche of the listening subject, and the cultural context in which music is produced, reproduced, and consumed. Post-Lacanian psychoanalysis can suggest how music envelops the body at our organ of parallel processing—the skin. Applications of post-Lacanian psychoanalysis to ideological interpellation can connect psychoanalysis to culture. Music theory can ground these considerations in precise de-tails of musical textuality.

This is my second book on music, psychoanalysis, and culture. My first, *Listening Subjects: Music, Psychoanalysis, Culture*, listened to classical and popular musical texts from post-Lacanian psychoanalytic, musical-theoretical, and musical-historical perspectives. It succeeded in bringing musical texts and musical contexts together within each chapter, but there was no large-scale unity to the argument, and the discursive technique relied on making and supporting too many one-to-one correspondences between a detail of music and a psychoanalytic detail, such as the sonorous envelope, the acoustic mirror, the object *a*, the Real, and so on. When *Listening Subjects* was published, I began to imagine a second book that would focus on Freud and Lacan as primary sources, avoiding one-to-one correspondences between musical and psychoanalytic details; would tell a story of historical modernism writ large in music (late eighteenth century to the present); and would theorize an aspect of German culture.

Why Germany?

I come from a German-Jewish background. My great-uncle Joseph Schwarz was a leading opera baritone and lieder singer in Germany and Austria during the first two decades of the twentieth century. He studied at the Vienna Academy of Music and died in 1928. He is buried in a well-known mausoleum in the Jüdischer Friedhof Weißensee in the former East Berlin. The cemetery embodies much of late nineteenth-, twentieth-, and even twenty-first-century Jewish culture in Berlin. Gravestones celebrate the professions many Jews held in public service in the late nineteenth and early twentieth centuries. There is a large monument to Jews who died fighting for Germany in World War I, and there are graves from the current Jewish community in reunified Berlin. My great-uncle's grave has many columns supporting a roof and window that can be opened into a tiny attic. Several Jews hid from the national socialists in that space and survived the entire war in Berlin.

One of Joseph's brothers was my grandfather, Jules Schwarz. Jules was also a baritone, and he sang with pride for the German troops during World War I. After the war, he sang for the opera in Graz, emigrating to the United States in 1926. Like many German Jews of his generation, my grandfather loved the German language and culture. The trauma of surviving World War II in the United States meant not only that he lost many family members in the Holocaust but also his connection to Jewish culture in Germany. George Schwarz (a cousin of Jules and Joseph) managed to leave national socialist Germany in the 1930s, reaching Shanghai and then Paris after the war.

Jules married Doris Sklarinksy in the United States. They had three children: Marilyn (who died in early childhood), Terry (who died in 1976), and Joseph (my father). My father has dedicated his life to painting and continues to paint in North Carolina. For many years, he has been working on a large canvas, *In Memoriam,* which depicts bodies of Jews piled high, awaiting incineration. I have been inspired over the years by my father's dedication to his art, his relentless attention to the craft of visual composition, and the project of giving form to the experience of assimilated American Jews in the postwar period. He has also taught me how to see beauty in unusual places.

I have lived, worked, and studied in Germany. I was married for many years to Marie-Luise Gättens from Hamburg. Our son has lived in Germany and attended a gymnasium. My work theorizing both magnificent and dark sides of German culture is very much a product of my family history.

Looking Awry/Listening Awry

In his book *Looking Awry,* Slavoj Žižek asserts that "what is at stake in the endeavor to 'look awry' at theoretical motifs is not just a kind of contrived attempt to 'illustrate' high theory, to make it 'easily accessible,' and thus to spare us the effort of effective thinking. The point is rather that such an exemplification, such a mise-en-scène of theoretical motifs renders visible aspects that would otherwise remain unnoticed."[1] More specifically, Žižek reads a passage from Shakespeare's *Richard II* (act 2, scene 2), in which the queen and Bushy, the king's servant, are speaking. The queen is anxious about the king's fate, and Bushy is trying to console her, saying that her tears are distorting her vision. Žižek is interested in two levels of metaphor in Bushy's words to the queen. Žižek points out that on one level Bushy suggests that the queen's worries have needlessly multiplied themselves like reflections in cut glass; once viewed directly and straight ahead, they clear. On a second level, Žižek suggests that, like an anamorphotic image, things seem confused when looked at straight ahead and only attain internal consistency when looked at awry:[2]

On the level of the first metaphor, we have commonsense reality... a
thing split into twenty reflections by our subjective view, in short, as a
substantial "reality" distorted by our subjective perspective. If we look at
a thing straight on, matter-of-factly, we see it "as it really is," while the
gaze puzzled by our desires and anxieties ("looking awry") gives us a
distorted, blurred image. On the level of the second metaphor, however,
the relation is exactly the opposite: if we look at a thing straight on, i.e.,
matter-of-factly, disinterestedly, objectively, we see nothing but a form-
less spot; the object assumes clear and distinctive features only if we look
at it "at an angle," i.e., with an "interested" view, supported, permeated,
and "distorted" by *desire*. (*Looking Awry* 11–12; emphasis in the original)

This book listens awry by understanding musical meaning partici-
pating both at the level of purely objective, internal properties of a work
and in conditions in social space that made it possible for such principles of cohesion to come into being in the first place. This book listens
awry by cutting against the grain of a fixed relationship between text
and context (subordinating one to the other). The book listens awry by
bringing out contrasts of genre from one chapter to another; it shifts
from more public issues in one chapter to more private issues in the
next; it emphasizes an archival, historical approach in one chapter and
an aesthetic one in the next; it has few musical examples in one chapter
and many in the next; it addresses high art in one chapter and popular
music in the next. Such an oscillating approach simply "happened" over
the years of this book's writing. In writing these prefatory remarks, it
seemed to me that these points of contrast created discursive friction
enabling a reader to both grasp each chapter's argument and the evidence
upon which that argument is based against the relief, as it were, of the
strategies of other chapters.

Many ideas appear again and again throughout the book: the other/
Other binary, trauma, the Jew, and the look/gaze binary, to name a few.
The other (with a lowercase *o*) denotes an Imaginary projection of the
self onto a person who is at once part of the self and a part of the social
space against which the self must be protected; the Other (with an uppercase O) denotes a Symbolic embodiment of irreducible alterity inherent
to Law, Language, and the structure of social space itself. In the history
of the conductor, the idea of the masterwork and the need for perfection of musical performance opens a space of the Other at the heart of
the musical text and musical performance. Modernist perfection implies
that an agency larger than any individual is looking for perfection. The

dimension of the sublime in Schubert suggests the embodiment of a contact with the inscrutable Other; in the writings of Kant, the sublime is often connected to God and to the immensity of nature. The discourse of psychoanalysis, as well, circulates around how the psyche organizes itself in relation to the demands of the Other. In German war songs, the other embodies that which must be purged from German social space. In *Parsifal*, the other is embodied in Kundry, whose seductions have stained the community of the Knights of the Grail. The call of Titurel is the call of the Other to purge social space.

Trauma runs throughout the book as well; it is inherent in discussions of the sublime in the late eighteenth and early nineteenth centuries. Moving from the beautiful (that formal design of an object that can and must be communicated in social space) to the sublime (that block in the subject evoked by an inability to process the impact of immense forces in nature or infinite numbers) always suggests confronting a breach. Traumatic breach underwrites much of the discourse of the hysteric that turns into the discourse of psychoanalysis in the late nineteenth century. There is the trauma of national socialism and its aftereffects. Trauma is at the core of *Parsifal*. Amfortas's wound embodies the stain at the heart of the community of the Knights of the Grail. The wound is extraordinarily embodied in Syberberg's film as a piece of flesh external to Amfortas's body that changes shape each time it appears.

Judaism also appears throughout this book. One of the most important professional conductors in Germany was Felix Mendelssohn, grandson of Moses Mendelssohn, a significant German-Jewish scholar in German history. The Jew appears in the discourse of the hysteric as particularly vulnerable to symptoms. The Jew appears in German war songs, from proud citizen of Germany in World War I, singing songs in the trenches with non-Jews, to the other that must be purged in the war songs of World War II. The Jew appears in the discourse of nineteenth-century anti-Semitism in which the writings of Richard Wagner played an important role. In his infamous "Das Judentum in der Musik," Wagner singles out Mendelssohn as an example of a composer condemned to surface impressions because his Judaism kept him from sending roots into the soil of Germany.

The book also discusses the look/gaze binary. Eye contact produces a look; looks seeing other looks (or imagining them) produces the gaze, according to Lacan. The conductor is that oddly mute musical virtuoso who in modern orchestral performances communicates always just ahead of the beat what an orchestra is supposed to do. He looks at his musicians who look at him; the audience imagines those looks, sees them at an angle or imagines them (depending on where they are sitting), (re)producing the entire spectacle to his/her inner eye as gaze. A gaze can be embodied in music when notes seem to look at us, as in Schubert's "Die Stadt" and other songs. The gaze is connected to the ideé fixe of the traumatized subject; the gaze is embodied in the music of Anton Webern's *Sechs Orchesterstücke*, op. 6, no. 4, which concludes with a single, reiterated musical "scream" (Webern describes this piece as a musical representation of coming to terms with his mother's death). In German war songs (particularly of World War II), the music is powered by a logic of sadism, according to which the subject acts in the service of the Other whom he imagines is gazing at him, goading him to action. *Parsifal* is all about the gaze—in Wagner's opera and in Syberberg's film. To pick just one example, the audience sees Parsifal seeing Amfortas seeing the Knights who see him fail to perform his office of the Grail ceremony. Such a thickly imbricated knot of looks and their symbolic significance produces the gaze of the work writ large.

In the first chapter, "The Rise of the Conductor and the Missing One," I examine archival sources that describe how orchestras were conducted in the eighteenth century. It was standard practice in the eighteenth century to have two "conductors" in a performance of orchestral music— a concertmaster (usually but not always the first chair, first violin) and a Kapellmeister (a surrogate for the composer playing at a keyboard instrument). There were no concert halls as we know them today; music was played in opera houses, taverns, and churches. There was no standard layout of an orchestra; clear orchestral "choirs" (strings, brass, winds, percussion) emerged in the early nineteenth century. Chapter 1 includes diagrams of early orchestral layouts to show how the modern orchestra emerged and how the single conductor finally took his place at the front of the orchestra with his back turned to the audience.

I found that the mid- to late eighteenth century was a time during which the idea of the masterwork entered Western music history. Early revivals of Handel's *Messiah*, in particular, form a beginning of the canon and the aesthetic of masterworks to be faithfully performed in public. Contemporary writers were aware that music was being generated by a new kind of artist—the genius—whose works embodied difficult effects that were no longer self-evident to a group of musicians led by a concert-master beating time with his bow and a Kapellmeister playing a keyboard, filling in harmonies as needed.

Chapter 1 examines a late symphony of Haydn and a contemporary account of anxiety relating to a detail of the work's complexity that is symptomatic of the reception of orchestral music at the time. The chapter compares the gaze of the singular, modern conductor with the Lacanian gaze. With the phrase "the missing One," I suggest that such elements produce a void at the heart of the modern musical masterpiece. Into this space the conductor steps to call the masterwork into being through his gaze and gesture.

In the second chapter, "Franz Schubert's 'Die Stadt' and Sublime (Dis)pleasure," I move from the public world of the conductor into the private world of the art song. I begin with a discussion of the sublime in the eighteenth century, moving from general aesthetics to specific writings that discuss the sublime in music. I am especially interested in the writings of Christian Friedrich Michaelis, who argues that there is not only a correlate of the Kantian mathematical and dynamical sublime in music (for Michaelis, a "masculine" sublime) but a quiet, "feminine" sublime as well. Recent musicological scholars (such as Jeffrey Kallberg, Lawrence Kramer, and Charles Rosen) have discussed various registers of delicacy in Romantic music. With the support of Michaelis and contemporary musicologists, I suggest that selected songs of Franz Schubert embody a sublime of the delicate.

For me, this sublime of the delicate relies on a tension between conventional musical materials that unfold in time and elements of the music that "tug" at that very conventionality. As examples of conventional musical materials, I mean conventional antecedent-consequent phrase structure, harmonic progressions that prolong the dominant, long-range melodic shape that always stretches out the tonic note to an apex followed by a final descent. As examples of elements of the music that "tug" at that conventionality, I mean notes that sound over and over again, seeming to gaze at the listener as well as structures that seem to "move" but in fact cycle back on themselves, going nowhere.

In this chapter, I discuss "Die liebe Farbe," "Der Wegweiser," and "Ihr Bild" for an introductory look at the book's crucial distinction between reiteration and repetition. Repetition serves symbolic mastery; it implies a series. Reiteration, like a cursor on a screen, goes nowhere; it simply

registers over and over again. The chapter culminates in a detailed reading of one of Schubert's most reiterative works: "Die Stadt." The work
sets a Heine text about a disappointed lover gazing at a town in the distance where he has lost what is most dear to him; I show how the music
embodies the fixed gaze of Heine's narrator.

In the third chapter, "Music and the Birth of Psychoanalysis: Anton
Webern's Opus 6, no. 4," I offer a synoptic overview of the history of
the discourse of the hysteric in the nineteenth century as it evolves into
the discourse of psychoanalysis. Although I touch on developments in
England and America, the focus of this survey moves from the French
school (which viewed hysteria as a sign of degeneration) to the German
school (which viewed hysteria as the product of a traumatic symptom
registered on the body). I am particularly interested in theories of trauma
and how they enter Western discourse in the age of industrialization
and increasingly mechanized warfare.

The survey of the birth of psychoanalysis provides a context with
which to understand Webern's *Sechs Orchesterstücke*, op. 6, no. 4 (sub-
titled "Marcia funebre"). In the music, I find a delicate but powerful
"tonal" element—a large-scale organization of the work around a single
note, D-natural. Like Kandinsky's abstract paintings of the period in
which traces, signifiers of representational shards, can be seen, so, too,
in this highly expressionist, atonal work, the faintest outlines of an obsessive D-natural-ness can be heard.

In the fourth chapter, "Left! Right! Left! Right! Music, Bodies, Fascism,"
I show how national socialist musicians skillfully turned the entire history of German classical and popular music to the right. The title of the
chapter condenses this left-to-right political and musical conversion and
opens with a look at how music functioned in national socialist Germany.
It then moves to war songs from World War I, with texts written by a
wide variety of writers (ranging from progressive poets to a descendant
of Felix Mendelssohn), including men and women articulating a range
of patriotic sentiments. The music of World War I songs is simple met-
rically and melodically, suggesting folk songs. For the music of World
War II songs, a profound change occurs. Their texts are appropriated
from a wide range of music from Lutheran chorales, folk songs, socialist
worker songs, and explicitly national socialist propaganda songs, and the
music often uses uneven rhythms and odd combinations of rhythms.

Many melodies are in modes (with archaic connotations); some are in keys (with modern connotations).

I focus in this part of the chapter on a single volume of songs that appeared in 1934, published by Bärenreiter and titled *Wohlauf Kameraden! Ein Liederbuch der jungen Mannschaft von Soldaten, Bauern, Arbeitern und Studenten.* This book contains intriguing juxtapositions: folk songs with songs celebrating Hitler along with updated versions of Lutheran chorales with calls to war against the enemy. There are three different versions of "Brüder zur Sonne zur Freiheit," with texts embodying varying degrees of hatred of the other. The chapter builds to a discussion of one of the most often-sung songs of the SS, "Volk ans Gewehr," a song that incorporates a Klezmer-like opening melody and a call to purge German blood of foreigners and Jews.

In the fifth chapter, I break the chronology by looking at twin versions of *Parsifal,* first the opera of Richard Wagner (1882) and then the film version by Hans-Jürgen Syberberg (1982). I examine how Wagner adapted Wolfram von Eschenbach's epic into his libretto and discuss nineteenth-century German anti-Semitism and Wagner's role in that discourse both as author of "Das Judentum in der Musik" and as composer, with specific reference to the implicitly Jewish qualities of Kundry recognized by Wagner himself (via Cosima in her diaries).

I first began this chapter inspired by the exquisite beauty and power of the Transformation Music in act 1 that renders the moment of transformation of the main character Parsifal as he leaves behind the innocence of childhood and begins to understand his place as redeemer in the social order. I focus on one musical detail in the Transformation Music: a major third that descends a half-step as a crucial element in the opera, tracing it into act 2 and to the scene in act 3 in which he redeems the community of the Grail.

The chapter and the book conclude with *Parsifal* told again, this time in the film of Hans-Jürgen Syberberg, who sets the entire opera in his film, with extraordinary interventions. He has an introductory scene before a visual representation of Wagner's *Vorspiel.* With the exception of only one scene, the entire film takes place in an interior space on a huge death mask of Wagner. The crucial Grail scenes take place inside Wagner's head, and Syberberg sets the powerful Transformation Music of act 1 to Parsifal moving through passageways lined with flags of German history moving in reverse chronological order. This is symptomatic of Syberberg's entire range of psychic trajectories—regression to a fantasy of bliss before sexual difference, to name just one.

This fantasy of regression is important for Syberberg; he splits Parsifal in two. Parsifals I and II are intertwined in an egglike union at the outset of the film. They split, and Parsifal I (a "boy" with feminine attributes) performs all of the action of act 1 and most of the action of act 2 (through Kundry's failed seduction); at the end of act 2, Parsifal II (a "girl" with masculine attributes) emerges. At the crucial Grail ceremony of act 3, the two Parsifals sing in unison of the redemption of the community of the Grail.

Syberberg raises a commonplace in filmed versions of opera to a self-conscious aesthetic device. He has all of his characters' voices (even those who actually sing their parts) added to the film in postproduction. Thus the film is visibly silent. The only diegetic sound in the entire work is water that we first hear in Titurel's grave/cave, as he utters the ominous question/demand "Mein Sohn Amfortas, bist du am Amt?" in act 1, and the sound of water as Parsifal II passes a fountain on the way to the Grail ceremony in act 3. The chapter concludes with a consideration of the role of puppets in the film and a consideration of Syberberg's reactionary aesthetics in the context of Federal Republic politics.

Intellectual Debts

I owe an intellectual debt to Lydia Goehr for conceiving the period from the late eighteenth century to the late twentieth century as "modern." Goehr writes that historical modernism in music involves both continuity and discontinuity of practices around 1800: "emergence is not a pre-determined process showing the inevitability or predictability of the rise of a given concept. It is rather a contingent, retroactively discovered, bonding and roping process."[3] "Prior to 1800 there were functioning concepts of composition, performance, and notation in musical practice, just as there were after that time. This is the continuity. The discontinuity lies in the fact that their significance, and the conceptual relations in which these concepts stood to one another, differed across the two time periods" (Goehr 108).

For my questioning the benevolence of the Enlightenment, I owe an intellectual debt to Michel Foucault, who describes discourses that arose in historical modernism in terms of disciplinary institutions—the modern hospital, the prison, the modern school, systems of grammar, and developments in science. Foucault's genius in these writings is to reveal coercive currents beneath the benevolent appearances of the Enlightenment. It is fascinating to read of the history of the Salpêtrière asylum in Paris in light of Foucault's writings on the hospital. My sense of history as punctured by gaps owes a debt to Foucault's *Archaeology of Knowledge*, in which he offers a theory of modern history as a series of ruptures beneath an apparently unbroken, diachronic surface: "discourse is snatched from the law of development and established in a discontinuous atemporality. It is immobilized in fragments: precarious splinters of eternity."[4]

I am indebted to Harold Bloom for his notion that the modern masterwork comes into being as a response to anxiety.[5] Bloom discusses "strong poets" whose works negotiate revisionary "ratios" in relation to powerful antecedents. I locate the origins of the modern masterwork in an undercurrent of anxiety in late eighteenth-century writers who feel that music is becoming too difficult to play and that greatness is beginning to lie not only in clarity but in elusive works of genius.

Thesis IX of Walter Benjamin's "Theses on the Philosophy of History" has guided this book along every stage of its realization. There are no one-to-one correspondences between Benjamin's paragraph and *Listening Awry,* but I have been guided by Benjamin's vision of history and the extraordinary humanity of his words. I quote the thesis in its entirety:

A Klee painting named "Angelus Novus" shows an angel looking as though he is about to move away from something he is fixedly contemplating. His eyes are staring, his mouth is open, his wings are spread. This is how one pictures the angel of history. His face is turned toward the past. Where we perceive a chain of events, he sees one single catastrophe which keeps piling wreckage upon wreckage and hurls it in front of his feet. The angel would like to stay, awaken the dead, and make whole what has been smashed. But a storm is blowing from Paradise; it has got caught in his wings with such violence that the angel can no longer close them. This storm irresistibly propels him into the future to which his back is turned, while the pile of debris before him grows skyward. This storm is what we call progress.[6]

Acknowledgments

I thank Lisa A. Raskin, dean of the faculty at Amherst College, for major funding that allowed me to conduct basic research toward the formulation of the central thesis of this book and the first chapter.

I thank Provost Howard Johnson of the Office of the Provost, University of North Texas, for two Junior Faculty Summer Research Fellowships and a Faculty Research Grant, which made much of the research for the book possible. Thanks also to Art Goven and Lloyd Chesnut, vice presidents for research and technology transfer, for their support.

Special thanks to Dean James C. Scott of the College of Music at the University of North Texas for his support of this book. Thanks as well to Jon C. Nelson, associate dean for operations, for support that enabled me to acquire software for the production of musical examples. Thanks to Joán Groom, music theory coordinator, for her support and flexibility in adjusting my teaching assignments during the research and writing of this book.

Thanks to my editor Richard Morrison at the University of Minnesota Press for his support and firm guidance during the long process of seeing this book through from early drafts to finished manuscript. Special thanks to Cindy McTee for her invaluable support and astute readings of several stages of the manuscript's composition. Thanks to good and brilliant friends who have helped make my life richer: Anahid Kassabian, Eric L. Santner, and Antonia Lant. Thanks to Reiner Krämer for his precise revisions of my German-to-English translations. Late thanks as well to Jeff Hodges of the College of Music for ideas leading to my Peter Gabriel/Primus chapter in *Listening Subjects.*

My gratitude also to my son Jakob for his patience and support during the writing of this book. Thanks as well to Amy for her love and support.

CHAPTER ONE

The Rise of the Conductor and the Missing One

In the eighteenth century, orchestras in Germany, England, France, and Italy performed symphonies with at least two "conductors."[1] The composer (or his surrogate)[2] sat at a keyboard or harpsichord filling in harmony, and the concertmaster sat or stood at the head of the first violin section beating time.[3] This is the well-known "double direction" of eighteenth-century, European orchestral performance.[4] Throughout the late eighteenth century, the roles of these conductors underwent a series of gradual transformations, leading to the emergence in the early nineteenth century of the single conductor of the modern era.[5] I would like to understand this conversion of double direction into single direction in both musical-historical and psychoanalytic terms.[6] I will focus on developments in German-speaking countries.[7]

A Historical View

Social spaces in Germany and the structure of the orchestra itself changed from the late eighteenth to the early nineteenth century. Where, earlier, orchestral music functioned in courts and the church, now orchestral music began to be played to the new and rising middle class. Isolated, single concerts transformed into the modern subscription series, and concerts moved from the church, theater, opera house, and tavern to the new, modern concert hall.[8]

The symphony orchestra became standardized into choirs of clearly defined sections (strings, winds, brass), with a relatively fixed number of players in each section. These sections were laid out on stage in a wide variety of configurations that became standard in the early nineteenth century.[9] The individual music stand became the standard platform from which performers projected music to the audience in the new space of the concert hall.[10]

The idea and ideology of the genius developed during this period.[11] Works of great composers contained difficult musical effects that required coordinated execution in performance. Standardized procedures of orchestral rehearsal became the norm.[12] Single movements and opera excerpts were played less and less frequently in favor of performances of entire instrumental works. The concertmaster gradually ceased playing his violin while conducting orchestral performances and instead beat time (with audible time-beating declining in favor of silent time beating) with his bow, a baton, a roll of paper, or a handkerchief.

By the early nineteenth century, the Kapellmeister and the concertmaster merged into the single modern conductor, who made music with his back turned to his audience. This turn might seem to be a turn *away* from the audience, but I would like to understand it as a turn *toward* a new kind of textuality in music in the early years of historical modernism.

A Psychoanalytic View

This 180-degree conversion of the conductor away from his audience toward his players connects the history of the conductor to the mirror phase of Lacanian psychoanalysis.[13] The imaginary plane that both separates and connects audience and performer in the modern concert hall is like a mirror.[14] Lacan has shown how the mirror phase connects the developing subject to an ideal self reflected in the (m)other's face in a complex and kinetic series of identifications and (mis)identifications. The mutually exclusive binary categories of mirror identification and (mis)identification underwrite elemental components of subjectivity reflected by a wide variety of structures in social space.[15]

The mirror phase is embedded in the practice of a conductor walking out onto a stage and facing an audience, and, crucially, making eye contact with it. He has taken his place in the imaginary plane that both connects and severs him from his audience. This is the dimension of specular identification between conductor and audience.[16] Having made eye contact, the conductor turns his back on the audience. The audience directly sees the musicians looking at the conductor and indirectly sees the conductor looking at the musicians. This moment is the appearance of the gaze. Eyes look; when eyes look at eyes looking, the gaze opens—a structure of displaced, transposed looks in the visual field of the Other.[17]

Space opens in the modern musical text at precisely the moment the modern musical text itself comes into being. In one prolonged and complex historical "moment," music becomes too complex for a coherent performance under the conditions of double direction. At such a moment, the emerging complexity of music has already produced a new kind of meaning that demands a new kind of musician. The modern, single conductor creates the illusion of coherence over and over again, from one performance of a great masterpiece to another, pulling the elements of music together around a vortex of silence through gaze and gesture.[18]

Eighteenth-Century Double Direction and the Orchestra

Eighteenth-century orchestras played in theaters, churches, and concert halls, with opera orchestras tending to be larger than court orchestras (Galkin 35).[19] Schünemann suggests that on average the eighteenth-century orchestra had from four to twenty violins with "corresponding winds"; apparently the other instruments were not even counted on a systematic basis (Schünemann 183). Schünemann points out that there were occasionally very large orchestras, many formed to perform and celebrate one of Western history's first great composers—Handel.[20] The 1786 Handel celebration in Berlin had an orchestra of thirty-eight first violins, thirty-nine second violins, eighteen violas, twenty-three celli, fifteen basses, plus winds; other massive performances honored Handel in London (1784) and Stettin (1785) (Schünemann 183). The number of players in an eighteenth-century orchestra thus varied widely from place to place and from occasion to occasion. And, from one eighteenth-century orchestra to another, the placements of instruments on stage also varied widely. The fluidity of the number of musicians in an orchestra and placement of instruments on stage has much to do with the double direction of the eighteenth-century orchestra and the gradually evolving roles of these two conductors. I shall examine the nature of eighteenth-century double direction with special attention to the placement of instruments on stage, the nature of the stages themselves, and the relationships among musicians on stage and the audience.[21]

Heinrich Christian Koch defined the Kapellmeister in his *Musik-Lexicon* of 1802 as associated with the composer or as the composer's surrogate. He has the score with him during rehearsal and performance and fills in harmonies as required, cues entries, and holds together all aspects of a work's performance and rehearsal, including determining the number and placement of performers (Galkin 157–58).[22] As early as 1703 Sébastien de Brossard included in his *Dictionnaire de musique* an entry under "Capo," suggesting that the French equivalent of the German Kapellmeister was, in his view, a teacher of the members of the orchestra (quoted in Galkin 145). Schünemann reports that Rousseau, Junker, Petri, and Hock agree that the basses should be placed next to the keyboard or harpsichord. As a result, the basses could take the beat from the Kapellmeister and transfer it to the rest of the orchestra. The proximity of basses to the keyboard is reflected in a number of sketches that have survived depicting the layout of eighteenth-century orchestras. Figure 1 is adapted from a sketch from Max Seiffert that shows a Kapellmeister at the middle of an orchestra, with no audience shown. The celli and basses are very close to the Kapellmeister ("a" and "b" in the sketch).[23]

An arrangement that more closely resembles the modern binary of audience/performer can be seen in the sketch of the Gewandhaus orchestra (Figure 2). Notice that a horizontal line separates the performers from the audience in the sketch; there are celli in front of the Kapellmeister. Their backs were probably turned to the audience since their function was to communicate the beat provided by the Kapellmeister to the rest of the orchestra.

Another common feature of the eighteenth-century orchestra was to have, in addition to the basses, the concertmaster close to the Kapellmeister. According to Koch, the concertmaster was responsible for placing, tuning, and organizing the practical needs of a performance.[24] Koch says it is far more important for him to be a well-rounded and experienced musician than an accomplished soloist. The concertmaster is usually the first chair, first violin (Galkin 176–77).[25] Figure 3 shows the Bachmann Liebhaberkonzert of Berlin (with the concertmaster marked with a "b+").

In Figure 3, an ascending stage is indicated, and you can see basses ("e") both near the Kapellmeister ("a") and against the far wall to the left. In addition you can see the concertmaster separated from the other first violins. What strikes the eye about the Seiffert, Gewandhaus, and Bachmann Liebhaberkonzert orchestras is that the double direction is from the middle of the musicians. It is important to imagine how self-evident the presence of the double directors in the midst of the music

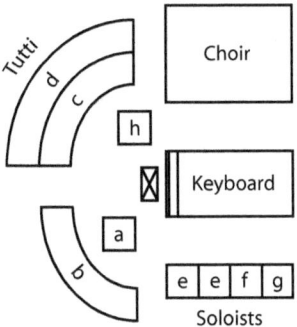

a = cello, b = bass, c = strings, d = winds,
e = violin, f = flute, g = cello, h = vocal soloist

Figure 1

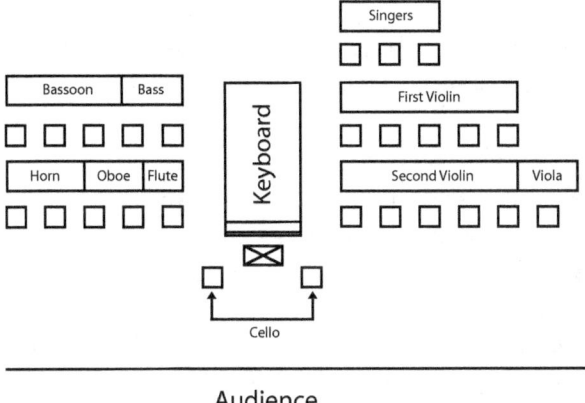

Figure 2

must have seemed to an eighteenth-century concertgoer. It is difficult, however, to get a clear sense of who sees whom from these sketches. A contemporary writer criticized the Bachmann Liebhaberkonzert arrangement, saying the concertmaster had his back to the Kapellmeister (Schünemann 189). Rellstab's Berlin Orchestra sought to correct this problem (Figure 4).

In Rellstab's arrangement, the concertmaster ("b+") can see the Kapellmeister ("a"), and there is a stand of basses ("e") near the Kapellmeister as well. Still, it would seem, given the placement of letters on the sketch, that the musicians were not all looking in the same direction.

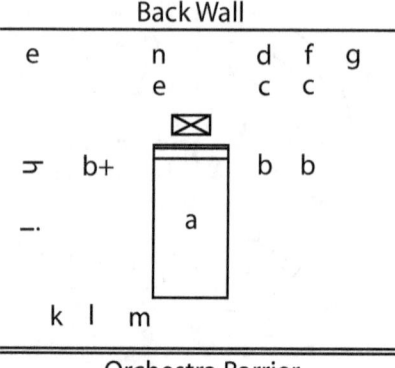

The stage is elevated from the main floor
and ascends toward the back wall.

a = keyboard; b = first violin; b+ = concertmaster;
c = second violin; d = viola; e = basses; f = oboe;
g = horns; h = bassoons; i = flute; k, l, m = soloist
and singers; n = choir

Figure 3

Quantz made a suggestion according to which no musician would
have his back to the audience (Figure 5).

Quantz's arrangement had the basses and concertmaster near to and
looking at the Kapellmeister without any musician's back turned to the
audience. Junker found Quantz's plan too spread out and wanted to
have the musicians surround the keyboard, according to the plan shown
in Figure 6.

Figure 7 shows Petri's plan for triple direction: the Kapellmeister at
the keyboard (called "director" in the sketch), the concertmaster to his
right (called "leader: first violin"), and the first-chair cello (called "leader:
celli") as a second concertmaster for the lower strings.

The orchestra that performed Handel's *Messiah* in Berlin in 1786
brings together these multiple directing agencies (Figure 8). There is a
director ("a") in front of the entire ensemble, a Kapellmeister ("b")
with celli and basses at each side ("e"), and a concertmaster ("c") just to
the left of the front of the Kapellmeister. Five musicians led the performance from the middle of an enormous ensemble of singers and musicians. This is very similar to the immense orchestra of the 1784 *Messiah*
performance in London.

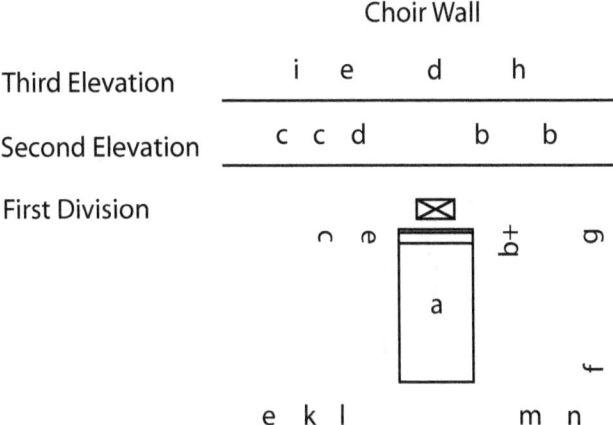

a = keyboard; b = first violin; b+ = concertmaster; c = second violin; d = viola; e = bass; f = flute; g = oboes; h = basoons; i = horns; k, l, m, n = solo singers and musicians

Figure 4

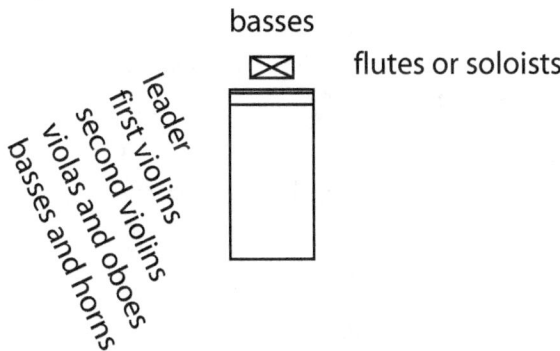

Figure 5

You can catch a glimpse of the modern orchestral arrangement in Junker's diagram (Figure 9) of the orchestra at Mannheim—famous for their uniform bowings and crescendo-decrescendo techniques (Galkin 72–73).[26] At Mannheim the Kapellmeister is the central focus of the orchestra at the center of an imaginary circle enclosing both the performers and, implicitly, the audience. The basses are close to the Kapellmeister as in so many eighteenth-century, double-direction orchestras. Junker's Mannheim diagram clearly shows that neither the winds nor strings are yet conceived as orchestral colors of their own.[27]

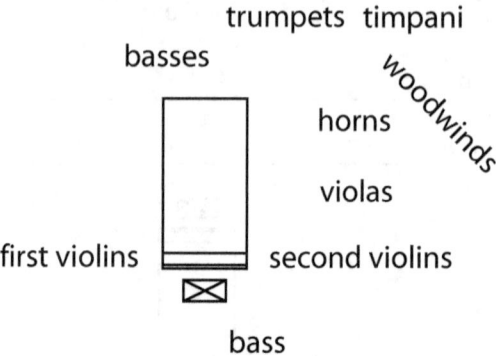

Figure 6

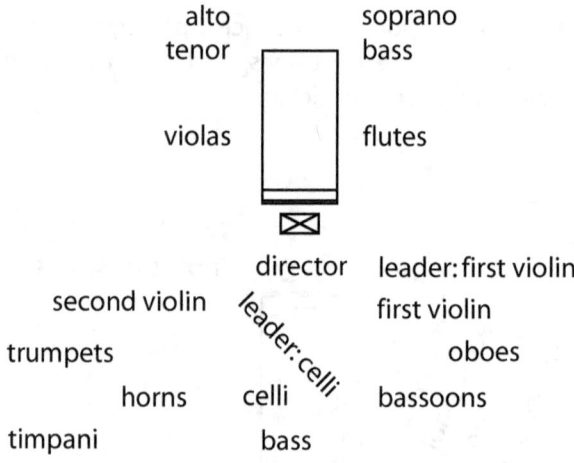

Figure 7

Reichardt's orchestra got rid of the keyboard—a bold step at the time (Figure 10). According to contemporary accounts, there were basses (omitted in the diagram) close to the Kapellmeister;[28] he conducted with a violin bow or baton with the concertmaster close by. The core of sound is clearly the strings with winds and brass at the edges. The conductor faces out toward the audience from the back of the theater wall. The omission of the keyboard is a profound gesture, taking leave of a powerful instrument of double direction.[29] Reichardt also added a special podium from which to conduct (Schünemann 257).[30]

The layout of the Hofkapelle in Vienna (Figure 11) shows the emergence of the winds as a clearly autonomous section of the orchestra. In

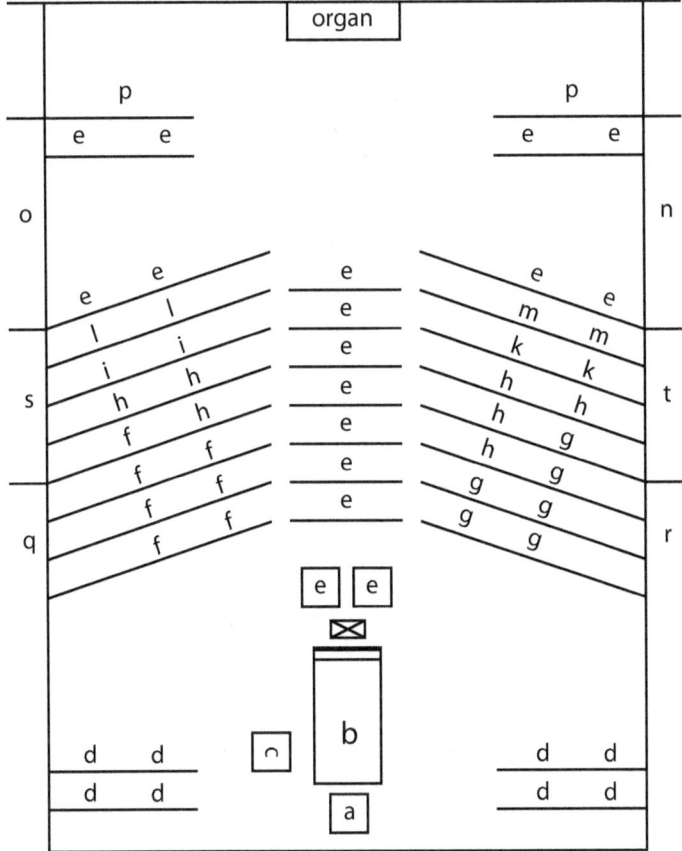

a = director, b = keyboard, c = leader of the violins, d = solo
vocalists, e = celli and basses, f = first violins, g = second
violins, h = violas, i = flutes, k = oboes, l = bassoons, m = horns,
n = trumpets, o = trombones, p = timpani, q = sopranos,
r = altos, s = tenors, t = basses

Figure 8

this diagram you can start to see the contemporary orchestral layout
emerging. There are clear choirs of strings, winds, and brass (although
the brass are split, with trumpets on one side of the organist and trombones and horns on the other). The conductor is at the center of the
orchestra on an elevated podium. The elevation helped the conductor
literally rise above the orchestra, to better be seen, of course, but the

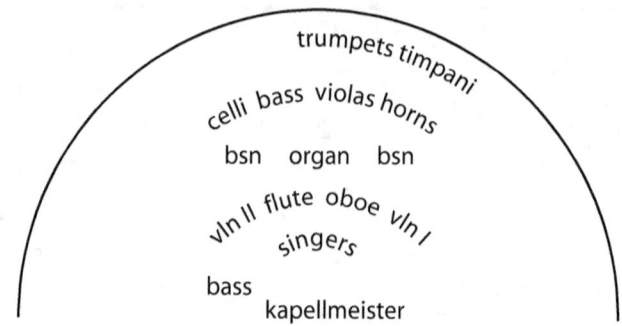

Figure 9

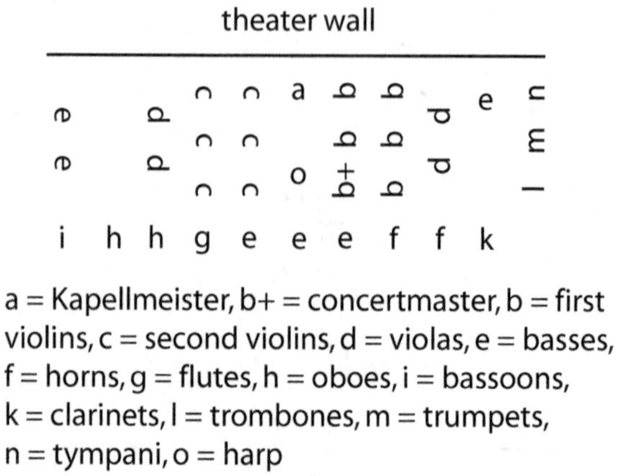

theater wall

a = Kapellmeister, b+ = concertmaster, b = first
violins, c = second violins, d = violas, e = basses,
f = horns, g = flutes, h = oboes, i = bassoons,
k = clarinets, l = trombones, m = trumpets,
n = tympani, o = harp

Figure 10

elevation also suggests a metaphorical rise in musical and aesthetic mastery and status. The concertmaster and the basses are still near one another.

A similar independence of the wind section can be seen from the diagram of an orchestra in Dresden (Figure 12). As with the Hofkapelle in Vienna, the strings, winds, and brass sections are clear. In addition, the conductor has moved to the very front of the orchestra and each level moving back from him to the wall of the hall is increasingly elevated.[31] Music is thus projected out toward the audience.[32] In the early nineteenth century, the orchestra gradually assumed its contemporary form. The orchestras of Mannheim, Leipzig, and Paris contained a roughly uniform one-to-eight ratio of winds to strings by the second

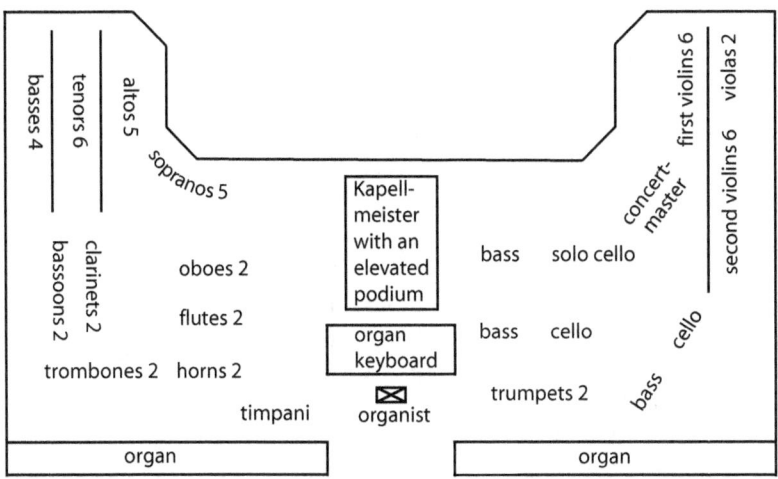

Figure 11

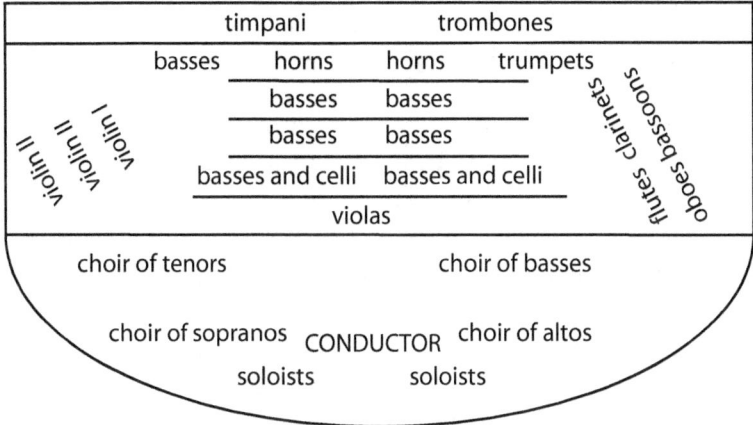

Figure 12

decade of the nineteenth century (Galkin 171–72). The contemporary orchestra attained a relatively stable strength and distribution of players in the early twentieth century.[33]

Complex Musical Works

On the one hand, the modern, singular conductor enabled the composition of a new kind of music for a new kind of performance; on the other hand, a new kind of musical performance of a new kind of music demanded his appearance. He is at once a *cause of* and an *effect of the cause of* the modern musical masterpiece. Musical works are whole and must be well executed in performance.[34]

Musical performances at the turn of the nineteenth century were often transparently bad, however. Here is an excerpt from a review of a performance of Mozart's Mass in C minor in Fulda published in *Die Allgemeine Musikalische Zeitung (AMZ)*:

> Although at such concerts it is customary to have the king's concert-master conduct, this concert was directed by a Benedictine monk from the Domkirche; he had neither a clean and solid bowing arm nor sufficient knowledge of the art of directing. He stood by the first violins and scratched away without having chosen a tempo. He kept playing on his untuned violin in complete ignorance of the orchestra, one piece after another, with no regard as to whether anyone in his section was playing C-natural or C-sharp. No instrument played with any other, and the whole production deteriorated into an everlasting mess of dissonances. Together with constantly reserved trumpets and false chords on the organ, one could barely recognize Mozart's work.[35]

Mozart's works generated in late eighteenth-century writers what we might now refer to as "anxiety."[36] In general, across the pages of the *AMZ*, Haydn is praised as the great master of clarity.[37] In the following passage, Mozart's "genius" is opposed to (an implicitly Haydnesque) "taste": "Our orchestra does not like to perform symphonies by Mozart. One can still not really get used to their spirit. The overtures did not have the expected effect and reinforced the opinion that Mozart, even though he is Haydn's rival, but a much less prudent rival as a composer of instrumental music, has proven to have more genius than he has taste."[38]

Writers for the *AMZ* felt particularly uncomfortable with the new compositional practice of giving independence to winds: "While the older composers use wind instruments only separately, sparingly, and almost always as reinforcements for the string instruments, the new masters use them in such different ways, almost too complex to enumerate. Soon they are filling up holes in sustained harmonies that cannot be covered by the melodic strings. Soon they form a second orchestra that works competitively with the main orchestra. Soon they are entrusted with the counterpoint to the melody led by the violins."[39] In the same article, the author argues that wind instruments are more powerful than string instruments in stimulating affective responses in listeners because "wind instruments are, from their nature, much more different from each other than string instruments. Their tone is more similar to the most Godly of all instruments, the human voice. They penetrate more quickly to the heart and stimulate according to their unique characteristics this or that emotion much more powerfully than string instruments, which have a more general and therefore less defined character."[40] The independent emergence of winds was a threat to be managed by the conductor, who could and would achieve balance and proportion of orchestral sonorities.[41]

What we call "program music" was a concern to writers for the *AMZ* as well: "We would like the opportunity at the end of this letter to express our opinion on painting symphonies. They seem odd, and we reject them since they cannot be reconciled with visual arts. Dittersdorf in Germany and Roseti in Italy were the first to attempt such compositions, in which the composer has not a fixed and determined purpose but rather a painterly one."[42]

The practice of including opera scenes and movements of symphonies undermined the sense of unity inherent in works of the late eighteenth and early nineteenth centuries. A writer for the *AMZ* addresses this concern: "The custom to perform single opera scenes and opera arias in public concerts has only become common in the last twelve to fifteen years: previously one rather performed whole works—not always oratorios and other great works, but especially large or small cantatas and the like. There are many reasons for the present custom. The first is in both the music and the world of the theater in which there is the demand for new and nothing but new pieces."[43] Later in the same article the author writes that performing excerpts out of context produces affect without a motivated connection to a source: "The story, the situation of the characters, the action, the states of mind of the characters—everything is gone. It is precisely the most admirable in real opera, the individual [in the music] that corresponds to the individual in the libretto, that is completely missing."[44]

A writer for the *AMZ* describes the negative effect of rubato on musical coherence:

They break violently through the limitations that art has received from nature, so that the best orchestra has a hard time following the labyrinth of motions, often guessing, to the most embarrassing effect in which the accompaniment of the voices does not tolerate any ease, and which is only possible by means of rests, which through ignorance is not seldom ascribed to bad intention. Some follow their petulance so far that they break out of their measures, adding one, two, three, even more quarter notes where none belong without regard to the barbaric effects of such liberties, whether they fit any longer in the harmony, whether one wrong note piles upon another; they feel justified doing whatever they wish, ignoring the principles of poet, composer, art, and artist in the pursuit of their individual impulses.[45]

Difficult Works

Around the turn of the nineteenth century, writers for the *AMZ* began to openly discuss the difficulty of music. In the following article in the *AMZ*, published March 4, 1801, an author wrote,

> Finally only the instrumental composer can be competent who knows how inner and outer tones work and how to bring them together according to valid, natural laws of tones, modes, keys, harmonies, rhythm, instrumentation, and so on, through study and genius. Such a composer will, during composition and performance, choose not simply the best-sounding music but will rather be true to a certain idea or emotion. To such a composer the question "Sonata, what do you want of me" can never be asked.[46]

The following extended discussion of a late Haydn symphony suggests an anxiety about musical coherence as well:

> One began with a symphony of Joseph Haydn, the third in D major of the six that were published in London. Whoever has listened to a great instrumental work will understand the correctness of expression, the precise coming together of the instruments that seem led by a single bow, especially, however, the pure tones of the violins, the clarity of the basses, and tenderness of the winds. What a beautiful impression this symphony also makes today! The not overly simple ideas of the first movement in 6/8 followed one upon the other naturally! They were performed as well by this orchestra as by a quartet of players who were used to performing with one another. The wondrous movements, and the rolling of the basses in the slow movement's minor section, the surprising instrumental play of instruments exchanging ideas in the minuet bear witness to the genius of limitless art who is equally great in smaller gestures. However, after the minor section in the finale allegro that is begun with such vigor, one voice after another moves in an imitative, fugue-like passage of contrasting ideas, and the listener, not always used

to hearing such a thing, is torn out of himself. People looked at each other, and it seemed as if order no longer reigned. Then after fifty measures of this deceiving game, everyone ordered himself again into a large, cadential motion which eventually came to a satisfying close, and we were placed back into the repose of our previous pleasure.[47]

The basic theme or idea for this movement is played by the first violin in measures 1–2, to the downbeat of measure 3. There is a metrical difference between the theme and the accompaniment. The accompaniment (second violins, viola, celli, and basses) play in four-square 2/4 meter, while the theme has a two-eighth-note *upbeat* plus one measure plus a beat into the next measure. The first violin's theme interlocks with the accompaniment throughout, and this interlocking must be absolutely precise (see Figure 13).

The music embodies a period of two antecedent-consequent phrases in D major. Haydn's wit can be heard in his definition of the V-I cadence through silence—the quarter-note rest on the downbeat of measure 7 in the bass presses the V of V E-natural right up against the A that concludes the section on the dominant.[48] There is an aspect of the orchestral writing in this movement that exhibits Haydnesque wit (see Figure 14).

In measure 23 the music (in D major) reaches the dominant, and measures 24–28 prolong a-natural[1] with a chromatically ascending wedge from b-flat[1] in measure 25, through b-natural[1] in measure 26, through c-natural[2] in measure 26, through c-sharp[2] in measure 27, through d-natural[2] in measure 27. Melodically this d-natural[2] is the goal of the chromatic wedge, and it signals the return to tonic and a return of the bouncy theme—brought out by Haydn's staccato markings. Measure 28 gives us an entire extra measure of d-natural[2]/a-natural[1] eighth notes. The first pair concludes the ascending wedge gesture and the second pair is the pick-up to the next phrase played by the flute.

The writer from the *AMZ* cited above is struck with wonder at the passage marked "Maggiore," or major, from measure 103 to the end. In this passage the main theme articulated *forte* on two upbeat eighth notes enters in a richly imitative texture (see measures 110 [bassoon, celli, and basses], 112 [second oboe and second violins], and 114 [flute, first oboe, and first violins]). The conductor would rehearse and control precisely such passages, which must have been very hard to lead from the first violin's chair (see Figure 15).

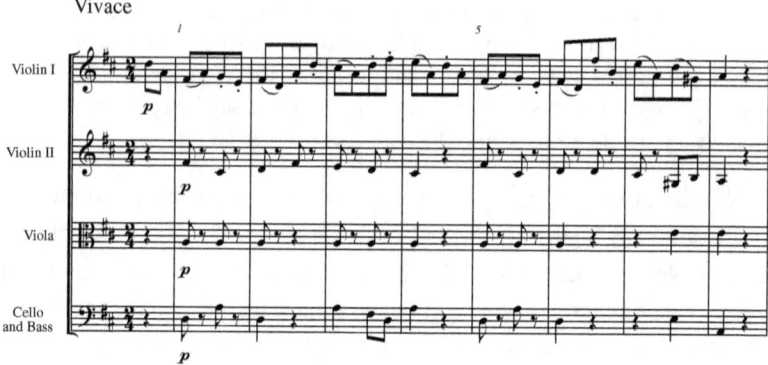

Figure 13

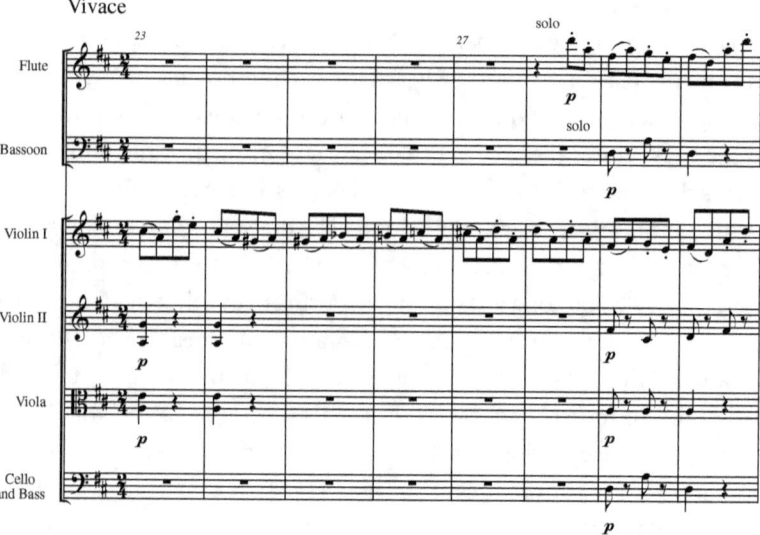

Figure 14

Haydn expands the one measure that had connected the conclusion of one phrase to the upbeat of the next to four full measures (measures 110–14 in Figure 15). After the imitative passage of the Maggiore music, Haydn intensifies the witty glitch in measure 178 in Figure 16.

Although the first violin plays the same pitches in measures 27–28 as in measures 177–78, the staccato markings in the latter and the doubling in the bassoon makes it sound as if the bassoon had usurped the flute's solo, coming in too early.[49]

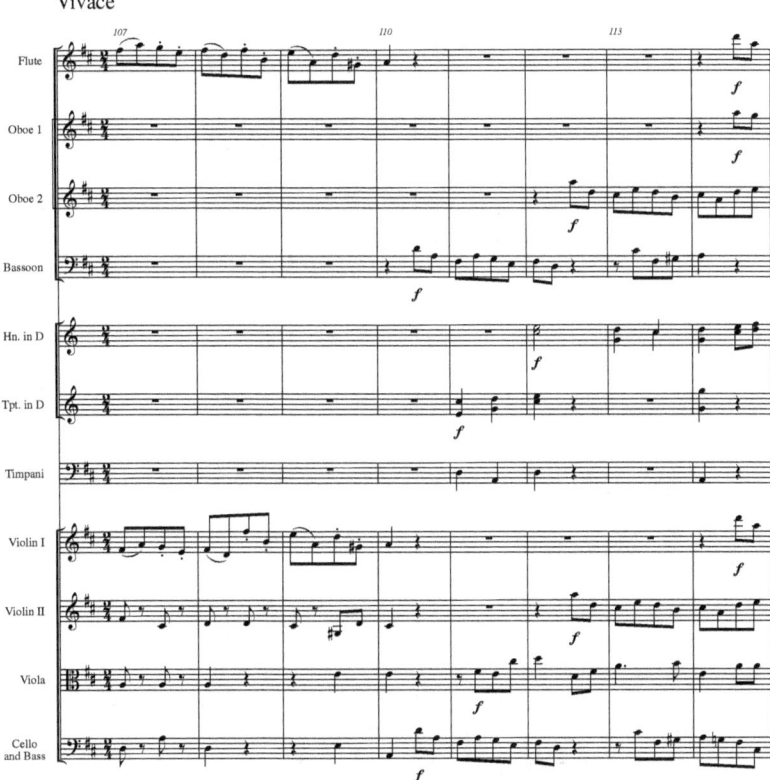

Figure 15

Toward the First Appearances of the Modern, Singular Conductor

Two extended passages from the *AMZ* embody the urgency for a new musician just beyond the horizon. The first is an extended critique of the conducting of the Viennese concertmaster Schupanzig:

> The great achievement of Mr. Schupanzig is certainly his distinguished
> playing, which contributes positively to his conducting. But with all due
> respect to his playing, we cannot agree with the widely held opinion that
> he is what one would call a great director. In order that this not seem like
> a gratuitous criticism, let us say to the educated man that Schupanzig is a
> skilled but limited practitioner, without knowledge of theory and compo-
> sition. The most skilled and practiced director, lacking in such knowledge,
> can, in our opinion do little more than play his part well and, when

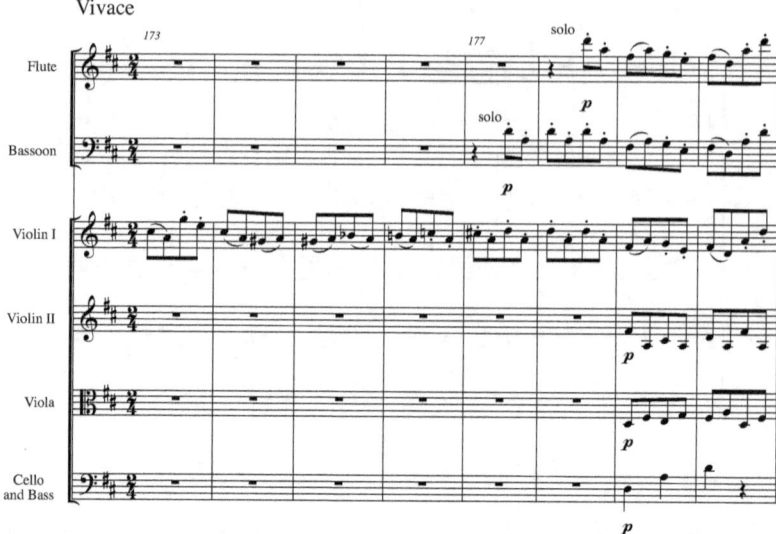

Figure 16

instability in tempo or another error in the orchestra occurs, dig into his instrument and stamp his foot on the floor. A great director, however, must do much more—he must keep the orchestra together in a way the audience does not notice; he must also improve the orchestra and bring the ensemble together without notice from the audience, should errors occur.[50]

This passage prefigures the essence of the singular, modern conductor, whose gaze is a central organizing source of musical meaning. The gaze is at once *seen* by the musicians, who get their cues from it, and, paradoxically, it is *unseen*, necessarily invisible at the heart of the music constantly being called into being.

The second passage is a wonderful description of orchestral performances in Amsterdam in which the author implicitly hears the realization of a masterpiece as the product of confronting and mastering complexity:

The music was performed, under the direction of Mr. Schmitt, with passion, power, precision, and delicacy, to the great pleasure of the educated listener. No symphony was performed until the completion of exacting rehearsals (which always occurred with full orchestral participation) until every attribute of the work was rehearsed to perfection. It is curious that the more difficult the work (as for example with the Mozart C major and G minor symphonies) the more passionate, powerful, and perfect was the performance.[51]

The author implicitly understands that the modern musical masterpiece does not spring to life despite its inherent difficulties but because of them. The ground is being prepared for the single, modern conductor.

Two Concerts

Carl Maria von Weber reorganized the layout of the orchestra for the January 14, 1818, production of Spontini's *La Vestale* in Dresden. Weber was director of the opera in Prague from 1813 to 1816, where had begun such a reorganization of the orchestra. The usual arrangement had the Kapellmeister in the middle of the orchestra with cello and bass reading the continuo over his shoulder, and trumpets and percussion far to the right, out of sight of the conductor. Weber wished to establish a clear line of sight between him and all musicians.[52] In response to a published letter critical of his innovations, Weber asserted that "the seating of the orchestra will depend entirely on the nature of the work performed, the main object being that no instrument should fail to be heard and that the conductor should have an equally good view of the stage and orchestra and be able, in his turn, to be clearly seen by everyone taking part" (Weber 249).[53] Later in the article, Weber explicitly relates his re-organization of the orchestra to the emergence of the conductor and the weakening position of both Kapellmeister and concertmaster: "The days are gone when the bass line in an Italian opera would contentedly bed down on the same note for eight or ten bars and after innumerable rehearsals was known by heart, so that it could safely be played from the score with the continuo player acting politely as page-turner or leaving even that to the leader" (250).[54]

La Vestale was repeated on the 17th and 21st of January 1818. The reviewer in the *AMZ* was very flattering: "One could not wish for a more fully realized performance from the singers as well as the orchestra. This was achieved through the unanimously acclaimed, lively, and penetrating direction of von Weber and Pollendro."[55]

Louis Spohr was a violinist, composer, and celebrated concertmaster in the early nineteenth century.[56] In 1820 Spohr conducted in London using a baton; the concert became well known as a milestone in the history of conducting. Here is an extended description of the event in Spohr's own words:

Meanwhile my turn had come to direct one of the Philharmonic concerts, and I had created no less sensation than with my solo play. It was at that time still the custom there that when symphonies and overtures were performed, the pianist had the score before him, not exactly to conduct from it, but only to read after and to play in with the orchestra at pleasure, which when it was heard, had a very bad effect. The real conductor was the first violin, who gave the tempi, and now and then when the orchestra began to falter gave the beat with the bow of his violin. So numerous an orchestra, standing so far apart from each other as that of the Philharmonic, could not possibly go exactly together, and in spite of the excellence of the individual members, the ensemble was much worse than we are accustomed to in Germany. I had therefore resolved when my turn came to direct, to make an attempt to remedy this defective system. Fortunately at the morning rehearsal on the day I was to conduct the concert, Mr. Ries took the place at the piano, and he readily assented to give up the score to me and to remain wholly excluded from all participation in the performance. I then took my stand with the score at a separate music desk in front of the orchestra, drew my directing baton from my coat pocket and gave the signal to begin. Quite alarmed at such a novel procedure, some of the directors would have protested against it; but when I besought them to grant me at least one trial, they became pacified. The symphonies and overtures that were to be rehearsed were all known to me, and in Germany I had already directed at their performance. I therefore could not only give the tempi in a very decisive manner, but indicated also to the wind instruments and horns all their entries, which ensured to them a confidence such as hitherto they had not known there. I also took the liberty, when the execution did not satisfy me, to stop, and in a very polite but earnest manner to remark upon the manner of execution, which remarks Mr. Ries at my request interpreted to the orchestra. Incited thereby to more than usual attention, and conducted with certainty the *visible* [Spohr's emphasis] manner of giving time, they played with a spirit and a correctness such as till then they had never been heard to play with.... The result in the evening was still more brilliant than I could have hoped for. It is true, the audience were at first startled by the novelty, and were seen whispering together; but when the music began and the orchestra executed the well-known symphony with unusual power and precision, the general approbation was shown immediately on the conclusion of the first part by a long-sustained clapping of hands. The triumph of the baton as a time-giver was decisive, and no one was seen any more seated at the piano during the performance of symphonies and overtures.[57]

Mr. Ries's act in 1820 London of actually handing Louis Spohr the score of a work to be performed stands as a crucial moment in the history of conducting.[58] The Kapellmeister had been the composer or the surrogate of the composer, and the changing of hands described by Spohr stands for the emergence of a new musician.[59]

Despite Spohr's 1820 milestone, it was Felix Mendelssohn who made the single conductor a permanent fixture of modern, orchestral musical performance. Mendelssohn was an important musician on many levels. He brought public awareness of the music of J. S. Bach to a new level with his 1829 Berlin performance of the *St. Matthew Passion* (Galkin 414). Mendelssohn was widely respected for his musical talents, his quiet, gentlemanly manners, and his rigorous rehearsal techniques. Mendelssohn routinely faced the orchestra, turning his back on the audience. We take this for granted today, but indications of performance practice throughout the early nineteenth century suggest that baton conducting first took place with the conductor *facing* his audience (Bowen 161). Although full of praise for Mendelssohn's musicality, Schumann was disturbed by the baton: "For my part, I was disturbed, both in the overture and in the symphony, by the conductor's baton, and I agreed with Florestan that in a symphony the orchestra must be like a republic, subordinate to no higher authority" (quoted in Bowen 161).

A much more negative reaction to the baton is described by Moritz Hauptmann in an 1836 letter to his friend Hauser:

> The accursed white-wooden baton irritated me, and when I have to see that thing dominate, all music vanishes. It is as if the entire opera is only there so that a baton can beat time to it, to mark all of its most delicate nuances with this little stick. Perhaps it is necessary, but if I think of the maestro sitting so peacefully at the keyboard and accompanying the recitative precisely, as if everything was happening on its own, I am in another sphere entirely, heavens away from our crude and barbaric present, in which all dignity seems naked and exposed. (quoted in Schünemann 260)[60]

The Singular Conductor and the Gaze

The transformation of double (and even triple) direction to the singular conductor has much to do with looking. Until the building of modern concert halls, music was performed in spaces (such as the church) that were not necessarily designed for musical performances, and musicians had to arrange themselves in and around a variety of obstacles. Musicians often could not see one another, the Kapellmeister, and/or the concertmaster. Carl Maria von Weber's innovations sought to correct this lack of visual organization of the orchestra, connecting the conductor to each musician along a single, unobstructed line of sight. If the single conductor (Spohr, Weber, Mendelssohn, and all other subsequent single conductors of the modern era) were simply "looking" at their musicians in order to attain a more tightly organized musical performance, I don't think their innovations would have generated the reactions reported above. The audience at the 1820 Spohr performance would not have twittered uneasily; Schumann and Hauptmann would not have been so disturbed by the baton; the writer from the *AMZ* quoting Rousseau quoting Bernard would not have felt so threatened by the sonata form.

The masterpiece, as it emerged in the late eighteenth and early nineteenth centuries in central Europe, required skilled, disciplined, and strenuous interpretation. Music was no longer happening as if on its own, to paraphrase Hauptmann's nostalgic wish for the simpler musical days of an earlier era. Since the musical masterpiece was no longer self-evident but required interpretation, since orchestras needed to be rehearsed and guided beat by beat and measure by measure through a score, since cues had to be given for entrances of solo instruments and orchestral sections, the essence of the masterpiece was outside the work itself. Music moved from score to conductor's eye and gesture to the musicians, to their instruments, to a concert hall, and to the body, ears, and eyes of each member of an audience. It is not only that the eyes and gestures of the conductor make the music of the masterwork sound; it is that the audience *sees* that the eyes and gesture of the conductor make the masterwork sound.

Music, Look, Gaze

In an attempt to understand how identities are constructed in social space, Jean-Paul Sartre discusses the look as follows:

> Every look directed toward me is manifested in connection with the appearance of a sensible form in our perspective field, but contrary to what might be expected, it is not connected with any determined form. Of course what *most often* [Sartre's emphasis] manifests a look is the convergence of two ocular globes in my direction. But the look will be given just as well on occasion when there is a rustling of branches, or the sound of a footstep followed by silence, or the slight opening of a shutter, or a light movement of a curtain.[61]

Sartre goes on immediately after this passage to discuss the significance of the look in an attack; thus the images that suggest a stealthy approach. Sartre is interested in exploring how seeing the look of the other fixes one in spatial and temporal relations in social space. For him, the look has two dimensions: a direct eye-to-eye contact and another level of social implication appended to that eye-to-eye contact. In "a rustling of branches, or the sound of a footstep followed by silence, or the slight opening of a shutter, or a light movement of a curtain" a wider field of visual apprehension is implied than simple eye-to-eye contact.

In his well-known reading of precisely this passage in Sartre, Lacan makes a crucial move. Sartre discusses a look, a returned look, and a set of object relations initiated in social space; Lacan asserts that "the gaze . . . is, not a seen gaze, but a gaze imagined by me in the field of the Other."[62] For Lacan, the gaze is often drawn not by the eye but by an object. In a famous example, Lacan tells the following story:

> One day, I was on a small boat, with a few people from a family of fishermen in a small port. At that time, Brittany was not industrialized as it is now. There were no trawlers. The fisherman went out in his frail craft at his own risk. It was this risk, this danger, that I loved to share. But it wasn't all danger and excitement—there were also fine days. One day, then, as we were waiting for the moment to pull in the nets, an individual known as Petit-Jean, that's what we called him—like his family, he died very young from tuberculosis, which at that time was a constant threat to the whole of that social class—this Petit-Jean pointed out to me something floating on the surface of the waves. It was a small can, a sardine can. It floated there in the sun, a witness to the canning industry, which we, in fact, were supposed to supply. It glittered in the sun. And Petit-Jean said to me— *You see that can? Do you see it? Well, it doesn't see you!*[63]

For Lacan, the gaze is that look solicited by a glint of light coming from an object (the sardine can) that seems to see you more than you see it. The gaze is, for Lacan, crucially outside; it adheres to objects. I quoted the passage at length because I don't think the passage would work as a story without all the discursive details: the frail craft, the fishermen's vulnerability to disease, the industry the fisherman were supposed to be supplying. A simple can floating in the water would not have suggested the gaze to Lacan. There needs to be a widely distributed network of economic and social relations embedded in the story for the sardine can to embody the gaze. The entire host of social relations is condensed into the can's glint of light that flashes at Lacan as gaze.

The single conductor, with or without a baton, has organized the space of performance so that each performer can meet his eye, so that each beat of the work can be communicated to each performer in each section of the orchestra, so that all important cues and entries can be mimed and perfectly executed. An audience member at a contemporary concert to whose back a conductor is crucially turned, imagines, or sees obliquely (depending upon where he/she is sitting), the conductor see his musicians.

Music, Gaze, Trap

Audience members, critics, and scholars have gotten used to the single conductor, who has by now become what Adorno might have called "second nature." But in addition to the conductor as gaze, I would like to explore the theatrical element of conducting, that is, the business of walking out on stage, facing and bowing to the audience, turning his back, and making eye contact with the musicians just before the music starts.

In an extended discussion of anamorphosis, Lacan reads Holbein's painting "The Ambassadors" from the point of view of a distorted image of a skull in the painting that can only be recognized as such when the viewer looks at the painting askew. There is a large body of anamorphotic art in both Eastern and Western culture that depends upon distortion "righted" by perception through a lens, a filter, a skewed perspective. The skewed image that must be viewed awry becomes a crucial component of the Lacanian gaze. Lacan concludes his reading of "The Ambassadors" with an extraordinary general statement about painting, tantalizingly dropped at the very end of his lecture: "This picture is simply what any picture is, a trap for the gaze. In any picture, it is precisely in seeking the gaze in each of its points that you will see it disappear."[64]

For Lacan the gaze disappears when we give ourselves over to a painting:

> The painter gives something to the person who must stand in front of his painting which, in part, at least, of the painting, might be summed up thus— *You want to see? Well, take a look at this!* He gives something for the eye to feed on, but he invites the person to whom this picture is presented to lay down his gaze there as one lays down one's weapons. This is the pacifying, Apollonian effect of painting. Something is given not so much to the gaze as to the eye, something that involves the abandonment, the *laying down* [Lacan's emphasis] of the gaze.[65]

For Lacan, in giving ourselves over to a painting, we lay down our gaze; to the imaginary invitation "You want to see? Well, take a look at this!" We say "yes!" Something similar happens in music once the conductor comes out on stage, faces us, makes eye contact with us, and then turns to the musicians, making eye contact with them. The audience lays down its gaze and looks in symmetrical rows of seats, in a visual field parallel to the visual field of musicians making eye contact with the conductor. Music has Apollonian and Dionysian components, more or less depending on the style of work being performed. The gaze organizes the eye contact of both the conductor and musicians, and of the conductor and the audience as we "first" see him see his musicians and "then" lay down our gaze in order to feast our eyes on the work.

Although in opera, music is a feast for both eyes and ears, it is on symphonic performances as a feast primarily for our *ears* that this chapter has focused. What disturbed both Schumann and Hauptmann has nothing to do with what is heard but with what is seen, as it is integrally connected to what is heard. One can close one's eyes at a performance and feast the ears, as if in answer to the imaginary question: "You want to hear something? Listen to this!" We answer "yes!" What happens when you open your eyes in an orchestral concert is not that you feast your eyes as if looking at a painting; you see instead the brute instrumentality at the heart of the modern musical masterwork. Music in Hauptmann's good old days had seemed to play on its own. With the late symphonies of Mozart, the symphonies of Beethoven, and the new generation of turn-of-the-nineteenth-century works, this instrumentality could not be overlooked, and a new professional musician had to stand in its place and transform the score of the masterwork into a coherent performance that sounded in social space. The "trap" is that which catches us at the threshold of the work whose internal consistency can no longer be taken for granted.

The gaze is connected to the missing One as follows. Music of the late eighteenth, early nineteenth century no longer unfolds as if on its own; the Kapellmeister no longer sits at his keyboard and accompanies a work, filling in harmonics and cues as needed, working together with a concertmaster who marks time with his bow. In the era of double and triple direction, the coherence of the work seemed singular, a principle to be grasped and executed. As long as pieces were organized around this singular coherence, the multiple direction could continue. But as works became more complex in the late eighteenth century and the notion of a history of canonic music demanded repeatable, perfect performance, a space, a void, a missing One emerged at the heart of the modern masterpiece. The gaze is the structure that emerged as the single, modern conductor stepped into the place of the missing One. It is gaze in two ways: first, our seeing the conductor seeing his musicians, and second, the existence of a visual, theatrical component of music, externalized in public space.

This chapter examined in German musical history the rise of the single, instrumental conductor as a large moment that marked the emergence, as if from within musical texts and practices, of a new form of alterity. The remaining chapters will explore aftereffects of this moment, at times within masterpieces of the canon, at times at the margins of social space.

CHAPTER TWO

Franz Schubert's "Die Stadt" and Sublime (Dis)pleasure

The previous chapter tracked the rise of the conductor through a wide range of developments in the late eighteenth and early nineteenth centuries, including the increasing complexity of orchestral music, technological developments in instrument design, the emergence of a canonical body of masterpieces, the idea of perfection in music execution, and the notion of a work that transcends the immediate conditions of its initial performance. In short, music was making and taking its place in the public life of late eighteenth- and early nineteenth-century middle-class life in Europe. At the same time, a new form of introspective, private music, the art song, was also making and taking its more interior place.

The art song developed out of the eighteenth-century solo song and the opera aria. What was new in the early nineteenth-century art song was (a) a lyrical intensity and experimentation of harmony and form, particularly in Schubert, that prefigure much later developments in music, and (b) song cycles that set to music poetry cycles, a new form in poetry. Cycles in both poetry and music were made possible by a new consciousness of fragments. The fragment is both a metonymic and metaphoric element of musical Romanticism. Metonymically, the fragment stands for the larger whole to which it points (like a piece of a puzzle); metaphorically, the fragment is a small, concise version of the impossible whole—incomplete, always contingent, open.[1]

The sublime is an aesthetic category of eighteenth-century thought concerned with the enormity of untamed nature and its effects on the subject, as well as with religious and aesthetic awe inspired by God and works of art. As will be shown, writers and composers in the late eighteenth century understood music (especially the large orchestral and choral works of Handel, Haydn, and Mozart) as sublime in their enormity and power. As a complement to the sublime of the immense work, I will argue in this chapter for a sublime of the delicate work, as embodied in Schubert's "Die Stadt."

The Sublime in Eighteenth-Century Aesthetics

The sublime was a well-known category of aesthetic thought in eighteenth-century Germany, France, and England.[2] According to Elaine Sisman, "the sublime came to the attention of the eighteenth century in a rhetorical guise, through the translation of a first-century Greek treatise, *On the Sublime,* a work of profoundly original literary criticism attributed to a certain Longinus (now thought to be a first-century work by an unknown author, sometimes referred to as pseudo-Longinus to distinguish him from the more famous third-century rhetorician)."[3]

Immanuel Kant's *Critique of Judgment* distinguishes between the beautiful and the sublime. Although the two are closely connected to one another,[4] there are profound differences between them. For Kant the beautiful is a representation of pure form that results in a restful contemplation; it therefore has nothing to do with emotion.[5] The sublime produces at once attraction and repulsion in the subject: "the feeling of the sublime is a feeling of displeasure that arises from the imagination's inadequacy, in an aesthetic estimation of magnitude, for an estimation of reason, but is at the same time also a pleasure, aroused by the fact that this very judgment ... is in harmony with rational ideas" (Kant 114–15).[6] Kant distinguishes between the mathematical sublime (numbers that are infinitely large or infinitely small) and the dynamical sublime (immense forces of nature).[7]

Kant's ideas of the sublime have a profoundly theological motivation:

Whatever arouses this feeling in us [our superiority over nature produced by the sublime], and this includes the *might* [Kant's emphasis] of nature that challenges our forces, is then ... called sublime. And it is only by presupposing this idea within us, and by referring to it, that we can arrive at the idea of the sublimity of that being who arouses deep respect in us, not just by his might as demonstrated in nature, but even more by the ability, with which we have been endowed, to judge nature without fear and to think of our vocation as being sublimely above nature. (Kant 123).[8]

In an understated relative clause, Kant leaves open the door to applying to art his ideas observed in nature: "If . . . we start here by considering only the sublime in natural objects (since the sublime in art is always confined to the conditions that [art] must meet to be in harmony with nature), then the distinction in question comes to this" (Kant 98). Kant focuses on nature throughout the *Critique*; there are references to architecture, to gardens, and, rarely, to music.[9] For Kant, the sublime is "*absolutely [schlecthin] large*. To be large *[groß]* and to be a magnitude *[Groeße]* are quite different concepts. . . . Also, saying simply . . . that something is large is quite different from saying that it is *absolutely large*. . . . The latter is *what is large beyond all comparisons* [Kant's emphasis]" (Kant 103). For Kant, the absolutely large is produced by a "catch" in the mind of the subject:

> [The sublime] is produced by the feeling of a momentary inhibition of the vital forces followed immediately by an outpouring of them that is all the stronger. Hence it is an emotion, and so it seems to be seriousness, rather than play, in the imagination's activity. Hence, too, this liking is incompatible with charms, and, since the mind is not just attracted by the object but is alternately always repelled as well, the liking for the sublime contains not so much a positive pleasure as rather admiration and respect, and so should be called a negative pleasure. (Kant 98)[10]

Music and the Sublime

The very works that were at the center of the new concept of the masterpiece in the eighteenth century were considered sublime to writers of the period. According to James Webster, "The musical sublime . . . developed in the period bounded roughly by the mid-1780s and the death of Beethoven: in Mozart's and Haydn's late orchestral music, in *Don Giovanni* and *The Magic Flute*, in Beethoven's 'heroic phase' and, later, the *Missa Solemnis* and the *Ninth Symphony*."[11] And Elaine Sisman points out that "it was van Swieten who suggested to Haydn that the words 'And God said "Let there be Light" and there was light' be set only once in *The Creation*. . . . Haydn's overpowering C-major tutti on the word 'Licht,' in its brevity, simplicity, sudden loudness, transition from darkness to overpowering light, and magnificence produces a sense of wonder and awe, transport and respect."[12]

Writing in the 1830s, Gustav Schilling claims, "The sublime is exclusively expressed in beautiful simplicity of layout and execution, and it makes its effect solely by means of its massive power. Thus we find the sublime in many large-scale sacred works by famous composers, especially in this case because the sublime easily flows over into the solemn and the splendid. . . . The Overture to Handel's *Messiah*, the 'Hallelujah' Chorus . . . are all sublime and hence beautiful."[13] For Schilling the sublime must contain a component of the beautiful, in order for it to be comprehensible.[14]

Johann Georg Sulzer discusses the need to attempt to measure the sublime: "We must have a yardstick by which we seek to measure the extent of the sublime, even if unsuccessfully. Where this yardstick is lacking, its grandeur evaporates or degenerates into mere bombast."[15]

While these writers understand the sublime in music generally, the early nineteenth-century writer Christian Friedrich Michaelis offers an account of how specific musical materials can evoke the sublime: "The maintenance of one fixed unchanging idea, and the holding and piling up of dissonances are techniques that are employed in music solely for two purposes: either to express the sublime or to intensify the music's impact and to give it bite . . . ; such procedures always cause a certain degree of unrest or pain, which in turn arouses our vital forces and enhances our vital forces when the unrest is assuaged."[16] Michaelis's language is Kantian in both the sense that the sublime combines an affective response of pleasure and discomfort, as well as the idea that the sublime impedes the flow of cognition in the subject. And further:

> The feeling of sublimity in music is aroused when the imagination is elevated to the plane of the limitless, the immeasurable, the unconquerable. This happens when such emotions are aroused as either completely prevent the integration of one's impressions into a coherent whole, or when at any rate they make it very difficult. The objectification, the shaping of a coherent whole, is hampered in music in two principle ways. Firstly, by uniformity so great that it almost excludes variety: by the constant repetition of the same note or chords, for instance; by long, majestic, weighty or solemn notes, and hence by very slow movement; by long pauses holding up the progress of the melodic line, or which impede the shaping of a melody.[17]

In an article from 1801, Michaelis discusses a masculine and feminine sublime. For him, the masculine sublime in music has quick modulations, stormy textures, and is outwardly restless; the feminine sublime is subdued, understated, simple:

First there is the well-known version of the sublime in music which I would like to call the "masculine-, or ode-like sublime," after the analogy with the human character, suggesting an image of the sudden, courageous, and powerfully extroverted activities of Man. Second, there is a sublime which could be called an elegiac sublime, which, with its still enormity [stillen Größe] and noble humility [edlen Zurückgezogenheit], can be compared to the feminine character. The motion of modulations in this type [of the musical sublime] is serious . . . quiet and moderate; there is a greater simplicity; forward motion is less bold, less sudden, than in the other type [the masculine sublime]. Depressed resignation [schwermütige Resignation] seems to determine its mood.[18]

Writing of the delicacy of Chopin's music, Franz Liszt uses language that suggests an affective response mingling pleasure mixed with aversion. Liszt suggests that the Chopin mazurkas evoke

flowers of mourning like those black roses of depressing fragrance, their petals dropping from fragile stems at the slightest breath; weakened flashes kindled by false vanities, similar to the shine of certain lifeless woods that glisten in darkness; pleasures without past or future snatched from chance encounters; illusions, unexplainable fancies that summon us to adventure like those tart flavors of half-ripened fruit that please while setting the teeth on edge.[19]

Schubert's Songs and Sublime Delicacy

In suggesting that the songs of Schubert selected here embody a dimension of the delicate sublime, I will focus on repeated pitches in "Die liebe Farbe" from Die schöne Müllerin, "Der Wegweiser" from Winterreise, "Ihr Bild," "Die Stadt," and "Der Doppelgänger" from Schwanengesang.[20] The history of common-practice music is full of instances of conventionally subdivided note values. Repeating notes is often a trivial example of simply extending a pitch, energizing a long-held note by an instrument that does not sustain very well. Repeated notes on the piano are frequently used for just this purpose. Notes in many baroque pieces are repeated by stringed instruments as a way of providing a full and rich sound (baroque bows are much "weaker" than modern bows that can sustain pitches easily). But there are examples, particularly in Schubert's songs, in which notes are repeated in ways that go well beyond conventional extension of pitches.

I believe there are two meanings to the word "repetition" that obtain to Romantic music in general, and particularly to the works of Schubert under discussion here. I refer to them as "repetition" and "reiteration." Repetition produces a series as in (1, 2, ...); reiteration produces the paradoxical notion of a parallel series as in (..., 1, 1, ...). Repetition produces a series that is teleological; reiteration goes nowhere.[21] *Repetition* serves symbolic mastery and representation (the Kantian "beautiful"); *reiteration* serves that which resists symbolization (the Kantian "sublime"). Through repetition, meanings change; through reiteration a moment tries over and over again to register in symbolic space and fails.[22]

I will suggest that reiterative pitches embody the gaze in the works at hand. I argued in the previous chapter that the gaze emerges in orchestral musical performance when seeing seeing occurs at a void in the heart of the modern symphonic masterpiece. In the vocal works below, the texts to which the songs are set are all about seeing ("Die Stadt" and "Der Doppelgänger" in particular); in these works the text is not only about seeing but seeing *blocked*, either literally (by the fog of "Die Stadt") or metaphorically (by the inability of the narrator to recognize his own double in "Der Doppelgänger.") Reiterated notes that set failed sight in these works "gaze" at us.

In "Die liebe Farbe" and "Der Wegweiser," the gaze is less directly an embodiment of failed sight. In "Die liebe Farbe," a single note is reiterated across the entire score, gazing at us as an embodiment of a narrator whose imagination fluctuates between celebration and a brutally dark premonition of death. Both of these affective states oscillate back and forth in iterations of the line "Mein Schatz hat's grün so gern." In "Der Wegweiser" the musical gaze is set as an embodiment of a narrator caught between registering "the signpost" as a literal sign pointing to a town and a metaphorical sign pointing to his own death.

"Die liebe Farbe"

"Die liebe Farbe" from *Die schöne Müllerin* is a strophic song in B minor. Wilhelm Müller's text is provided below in both German and English:[23]

> In Grün will ich mich kleiden,
> in grüne Thränenweiden:
> Mein Schatz hat's Grün so gern.
> Will suchen einen Cypressenhain,
> eine Haide von grünem Rosmarein:
> Mein Schatz hat's Grün so gern.

Wohlauf! zum fröhlichem Jagen!
Wohlauf durch Haid' und Hagen!
Mein Schatz hat's Jagen so gern.
Das Wild, das ich jage, das ist der Tod,
die Haide, die heiss' ich die Liebesnoth:
Mein Schatz hat's Jagen so gern.

Grabt mir ein Grab im Wasen,
deckt mich mit grünem Rasen:
Mein Schatz hat's Grün so gern.
Kein Kreuzlein schwarz, kein Blümlein bunt,
grün, alles grün, so rings und rund:
Mein Schatz hat's Grün so gern.

I'll clothe myself in green,
in green weeping willow:
my love does so like green.
A grove of cypresses I'll seek,
a heath of green rosemary:
my love does so like green.

Up, away to the merry hunt!
Up, away over heath and hedge!
My love so loves the hunt.
The game I hunt is death;
the heath I call Love's Plight;
my love so loves the hunt.

Dig me a grave in the grass,
cover me with green turf:
my love does so like green.
No black cross, no bright flowers,
green, all green, all round!
My love does so like green.

Schubert repeats each instance of the line "Mein Schatz hat's Grün so gern" saturating this strophic setting both with this line and the rich rhyme "Schatz hat's" (see Figure 17).

The work is in B minor prolonged by its dominant. All tonic-dominant pairings involve a common tone: scale degree five of any tonic triad is the same note as scale degree one of the dominant. But Schubert has f-sharp[1] as a sixteenth note in every measure of the work. It's hard to imagine a more obsessive, stuck note that gazes out at the listener. The note is embedded in the piano accompaniment from measures 1–4 and

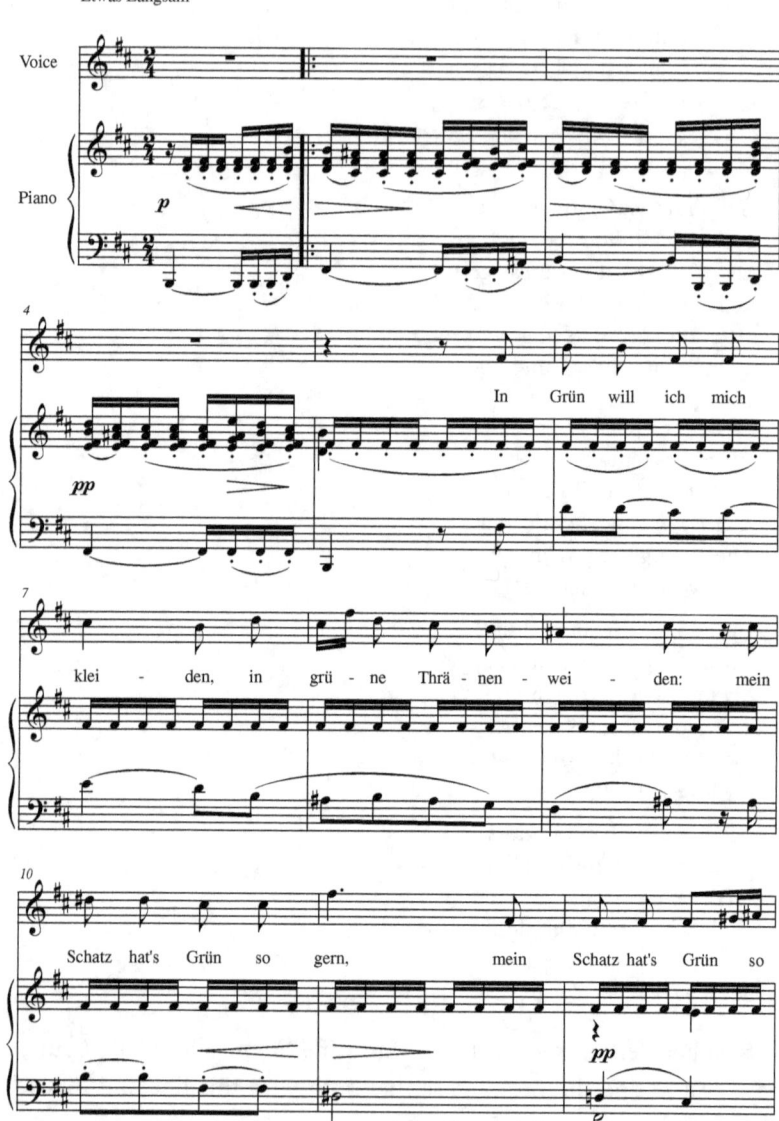

Figure 17

in the postlude from measures 23–26. The gaze is revealed as the voice enters; notice the f-sharp¹s almost all alone on the treble staff (piano right hand) from measures 5–21. I hear the f-sharp¹ of measures 5–21 stuck against the clear, diatonic motion from tonic B minor through its dominant to a perfect authentic cadence in measure 22. For me, the

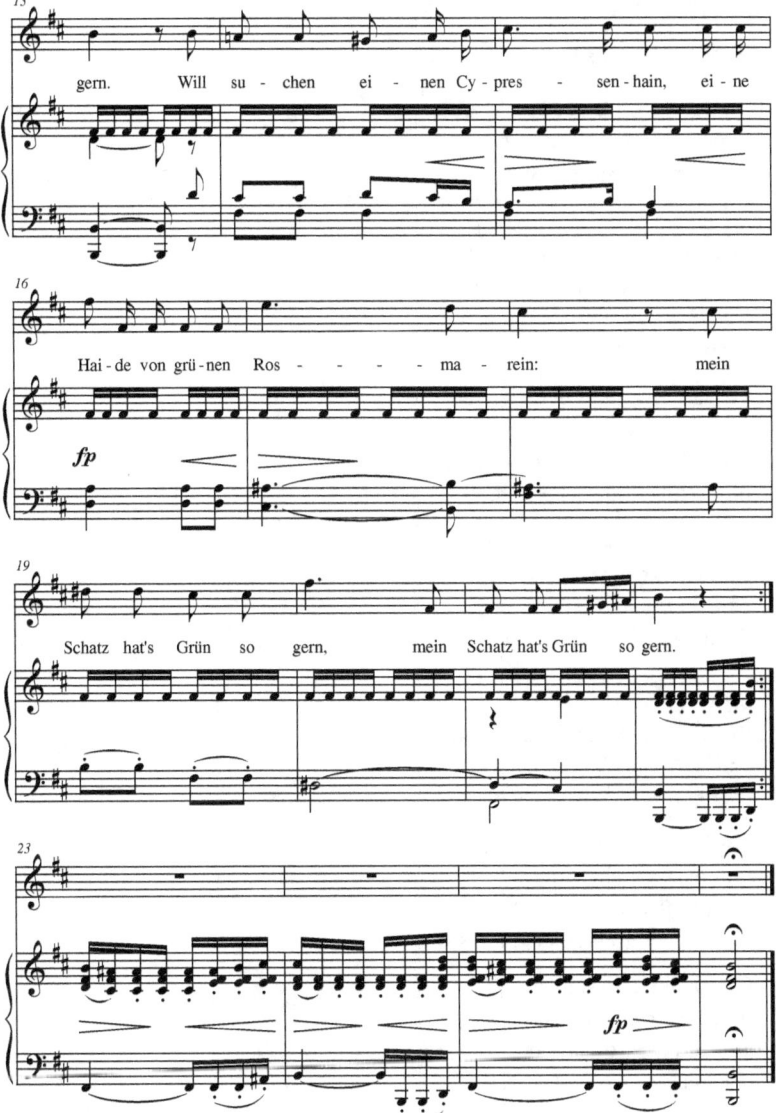

delicate sublime emerges here precisely between a conventional, diatonic harmonic motion (i V i in B minor) and a detail that tugs gently
at that very conventional motion (f-sharp^{1}s that saturate measures 5–21).
In exaggerating the role of f-sharp^1 in "Die liebe Farbe," against the conventional tonic-dominant polarity, Schubert evokes a sublime moment
at which the attention of the listener is "caught."[24]

"Der Wegweiser" from *Winterreise* (1827)

Wilhelm Müller's text:

> Was vermeid' ich denn die Wege,
> wo die andern Wandrer gehn,
> suche mir versteckte Stege
> durch verschneite Felsenhöhn?
>
> Habe ja doch nichts begangen,
> daß ich Menschen sollte scheun,
> welch ein törichtes Verlangen
> treibt mich in die Wüstenein?
>
> Weiser stehen auf den Straßen,
> weisen auf die Städte zu,
> und ich wandre sonder Maßen,
> ohne Ruh' und suche Ruh.'
>
> Einen Weiser seh' ich stehen
> unverrückt vor meinem Blick;
> eine Straße muß ich gehen,
> die noch keiner ging zurück.
>
> Why do I avoid the ways
> that the other wanderers tread,
> and seek out hidden paths
> over snowy rocky heights?
>
> For I have done nothing wrong
> that I should shun men —
> what foolish craving
> drives me into desolate places?
>
> On roads stand sign-posts
> pointing to towns,
> and I wander on and on
> restlessly searching for rest.
>
> One sign-post I see standing,
> immovable, before my gaze;
> one road I must travel, by which
> no one has yet returned.[25]

Müller's cycle tells the story of a narrator who leaves the house of his beloved and wanders a winter landscape that mirrors in its frozen desolation the interior alienation of the narrator. "Der Wegweiser" occurs

near the end of the cycle. The signpost is at once a literal signpost pointing the way to the social space from which the narrator is alien, and it is
a metaphorical signpost pointing to his own death (see the last stanza
of the work).

Schubert begins his setting of this text with a reiterated g-natural[1]
reminiscent of the reiterated pitches of "Die liebe Farbe." For the first
three lines of the last stanza ("Einen Weiser seh' ich stehen / unverrückt
vor meinem Blick; / eine Straße muß ich gehen"), Schubert sets a sequen-
tial, chromatic progression. I will point out the essential stasis of this
progression below (see Figure 18).

The progression shown in Figure 18 is characterized by semitonal
motion in the bass. It begins in measure 57 with a fully diminished
seventh chord (C-sharp in the bass); measure 58 is a second-inversion
G-minor triad (with D-natural in the bass); measure 59 is a root-position
dominant seventh chord (E-flat in the bass). These three chords provide the building block for this chromatic progression. In measure 60,
the fully diminished seventh chord returns, this time in first inversion
(with E-natural in the bass). Measure 61 is a second-inversion B-flat
minor triad (with F-natural in the bass). The next chord would logically
have been a root-position dominant seventh chord with F-sharp or
G-flat in the bass. Schubert omits this chord, and I have put the chord
in parentheses to show its omission. Measure 62 is a second-inversion,
fully diminished seventh chord (with G-natural in the bass). Measure 63
is a second-inversion C-sharp minor triad (with G-sharp in the bass).
Measure 64 is a root-position dominant seventh chord (with A-natural
in the bass) that Schubert uses as a dominant of the dominant to move
back to G minor.

If the progression had continued for four more measures, Schubert
would have ended up precisely where he began in measure 57. The slurs
in the example show that the entire progression projects horizontally, the
same fully diminished seventh chord presented vertically in measure
57. The progression goes nowhere; it is an example of a *Teufelsmühle* (or
"Devil's Mill").[26] The sublime dimension is opened (remembering
Sulzer's "yardstick") in the space between the diatonic tonic-dominant
polarity of the work (and its perfect authentic cadence in measure 67,
not shown in the figure) and the "Teufelsmühle" of measures 57–64 that
goes nowhere.

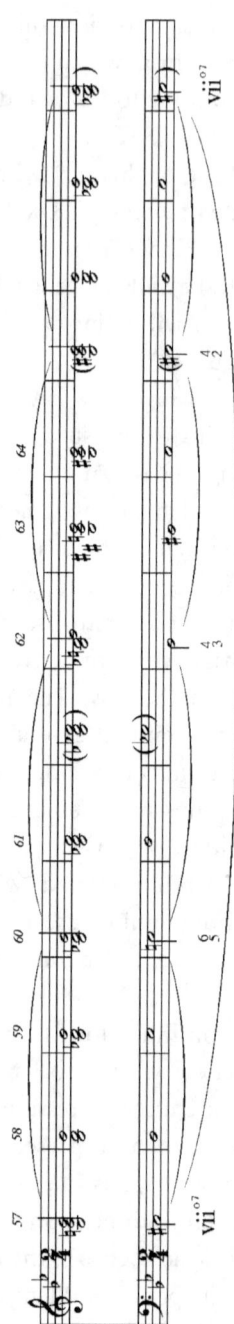

Figure 18

"Ihr Bild" from *Schwanengesang* (1828)

Schubert set six of the songs included in *Schwanengesang* to texts by
Heinrich Heine, a Jewish, German poet of the early nineteenth century
who imported the short line and simple imagery from folk poetry into
his high-art lyric. In much of his poetry, Heine explores in understated
lyric intensity issues of alienation from social space and from romantic
desire.[27] Heine's text:

"Ihr Bild"

Ich stand in dunklen Träumen
Und starrt' ihr Bildnis an.
Und das geliebte Antlitz
Heimlich zu leben begann.

Um ihre Lippen zog sich
Ein Lächeln wunderbar,
Und wie von Wehmutstränen
Erglänzte ihr Augenpaar.

Auch meine Tränen flossen
Mir von den Wangen herab.
Und ach! ich kann es nicht glauben,
daß ich dich verloren hab!

I stood darkly dreaming,
staring at her picture,
and that beloved face
sprang mysteriously to life.

About her lips played
a wondrous smile.
And as with sad tears
gleamed her eyes.

And my tears flowed
upon my cheeks,
And ah, I cannot believe
that I have lost you![28]

In *Listening Subjects*, I described Schubert's setting of this poem as an
acoustic mirror that fills with the image of the narrator's beloved. The A
section of the work is measures 1–14. As the poem moves from the narrator in dreams, to the image in the picture, to a hallucinatory evocation of

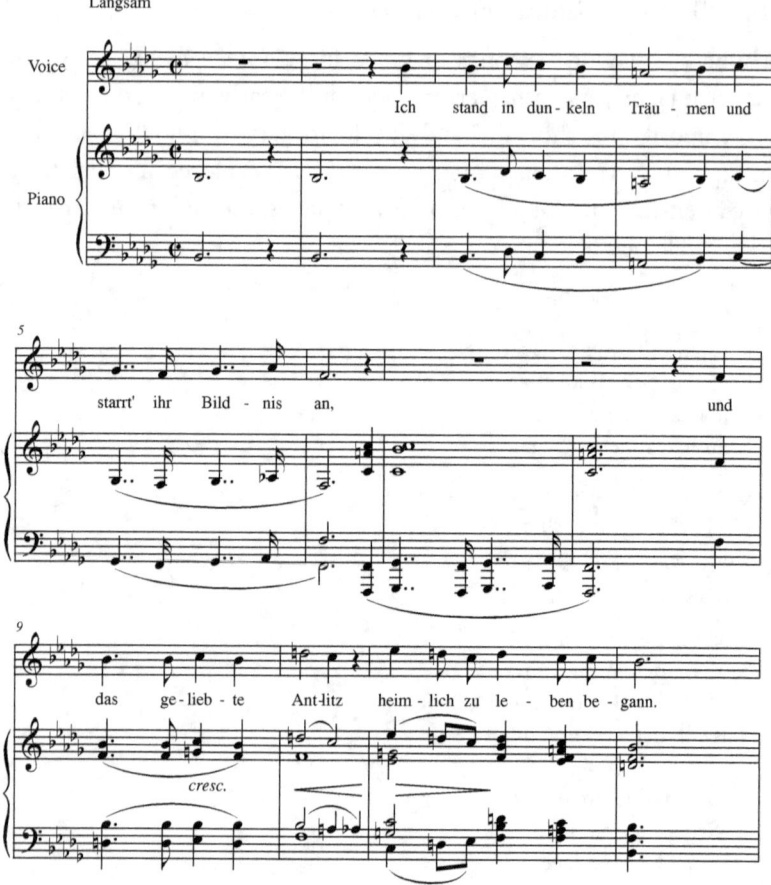

Figure 19

its coming to life, so, too, the music begins at the fringes of B-flat minor and fills to a full, four-part texture in B-flat *major* (measures 11–12; see Figure 19).

But the filling in of an acoustic mirror could have taken place if Schubert had written a single B-flat/b-flat octave at the outset of the work. In one of his first published essays, the music theorist Heinrich Schenker says the following about these two notes:

Since one can certainly not yet speak of these notes as a motive, the question arises, what purpose do these notes fulfill? Are we supposed to think that they introduce the key and give the singer his first note, or both? Whatever the case may be, we have got to ask why the master has the same note rearticulated when it would have been possible simply to hold one note for two measures. And in fact the solution to this riddle seems obvious. To repeat this tone in a slow tempo means to stare at it, and in doing so, we stand side-by-side the unhappy lover who stands "in dark dreams" staring at his beloved's picture.[29]

The poem is about the gaze with an implied inversion across the entire poem as the subject of the gaze at the beginning becomes its object at the end (the image in the picture/mirror vanishes and the lover ends up looking in horror at his own reflection). The reiterated B-flats at the outset of this work are like blinking eyes trying to make out what it only indistinctly sees.[30]

"Die Stadt" is the focus of this chapter. Heine's text:

Am fernen Horizonte
Erscheint wie ein Nebelbild,
Die Stadt mit ihren Thürmen,
In Abenddämm'rung gehüllt.

Ein feuchter Windzug kräuselt
Die graue Wasserbahn;
Mit traurigem Takte rudert
Der Schiffer in seinem Kahn.

Die Sonne hebt sich noch einmal
Leuchtend vom Boden empor,
Und zeigt mir jene Stelle,
Wo ich das Liebste verlor.[31]

On the far horizon
appears, as a misty shape,
the town with its spires,
shrouded in dusk.

A dank breeze ruffles
the grey waterway;
with dreary rhythm
the boatman rows my boat.

The sun rears once more
gleaming from the earth,
and shows me that place
where I lost my love.[32]

"Die Stadt" describes the poet being rowed down a river away from a city. The poem consists of three stanzas of four lines each, in relatively clear iambic trimeter rhymed xaxa / xbxb / xcxc. The first stanza describes the city from a distance, shrouded in the fog of evening. Reality and illusion bleed into one another as the poet describes the city *as if* an image of fog. The second stanza moves closer to the poet with a modern, imagistic description of the waters of the river wrinkling. The ancient connection between poetry and music is evoked in the reference to the sad rhythm of the rower in whose boat the poet leaves the city.[33]

The authoritative edition of Heine poems shows a discrepancy in the text here. The text Schubert set has "meinem Kahn" in the last line of the second stanza. The phrase "meinem Kahn" is also clearly visible in the facsimile edition of *Schwanengesang,* written in Schubert's own hand. Yet the authoritative edition of Heine poems shows that the phrase should read "seinem Kahn." The phrase "seinem Kahn" would have made it that much clearer that the narrator is alien to the social space around him.

In the third stanza, the sun comes out and shows the poet that he has lost what is most dear to him. The poet enters the poem in two breathless moments in the last two lines: "Und zeigt *mir* jene Stelle / Wo *ich* das Liebste verlor." Note how the imagery gets blinded in these lines. While there are single, understated adjectives in the first two stanzas, there are no adjectives in the third—a grammatical correlate of the purity of the imagery of painful revelation. From the beginning, the poem zooms in, from horizon to city, to towers, to the waters of the river, to the boat, to the rower, to the poet himself. Then suddenly the sun whites out everything in a flash. The city becomes "jene Stelle" or "that place," and the poet looses not "Das Geliebte," a specific person, but "das Liebste"—that which was most dear to him.

The Introduction

The song is a readily audible ABA' form with a six-measure introduction and a six-measure postlude.[34] The left hand of the piano begins the piece with thirty-second-note C-natural octaves for the first beat of measure one followed by a continuation of the low C-natural as eighth note followed by eighth rest for beats two and three. Without seeing the key signature, we hear a piece in C—subtly major, since the C-natural octaves will let the natural third sound (partial five of the overtone series). The "con pedale" marking will bring out this resonating overtone. Measure 2 is a reiteration of measure 1 much as the B-flats in mea-

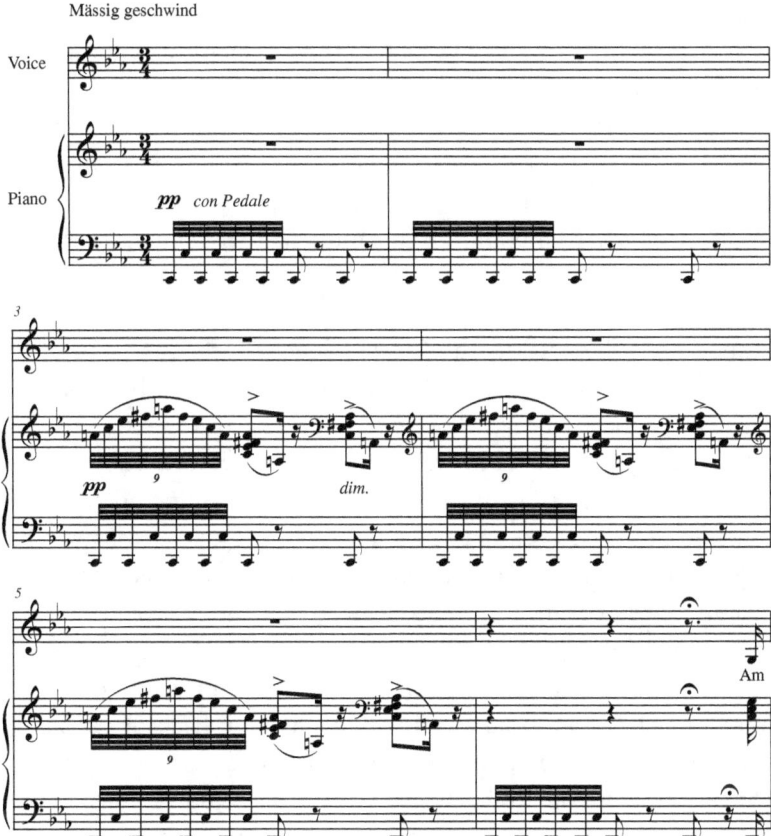

Figure 20

sure 2 of "Ihr Bild" are reiterations of the B-flats in measure 1 of that work. The octaves in both songs are like delimiters—pointers to a harmonic context that each song soon fills (Figure 20).

For measures 3, 4, and 5, the right hand of the piano overlays new material on the left hand. Upon the C-natural octaves, the right hand arpeggiates an F-sharp, fully diminished seventh chord. The nine-against-eight rhythm produces a blur of sound. Upon the eighth note C-naturals on beat two and three, the right hand plays an accented, fully diminished seventh chord followed by an A-natural sixteenth note. Upon the eighth note C-natural on beat *three*, the right hand plays the F-sharp, fully diminished seventh chord an octave lower followed by an A-natural sixteenth note, likewise an octave lower. Schubert's decision to write

those A-naturals as sixteenth notes insures that a brief silence will separate beat two from beat three, and beat three from the downbeat of the
next measure.

The right hand's music in these measures is reiterative like the left
hand's music. Measure 6 reiterates measure 1, getting stuck on the last
eighth rest of the measure. The fermatas on rests in measure 6 obliterate
the music's forward motion, as if the music were listening to itself.[35]

The A Section

Schubert sets the first stanza of Heine's poem in the A section of the
song from the upbeat of measure 7 through the first two beats of measure 14. Schubert sets each line of the poem to two-measure phrases
articulated by identical dotted-eighth rests in the vocal part.

The singer reads *leise* (quietly) before he sings his first note. The accompaniment had been marked pianissimo in measure 1. Pianissimo
suggests a demand to play very quietly; *leise* suggests a request to sing
quietly so as not to disturb someone or so that one can concentrate on
something hard to grasp (Figure 21).

The first two-measure vocal phrase moves from tonic to dominant
from the upbeat to measure 7 through the first two beats of measure 8.
The reiterated g-natural[1] embodies the narrator's gaze at the horizon.
The g-natural[1] is doubled by the top voice of the accompaniment an octave lower. The consonance of the phrase in C minor that shifts to a first
inversion chord in measure 7 is troubled by a highly dissonant a-flat[1] on
the downbeat of measure 8, like a ripple in what had been perfectly still
water. This A-flat sounds on the syllable "-zonte" of the word *Horizonte*
[horizon].

A-flat[1] comes into full acoustic view in the two-measure phrase from
the upbeat to measure 9 through the first two beats of measure 10. This
coming into view is embodied in the word *erscheint* [appears] on the
downbeat of measure 9. The vocal g-natural[1]/b-flat[1] on the syllables
"Nebel" stresses the a-flat[1] on the syllable "bild" as a double-neighbor
figure in measures 9–10. The music tonicizes the subdominant F minor
in measure 10 with the accompaniment's low C-natural that had begun
the piece in reiteration supporting a dominant seventh of subdominant
F minor in measure 9.

The subdominant F minor moves to the dominant for the third phrase
from the upbeat to measure 11 through the first two beats of measure 12.

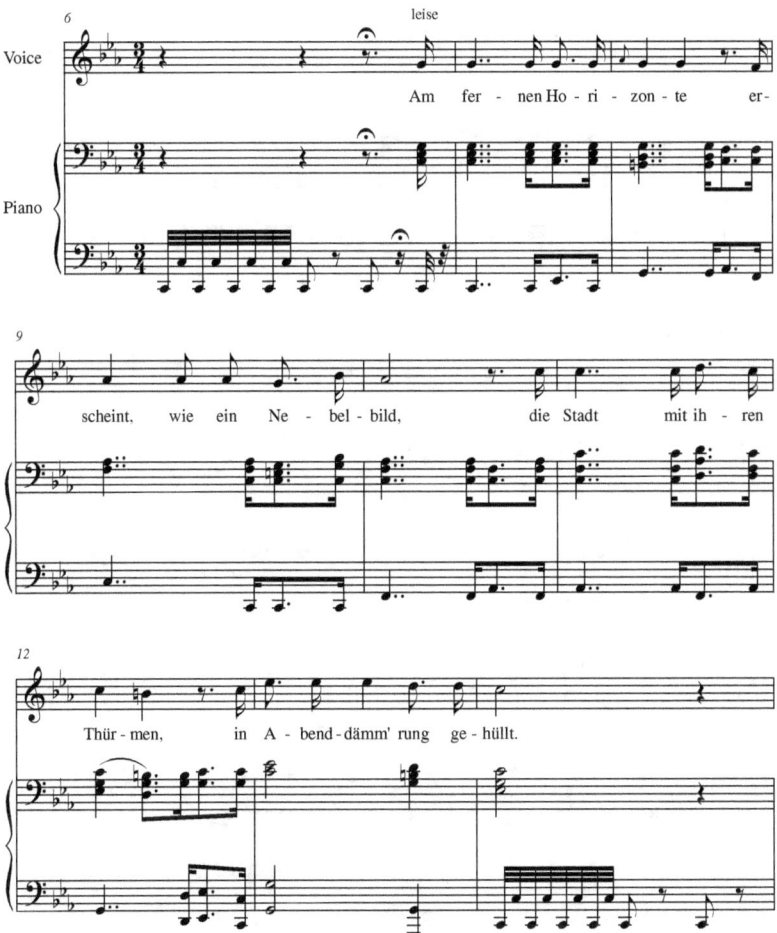

Figure 21

The vocal line stresses c-natural^2 with an upper neighbor note d-natural^2. The d-natural^2 in measure 11 sounds on the syllable "ih-" of "ihren" referring to the city with *its* towers. This bright, upper neighbor note is supported by a first inversion supertonic triad. This pointing gesture will become very important in the reworked material of the A section later in the work.

The fourth phrase of the A section from the upbeat to measure 13 through the first two beats of measure 14 brings the vocal line to its apex—e-flat^2 that descends elegantly through d-natural^2 to c-natural^2 in measures 13–14.

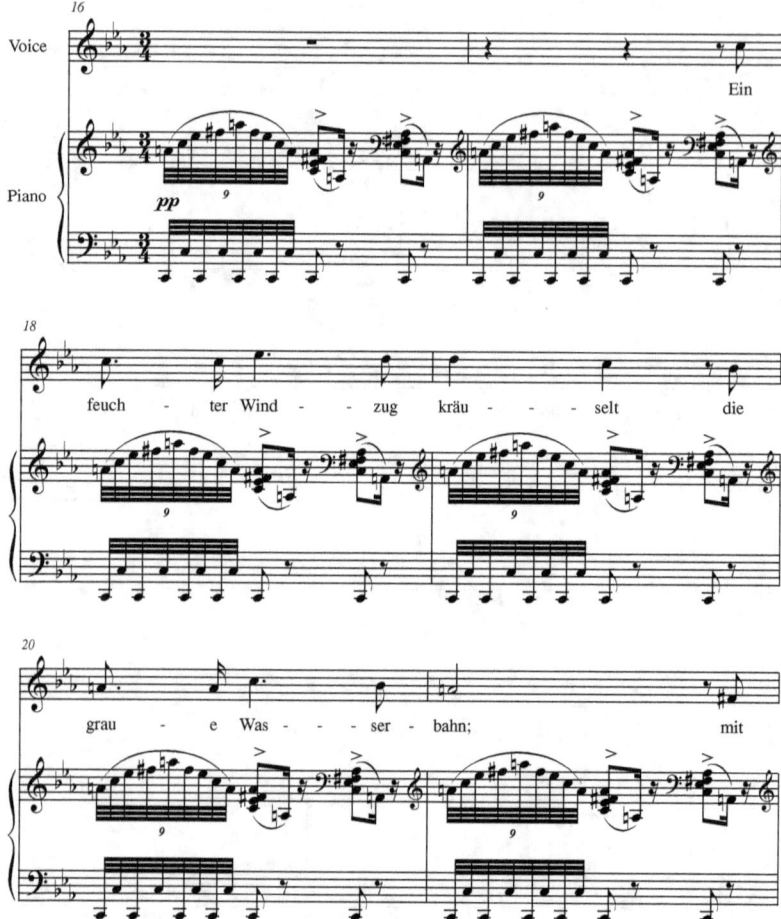

Figure 22

The B section

The B section of the song sets the second stanza of Heine's poem. The first stanza describes a city seen from the distance shrouded in fog; the second stanza zooms in quickly from the grey, wrinkled waters of the river to the slow measures of rowing in a boat. The grammatical and psychoanalytic subject of the poem has not yet been enunciated, although the rower is a surrogate for the subject who is about to appear (see Figure 22).

The entire accompaniment of the B section reiterates the music heard in measure 3—a musical correlate of the poem's imagery that zooms in to the immediacy of the implied subject's presence in a boat on grey,

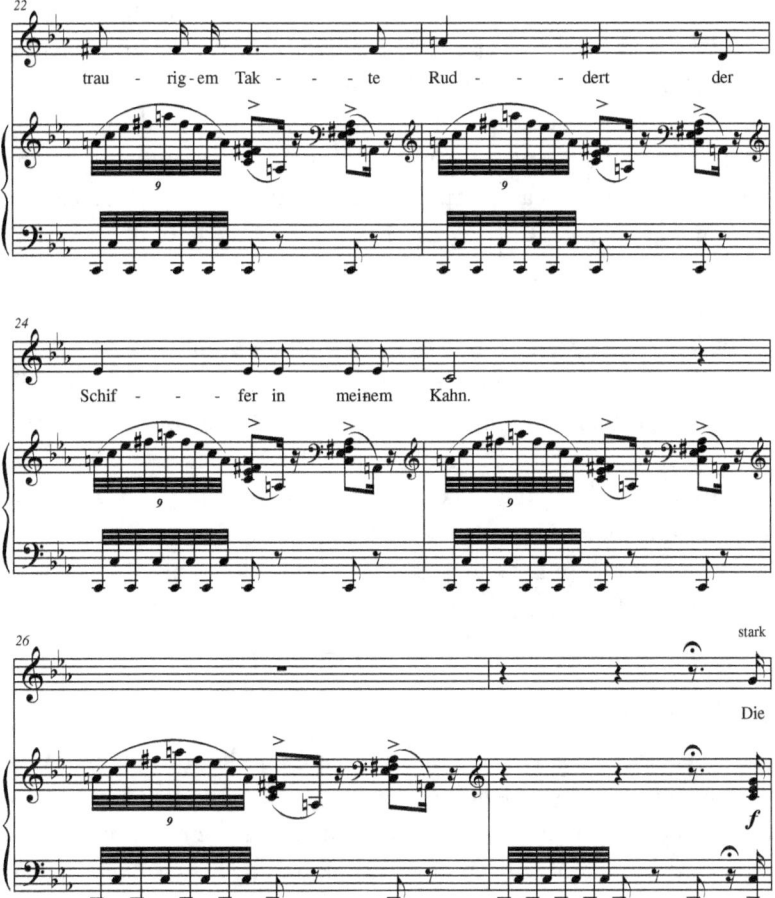

wrinkled waters. Schubert sets each line of the B section much as he
had each line of the A section, with short phrases separated from one
another by identical rests. In the A section the rests are dotted-eighth
rests; in the B section the rests are eighth rests. All four phrases of the A
section are exactly the same length: a sixteenth-note upbeat plus one
full measure plus two beats separated by a dotted-eighth rest. All four
phrases of the B section are not only the same as each other, they are
closely related to the lengths of the phrases of the A section: an eighth
note plus one full measure plus two beats plus an eighth rest.

The rising melodic motion of the A section cascades in a falling
motion in the B section. Like a gem slowly turned to show a single facet in
a new light, the vocal c-natural^2/e-flat^2/d-natural^2/c-natural^2 of measures

12–14 are stretched out over measures 17–19. The d-natural[2] on the downbeat of measure 19 is particularly lovely—the dissonant, accented passing tone "kräu-" of "kräuselt" wrinkles.

A rhythmically much weaker unaccented passing-tone b-flat[1] brings the second phrase down to a-natural[1] tentatively in measure 20 and more resolutely in measure 21. The rest of the vocal line skips passing tones and arpeggiates the fully diminished seventh chord downward to c-natural[1]—the voice's lowest note at the end of the B section in measure 25.[36]

The large-scale prolongation of the F-sharp, fully diminished seventh chord from the introduction across the entire B section is extraordinarily static. We had heard a similar, large-scale prolongation of a fully diminished seventh chord in the *Teufelsmühle* of "Der Wegseiser." The prolongation of the F-sharp fully diminished seventh chord in "Die Stadt" is much more bold. The only yardstick the listener has against which to measure its static, musical expanse is the bookend A and A' sections of the work and the perfect authentic cadences of measures 13–14 and 34–35 in C minor.[37]

The A' section

The A' section of the song sets the third stanza of the poem in which the sun comes out. The moment is one of recognition, sudden, unprepared, and blinding. The first-person pronoun enters the poem in two stages— in the dative "mir" of the penultimate line and the first-person singular "ich" of the final line. Grammar and psychoanalysis merge at the point at which the subject is enunciated (Figure 23).

Schubert sets this moment of recognition with a sudden shift in dynamic level from the *leise* of measure 6 to the *stark* of measure 27. The close-position harmonies of the A section that had been in the middle of the bass clef are raised an octave in the A' section with octave support that emerge right out of the C-natural octaves with which the piece had begun.

The first phrase of the A' section from the upbeat of measure 27 through the first two beats of measure 29 stresses the gazing g-natural[1] as in the A section, measures 7–8. While a-flat[1] had tentatively peeked out of the music in measure 8, a-flat[1] is a dissonant upper neighbor to g-natural[1] held for a full quarter note on the first beat of measure 29— a musical sneer on the syllable "ein-" of the word *einmal* (once).

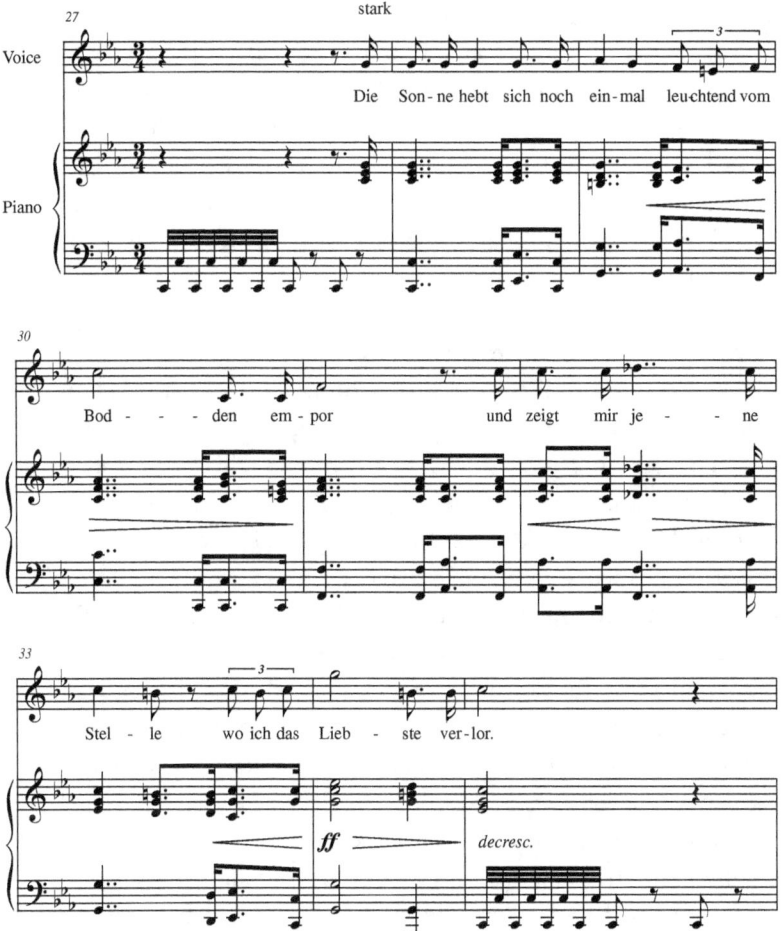

Figure 23

The second phrase moves from the upbeat to measure 30 through the first two beats of measure 31. Schubert represents the sun piercing the sky as if from the ground with the octave leap in measure 30 from c-natural² to c-natural¹.

The third phrase from the upbeat to measure 32 through the first two beats of measure 33 prolongs a subdominant (stained by a Neapolitan harmony to be discussed below) followed by a dominant harmony. Schubert marks the dramatic Neapolitan chord on the second beat of measure 32 for memory in a number of ways.[38] The d-flat² in the vocal line on the second beat of measure 32 is a chromatic version of the d-*natural*² of the third beat of measure 11. The d-natural^2 of measure 11 points to the towers of the city shrouded in fog; the d-*flat*^{2} of measure 32 points to a "Stelle," a site, a container of place.[39] The Neapolitan harmony is articulated by a crescendo and a shift in rhythm. Rhythmically, measures 7–12 and 28–31 begin with a double-dotted quarter note followed by sixteenth/dotted-eighth/sixteenth note. Schubert shifts the double-dotted quarter note to the second beat of measure 32 to articulate the Neapolitan.[40]

Leonard Meyer, in *Emotion and Meaning in Music*, argues that we expect patterns to continue. His debt to Gestalt psychology is well known. When patterns are disrupted, a structural gap is opened creating an emotional response. Schubert's rhythmic shift to emphasize "that place" with the Neapolitan is just such a structural gap. This gap remains open. Schubert does not reinstate the double-dotted quarter note followed by sixteenth/dotted-eighth/sixteenth note rhythm in the work.[41]

Harmonic theory of the Riemannian tradition teaches the Neapolitan as an altered subdominant. Schubert tonicizes the subdominant F minor with a dominant seventh chord in measure 30 leading to a root position subdominant on the downbeat of measure 31. This chord moves to the slightly less stable first inversion on the third beat of the measure. The sound of a root position triad shifting to its first inversion and then back again is a familiar sound in "Die Stadt" whose origins can be heard in measure 7 as the root position tonic harmony (C minor) shifts to a first inversion triad on the third beat of the measure.

Hearing the d-flat^2 of "jene" in measure 32 come right out of the subdominant that was tonicized in the previous measures makes sense. The sound of a root position triad on the first beat of a measure moving to a weaker first inversion chord on a weak beat is *reversed* here as a harmonic correlate of the rhythmic shift discussed above. In measure 32 the dotted-eighth/sixteenth note *first beat* of the measure (a first inversion subdominant chord) is followed by a double-dotted quarter note *second beat* (a root-position altered subdominant).

The fourth phrase moves from the upbeat to measure 34 through the first two beats of measure 35. The g-natural^2 at the top of the tenor's range tears open not only measure 34 but the entire vocal line. This is the only moment in the piece marked fortissimo by Schubert. Both voice and piano crescendo to it and decrescendo away from it. The facsimile that Schubert corrected on his deathbed is provided in Figure 24.[42]

measure 34

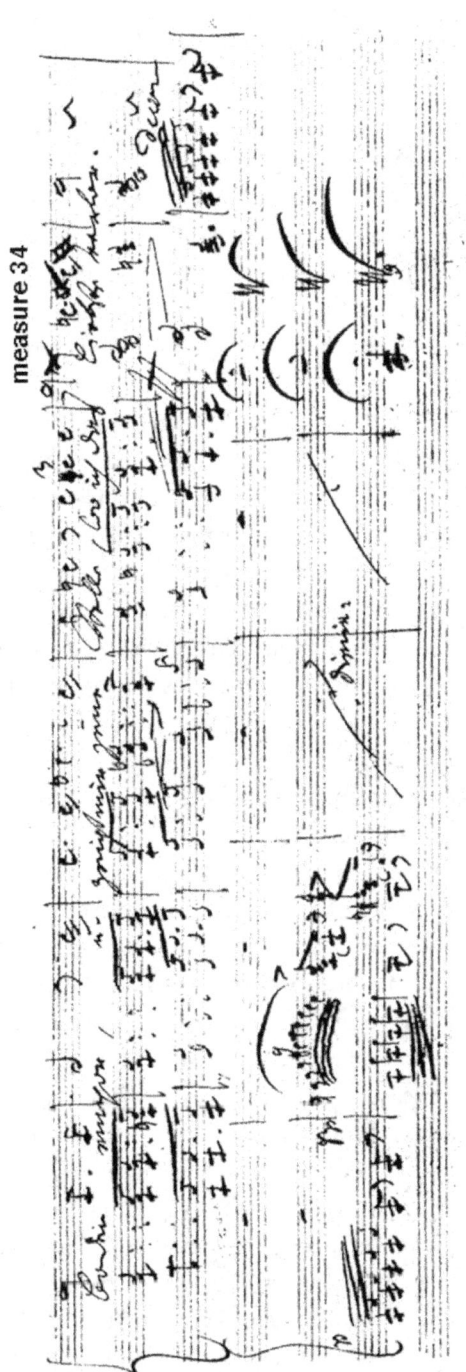

Figure 24

The autograph shows that Schubert had first set the words "Liebste verlor" in the vocal part to the pitches e-flat^2/d-natural^2/c-natural^2 (the crossed-out notes in measure 34). The sun comes out in the third stanza of Heine's poem to show the subject what he has lost (and in doing so, "who he is"—namely the subject of loss). Schubert's g-natural^2 on the downbeat of measure 34 connects back to the voice's initial g-natural^1 in measures 6–7 as a musical embodiment of shock lingering just beneath the surface of the narrator's gaze. See Figure 25 for a Schenkerian voice-leading sketch of the work bringing together these musical-analytical remarks.

The sketch offers no roman numeral description for the fully diminished seventh chord that is such a prominent sonority in the work—from measures 1–5, 16–25, and 37–39. The chord is nonfunctional—an embodiment of sublime delicacy in its reiterative insistence and lack of harmonic functionality. The chord is spelled as if it were a fully diminished seventh of the dominant, but it never moves to a dominant. It might be considered a fully diminished seventh chord built on the raised supertonic scale degree, but the chord does not contain a D-sharp (an enharmonically respelled E-flat). Stephen Slottow has suggested to me that the a-natural^1 of this chord moves to g-natural^1 of measure 6 as a diatonic version of the chromatic A-flat/G motion of measures 7–8 (vocal part) and measures 11–12 and 32–33.

I initially graphed the g-natural^1 of measure 6 as a half-note $\hat{5}$ to suggest an enormous, staring fifth scale degree that did not descend in the work;[43] g-natural^1 as $\hat{5}$ would then connect to the g-natural^2 of measure 34.[44] I have chosen, instead, to bring out both the static g-natural^1/g-natural^2 octave in the return of the A material (measures 27–35) within the context of a conventionally descending $\hat{3}$ line: e-flat^2 (in measure 34) is $\hat{3}$; d-natural^2 (in measure 34) is $\hat{2}$, c-natural^2 (in measure 35) is $\hat{1}$. The g-natural^2 (measure 34) functions as a cover tone over the fundamental line—connecting back to the g-natural^1 of measure 27, and, by extension, to the g-natural^1 of measure 6.[45] The dimension of the delicate sublime opens precisely in the space of the reiterative g-natural^1/g-natural^2 octave that covers up and is measured against (remembering Sulzer's "yardstick") the conventional descent. This structure of reiterative stuckness and conventional descent is embodied in the relationship between the voice and accompaniment in the work. The conventional fundamental line e-flat^2, d-natural^2, c-natural^2 is played by the *piano*; the *voice*

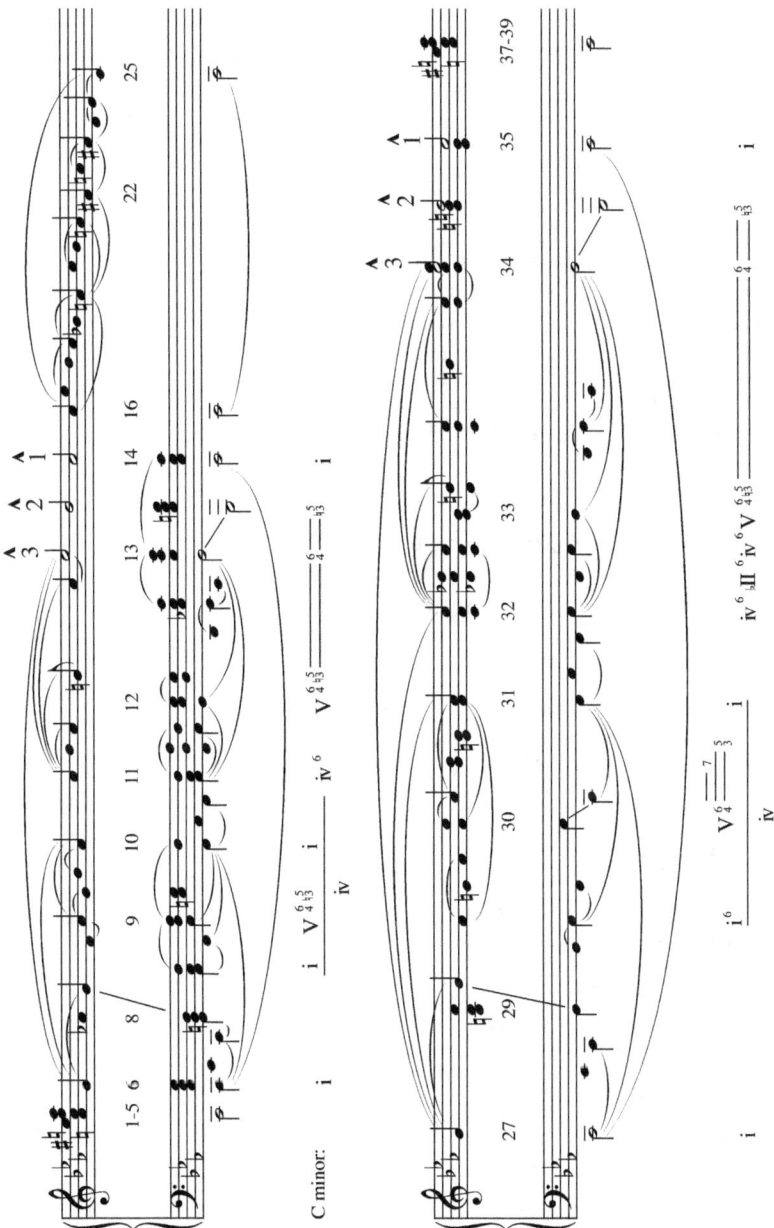

Figure 25

tears itself away from this line (with which it had sung in unison in measures 13–14) and reaches to the top of the tenor's range for the searing cover tone.

"Der Doppelgänger"

Heine's text:

> Still ist die Nacht, es ruhen die Gassen.
> In diesem Hause wohnte mein Schatz.
> Sie hat schon längst die Stadt verlassen,
> Doch steht noch das Haus auf demselben Platz
>
> Da steht auch ein Mensch und starrt in die Höhe
> Und ringt die Hände vor Schmerzensgewalt.
> Mir graust' es wenn ich sein Antlitz sehe,
> Der Mond zeigt mir meine eigne Gestalt!
>
> Du Doppelgänger, du bleiche Geselle
> Was äffst du nach mein Liebesleid
> Das mich gequält auf dieser Stelle,
> So manche Nacht in alter Zeit?

> Still is the night. The streets are at rest.
> Here is the house where my loved-one lived;
> long it is, since she left the town,
> yet the house still stands where it did.
>
> A man stands there too, staring up,
> wringing his hands in agony;
> horror grips me, as I see his face—
> the moon shows me my own self.
>
> Double! Pale companion!
> Why do you ape the torment of love
> that I suffered here
> so many nights in time past?[46]

I suggested in a note above that "Die liebe Farbe" is a study for "Der Doppelgänger." In the latter work, Schubert has an obsessive f-sharp^1 of measures 5–25 reach up to a dramatic f-sharp^2 on the word "Schmerzensgewalt" ("the violence of pain") in measure 31–32. The vocal line falls again to f-sharp^1 and rises to an excruciating g-natural^2 on the word *Gestalt* (form) in measure 41 (Figure 26).

The autograph shows that for the phrase "eigne Gestalt" Schubert first wrote f-sharp^2 followed by f-sharp^1 in measure 41 at the end of the

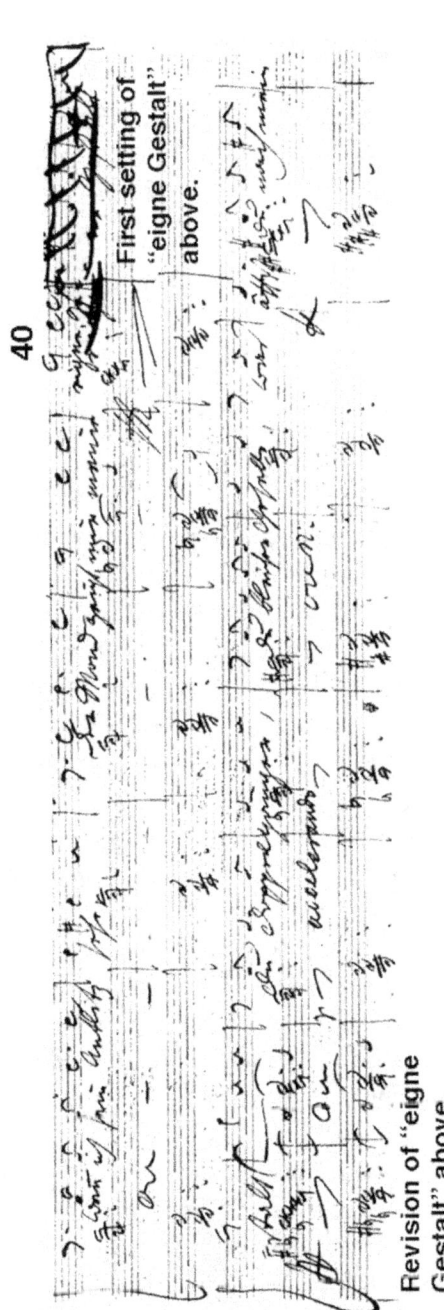

measure
40

First setting of "eigne Gestalt" above.

Revision of "eigne Gestalt" above.

Figure 26

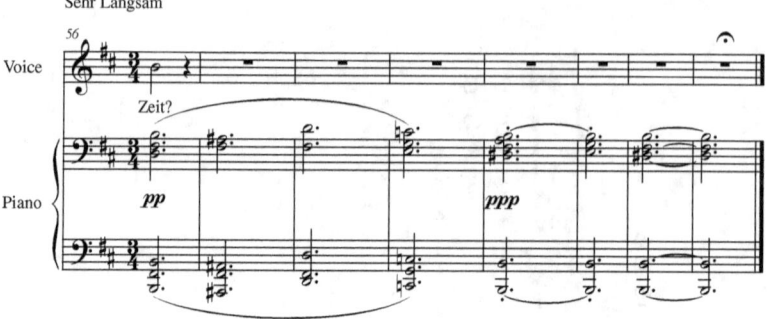

Figure 27

first system shown in the example. He scratched out this measure and wrote the g-natural[2] in its place in measure 41 at the beginning of the second system. This g-natural[2] is resolved by the f-sharp[2] of measure 52. The g-natural[2] also sinks into the postlude and resolves in an inner voice to the hint of E minor of measures 56–63. "Der Doppelgänger" ends evoking E minor with the final progression beginning with the C major of measure 59 sounding like the submediant of E minor. This chord is particularly lovely in its liberation of C-natural from its highly dissonant role in the work. C-natural had been a crucial note in the augmented sixth chords of measures 32 and 41; at measure 59 the note supports a completely consonant triad pointing to E minor.

B minor has always sounded in "Der Doppelgänger" as a B-natural$_1$ to B-natural octave divided by F-sharp (measures 1, 5, 9, 15, 19, 25, 29, 34, 38, and 43); in measures 60–63, however, the F-sharp is *gone*—a gesture of exquisite and liberating delicacy (Figure 27).

The delicacy of the open octaves with which the work ends is reinforced by the triple-piano dynamic marking and staccato markings—the only triple piano and staccato markings in the entire work.

I began this chapter discussing the sublime in Kant as mathematical (the endlessly large or the endlessly small number) and the dynamical (the overpowering presence of force in nature). I connected the Kantian sublime to music via Sulzer, Michaelis, and others. I suggested a dimension of the delicate sublime in Schubert songs that "catch" us between conventional meanings and reiterative elements that tug insistently at that very conventionality. This chapter's "catch" in the delicate sublime anticipates the ideé fixe of the discourse of hysteria in the next chapter.

The ideé fixe suggests that what we had thought of as "consciousness" actually consists of various *levels* of consciousness. Once nineteenth-century writers describe the unconscious as more than simply *not* conscious, the idea of split subjectivity emerges, leading to the discourse of modern psychoanalysis. The ideé fixe also prefigures traumatic experiences that mark the body and psyche of the subject.

CHAPTER THREE

Music and the Birth of Psychoanalysis

Anton Webern's Opus 6, no. 4

The last chapter described a certain "stuckness" in selected songs of Franz Schubert relating reiteration of pitches and chords, nonfunctional sonorities, and static progressions to the delicate sublime. These instances of music sticking might be seen, in the context of the present chapter, to prefigure the ideé fixe (hereafter referred to as the fixed idea) with which much of the discourse of hysteria (particularly in France) was concerned throughout the nineteenth century.[1]

This chapter will explore an early masterpiece of Anton Webern from perspectives that bring together a history of psychoanalysis and analysis of the musical work itself. The task of writing a history of psychoanalysis is of course immense and well beyond the scope of this chapter. What I will attempt, rather, is a history of the beginning of psychoanalysis in Western Europe, Britain, and America in the late nineteenth and early twentieth century. The closer one looks for such a beginning, the more the emergence of psychoanalysis recedes into the past, reaches into other modes of thought, and eludes one's grasp. I will focus on writings on hysteria for evidence of the basis of modern psychoanalysis—the existence of the unconscious and split subjectivity. Within discussions of hysteria, the element of traumatic shock runs as an undercurrent. An exploration of the writings of the period (particularly in France, Germany, England, and the United States) shows doctors fascinated by the relationships between ideas or states of mind and physical symptoms. The concept of the unconscious emerges gradually and quite tentatively in the writings of these men as they struggle to understand hysterical symptoms as products of genetics, heredity, degeneracy, accidents, traumatic experiences, and psychic states.[2]

I am interested in two things in writings on hysteria in the nineteenth century: (1) what was in the air in Webern's Vienna in the late nineteenth, early twentieth century as one aspect of the cultural context for one of his most powerful, oddly personal, and exquisite orchestral compositions, and (2) how writers of the period understood traumatic shock as at once the product of industrialization and the modernization of the workplace and the more interior scars left by accidents, diseases, and psychic shocks. I will then focus the discussion on Webern's *Orchesterstücke*, Opus 6, no. 4, "Marcia funebre."

The following roughly chronological overview of theories of hysteria and traumatic neuroses reaches beyond German culture to show that psychoanalysis evolved out of the discourse of hysteria in a broadly Western European and American context. The French theories of hysteria are based on various forms of *weakness*; the German theories are based on *ideas* that become imprinted on the body; and the English and American theories focus on dual consciousness and traumatic shock.[3] The emergence of the unconscious as more than simply "not" conscious or a repository of reflexes in the body took place gradually in all of the writings under discussion.

France

Representations of possession linked to women can be found across the entire expanse of Western history. According to Pierre Janet, writings of "possessions, choreas, epidemics of tarantism" can be found among the ancients.[4] Tourette locates the origin of hysteria in the following passage from Plato: "The uterus is an animal, hungry for children. If it remains unfruitful for an extended period after puberty, an infection ensues which spreads throughout the entire body, stopping the bronchial tubes and bringing utmost danger to the entire body."[5] According to Tourette, representations in art from the ancients to his day point to the continual presence of hysteria in Western consciousness, from a fifth-century ivory book cover showing a possessed woman being healed by Christ, to a sixth-century drawing of a woman "stiff" with the agonies of exorcism, to an eleventh-century bas-relief of a woman bent back in the throes of possession, and finally embodied in the practices of witch burning in France in the sixteenth and seventeenth centuries (Tourette 2–7).

Tourette suggests that, in 1618, Charles Lepois was one of the first to use the word *hysteria* to refer to a pathological disease affecting women. Lepois understood hysteria as a disease caused by pathology in the uterus that goes, literally, to the head of the patient (Tourette 8–9).[6] Tourette discusses the importance of the British writer Sydenham, who in 1681 argued that hysteria appears in both men and women as emotions ("Lebensgeister") that become located in a particular organ or part of the body (Tourette 10). In the eighteenth century, Tourette finds two doctors—Stahl (1724) and Hoffman (1730)[7]—who understand hysteria as caused by retention of the egg in the uterus.

The Salpêtrière asylum in Paris became the place where French theory of hysteria grew out of the practical work of caring for large numbers of women who, for a wide variety of reasons, were separated from Parisian social space of the nineteenth century.[8] Tourette considers Georget's work at the Salpêtrière crucial for the understanding of French theories of hysteria. In a treatise published in 1821, Georget is one of the first (according to Tourette) to acknowledge the "état second" [second state] characteristic of the hysteric.[9]

Charcot arrived at the Salpêtrière in 1862 and later began passing along his teachings to students through lectures and a few published papers (Tourette 17).[10] Charcot determined through observation of his patients at the Salpêtrière that the most common form of hysteria was the convulsive attack, and he sought to discover its rules and structure. By 1868, Charcot had arrived at an understanding distinguishing between hysteria and epilepsy (Tourette 17–18). In "Hysterie und Entartung beim Manne," he discusses male hysteria as the product of both mental and physical degeneration. Charcot mentions explicitly that hysteria can be brought on by misery, prefiguring later theories of the trauma of the everyday.[11]

Tourette worked closely with Charcot at the Salpêtrière, and their theories of hysteria largely coincide. For both, the primary cause of hysteria is weakness of body and spirit brought about by hereditary traits; for both, a secondary cause of hysteria can be the so-called agents provocateurs—or opportunistic trigger ("Gelegenheitsursachen") (Tourette 30). Agents provocateurs occupy the imagination of more and more writers throughout the second half of the nineteenth century.[12] These primary and secondary causes are central to French theories of hysteria in the nineteenth century.[13]

Tourette is acutely sensitive to the secondary causes of hysteria—the agents provocateur of opportunistic experience, particularly traumatic shocks. He points to the pioneering book of Mosso, who wrote at length of the role of fear in hysterical symptom formation.[14] For Tourette, repeated traumatic experiences can lead to hysterical symptoms, so he urges education without physical abuse (42–43) and domestic child rearing without exaggerated fear of punishment (43). Tourette sees an important difference between "nervous shocks" that are not dangerous and traumatic shocks that can be life-threatening.[15] He points out that in the late nineteenth century, theories of hysteria in relation to traumatic shock became more numerous due to the demands of victims of accidents to offer proof of diagnosis of injury in court cases (50).

Another student of Charcot, Pierre Janet, wrote at great length on hysteria, focusing on hypnotism and the fixed idea.[16] For Janet, while normal people process a continuous flow of experiences, hysterics fix on one; this fixation produces hysterical symptoms (225); for Janet, fixed ideas "install themselves in the mind in the fashion of a parasite" (267). According to Janet, fixed ideas are "those complete and automatic developments of an idea which take place outside the will and personal perception of the subject" (251). For Janet, such suggestions come from the "subconscious," and the way to get at them is through an artificially induced form of suggestion controlled by the doctor.[17] Hypnosis was seen as a technique with which the doctor could bring a patient back to a prior state with the hope of relieving the fixed idea and freeing the patient of the symptom.[18]

I would like to focus on the dual consciousness prefigured by the French notion of "état second" in the nineteenth century and the idea of "subconscious." Janet's "sub-conscious" is a place of actions "that . . . are not simple, mechanical reflexes; they are *intelligent acts* [emphasis Janet's], which can be understood only if we admit, as present in the mind of the subject, sensations, remembrances, and even complicated reflections" (254). For Janet, fixed ideas brought on by suggestion split consciousness and hide from the patient the causes of the symptom: "[a] tendency to suggestion and subconscious acts is the sign of mental disease, but it is, above all, the sign of hysteria" (277). And, weakness of body and mind produce hysterical symptoms according to Janet and French theory in the mid-nineteenth century.[19]

Alfred Binet is another student of Charcot whose work is based on the idea that a basic feature of hysteria is weakness: "The hysterical subject, as I, with many other observers, conceive him, is an exhausted subject."[20] Binet describes the unconscious that is characteristic of both normal people *and* hysterics alike as follows:

> For we are all possessed of an unconscious element, we all receive sensations of which we have no clear perception. Moreover modifications are continually taking place within us, which transmit unconscious impressions to our brain. And these divers obscure impressions are capable of suggesting ideas which appear all of a sudden in the light of consciousness, without our being able to guess at their origin. Perhaps our ideas most frequently originate thus, for they seem to summarize a work that goes on in the night of the unconscious.[21]

And further, Binet says,

> we perceive that the separation of the two consciousnesses does not interrupt all communication between them. The associations of ideas, of images, perceptions, and movements, that is, of all that pertains to the sphere of lower psychology, is preserved nearly intact; and hence an idea in the first consciousness provokes a movement in the second, and inversely, a sensation perceived by the second consciousness can awaken an idea in the first consciousness. (Binet, *On Double Consciousness*, 33)

Germany

While the French writers on hysteria have Charcot as a single major influence, Paris as a place of origin, and the Salpêtrière as an institution of origin, the German writers have no single, major figure and no primary city or institution from which to study hysterics. German writers on hysteria in the nineteenth century abandoned the French theories based on weakness as cause. P. J. Moebius turned decisively away from the idea that hysteria was caused by infection of the uterus and was particular to women. For Moebius, "all ill [krankhaft] changes in the body are hysterical to the extent that they are caused by illusions [Vorstellungen]."[22] Moebius discusses the relationship between normal changes in the body caused by ideas and pathological changes in the body caused by hysterical symptoms as follows: "crying, laughing, blushing, salivation, vomiting from disgust, cold sweats of anxiety, diarrhoea from fear, stiffness from shock. . . . Hysteria occurs when such conditions are triggered too easily or with too great a force by ideas [Vorstellungen]" (67).

For Moebius there is a continuum connecting normal and abnormal states of mind: "Hysteria is simply ill [krankhaft] intensification of a condition that is present in everyone. . . . Hysteria has absolutely nothing to do with the idea of exhaustion as it is applied to such conditions as neuraesthenia" (69).

In an article published a few years later, however, Moebius does ground hysteria in some form of degeneration, usually from an inherited predisposition: "Hysteria is always an endogenous disease [endogene Krankheit], which is to say that its main condition is a certain degree of degeneration [Entartung]."[23] Moebius thinks that in cases in which one is not born with such a predisposition to degeneration, acquired causes can include infectious diseases, alcoholism, and excessive stimulation [langdauernde Überreizung] (18). He also understands traumatic neuroses deriving from accidents caused by the accidents themselves and the fear of such accidents in laborers such as railway workers whose lives are just one false step away from injury (19). Thus Moebius has not entirely freed himself from the French notion of degeneration as essential to hysteria. He claims, on the one hand, that weakness has nothing to do with hysteria, and on the other, that hysteria is always the product of a predisposition.[24]

August Forel goes beyond Moebius in granting the possibility that hysterical symptoms can occur in perfectly healthy people. For him, acquired hysteria is completely plausible, although he still holds on to the idea that predisposition is a powerful precondition: "After physical trauma [physichen Traumata], after exhausting pain [erschöpfenden Leiden], even those without visible cause [nachweisbare Ursache], we see the appearance of acute, treatable hysteria, even in patients who had previously manifested absolutely no trace of pathology."[25] Forel's theories move away from the idea that hysteria is a disease to the idea that it is a structure governed by three principles:

1. Hysteria is not a closed disease [abgeschlossenes Krankheitsbild] but rather a pathological complex of symptoms or a syndrome. 2. This complex of symptoms can be either constitutional or acquired, and usually the two are combined with the first dominating. 3. This complex of symptoms reveals itself through a pathological suggestibility or auto-suggestibility. (93)

In a short article that appeared a year before his major study of hysteria with Josef Breuer, Freud uses the same language as Forel in referring to hysteria as a complex of symptoms. Freud distances himself from Janet, saying that the root cause of hysteria is a dreamlike, hypnoid state that leads to a splitting of consciousness. For Freud this hypnoid state is brought about not by a splitting of consciousness (Janet) but by an act of will: "the splitting of consciousness [die Spaltung des Bewusstseinsinhaltes] is the result of an act of will of the patient [die Folge eines Willensactes des Kranken]." Freud is quick to say that he does not think a patient intends to be hysterical and to have his or her consciousness split, but rather that the will of the patient misses its mark in seeking to master the hypnoid state, and a splitting of consciousness results.[26]

Freud discusses three forms of hysteria in which split consciousness works differently. The first form is hypnoid hysteria [Hypnoidhysterie], in which there is a hypnoid state and a splitting of consciousness accompanied by symptom formation. The second form is defense hysteria [Abwehrhysterie], in which acquired pathology develops that is not a product of inherited degeneracy. The third form, retention hysteria, [Retentionshysterie] is described as follows: "In the third form of hysteria . . . split consciousness plays a very small, perhaps nonexistent role. It is seen in cases in which only the reaction to traumatic stimuli remains [die Reaction auf traumatische Reize unterblieben ist], which are abreacted and cured, the pure retention hysteria" (364).

In his *Studies on Hysteria* (1893–95), coauthored with Breuer, Freud allies himself closely with Binet and Janet, linking hynoid states and double consciousness in hysteria.[27] Freud also approaches hysteria as acquired pathology resulting from traumatic experiences: "Our experiences have shown us . . . that the most various symptoms, which are ostensibly spontaneous and, as one might say, idiopathic products of hysteria, are just as strictly related to the precipitating trauma as the phenomena to which we have just alluded and which exhibit the connection quite clearly" (4). Freud goes on to say that some patients show symptom formations in hysteria that are symbolic: "[other cases exhibit] a 'symbolic' relation between the precipitating cause and the pathological phenomenon—a relationship such as healthy people form in dreams. For instance, a neuralgia may follow upon mental pain or vomiting upon a feeling of moral disgust. We have studied patients who used to make the most copious use of this sort of symbolization" (5). In this language Freud is anticipating his own work in dream interpretation, to be published only a few years later.[28]

Freud mentions quite clearly in *Studies on Hysteria* the powerful role of language in the psychoanalytic cure: "For we found, to our great surprise at first, that each individual hysterical symptom immediately and permanently disappeared when we had succeeded in bringing clearly to light the memory of the event by which it was provoked and in arousing its accompanying affect, and when the patient had described that event in the greatest possible detail and had put the affect into words" (6). Freud's understanding of hysteria and its traumatic "origins" thus rest on the splitting of affect from symbolization—a process retrospectively reinstated in what will be dubbed "the talking cure" of psychoanalysis.

In these pages Freud writes his famous sentence "Hysterics suffer mainly from reminiscences" (7). The long sentence that precedes this one is "We may reverse the dictum 'cessante cause cessat effectus' ['when the cause ceases the effect ceases'] and conclude from these observations that the determining process continues to operate in some way or other for years—not indirectly, through a chain of intermediate causal links, but as a *directly* releasing cause—just as a psychical pain that is remembered in waking consciousness still provokes a lachrymal secretion long after the event" (7; Freud's emphasis). Put simply, when the traumatic effect ceases, the cause ceases. What precisely continues to operate in the subject of hysteria brought on by trauma is at once a memory of traumatic events and a lack of completely successful symbolic, verbal abreaction (through autosuggestion or psychoanalytic cure). Freud's understanding of symbolic abreaction relates to an inability to forget. He speaks of the normal "fading away" of memories, which in hysterical subjects actually becomes stronger and stronger. In such cases "these memories correspond to traumas that have not been sufficiently abreacted" (10).

For Freud there are two conditions under which hysterical symptoms brought about by traumatic experiences do not "wear away" normally. In the first "are those cases in which the patients have not reacted to a psychical trauma because the nature of the trauma excluded a reaction, as in the case of the apparently irreparable loss of a loved person or because social circumstances made a reaction impossible or because it was a question of things which the patient wished to forget, and therefore intentionally repressed from his conscious thought and inhibited and suppressed" (10).[29] And "the second group of conditions are determined, not by the content of the memories but by the psychical states in which the patient received the experiences in question" (10). In conclusion, Freud argues that "it may therefore be said that the ideas which have become pathological have persisted with such freshness and affective strength because they have been denied the normal wearing-away process by means of abreaction and reproduction in states of uninhibited association" (11).

In discussing the repression of an insult as a traumatic experience, Freud's coauthor Breuer points out that "if the original affect was discharged not in a normal but in an 'abnormal' reflex, this latter is equally released by recollection. The excitation arising from the affective idea is 'converted' (Freud) into a somatic phenomenon" (206). And further: "The experiences which released the original affect, the excitation of which was then converted into a somatic phenomenon, are described by us as *psychical traumas* [Breuer's emphasis], and the pathological manifestation arising in this way, as hysterical symptoms of traumatic origin" (209). We have seen above how Freud and Breuer use the terms "unconscious" and "repressed" for the first time in this joint publication; Breuer refers as well to the idea of overdetermination with regard to the complexity of factors leading to hysterical symptom formation: "there must be a convergence of several factors before a hysterical symptom can be generated in anyone who has hitherto been normal. Such symptoms are invariably 'overdetermined,' to use Freud's expression" (212).[30]

Freud stated that the hysteric "suffers from reminiscences"; such reminiscences, however, can also be unconscious ones that are repressed from an initial moment of traumatic shock, as the following example from Breuer shows:

> a girl of seventeen had her first hysterical attack . . . when a cat jumped on her shoulder in the dark. The attack seemed simply to be the result of fright. Closer investigation showed, however, that the girl, who was particularly good-looking and was not properly looked after, had recently had a number of more or less brutal attempts made on her, and she herself been sexually excited by them. (Here we have the factor of disposition.) A few days before, a young man had attacked her on the same dark staircase and she had escaped from him with difficulty. This was the actual psychical trauma, which the cat did no more than make manifest. (213)

This language prefigures Freud's structural analysis of dreams to be published a few years later.

In the following passage, Breuer achieves a description of the unconscious, bringing all of the above-mentioned factors of hysterical symptom formation together:

"Hysterics suffer mainly from reminiscences" (p. 7 [citation Breuer's]). But if this is so—if the memory of the psychical trauma must be regarded as operating as a contemporary agent, like a foreign body, long after its forcible entrance, and if nevertheless the patient has no consciousness of such memories or their emergence—then we must admit that *unconscious ideas exist and are operative.* (221; Breuer's emphasis)[31]

Breuer refutes the French notion of weakness as an essential characteristic of hysterics: "Janet regards a particular form of congenital mental weakness as the disposition to hysteria. In reply, we should like to formulate our own view briefly as follows. It is not the case that the splitting of consciousness occurs because the patients are weak-minded; they appear to be weak-minded because their mental activity is divided and only a part of its capacity is at the disposal of their conscious thought" (231). And further: "In complete opposition to Janet's views, I believe that in a great many cases what underlies dissociation is an excess of efficiency, the habitual co-existence of two heterogeneous trains of ideas" (233). Breuer gives an example (though purely speculative and theoretical, as he acknowledges at the end of the passage) of how split consciousness might develop in a series of complex responses to a traumatic experience:

During the first few days after a traumatic event, the state of hypnoid fright is repeated every time the event is recalled. While this state recurs more and more often, its intensity so far diminishes that it no longer *alternates* with waking thought but only exists side by side with it. It now becomes continuous, and the somatic symptoms, which earlier were only present during the attack of fright, acquire a permanent existence. I can, however, only *suspect* that this is what happens, as I have never analysed a case of this kind. (235; Breuer's emphasis)[32]

England and America

Frederic W. H. Myers wrote at length in 1892 of a "subliminal consciousness."[33] Myers's task is "to indicate some ways in which the working of our ordinary, familiar faculties is reinforced by impulses or messages from the consciousness which exists below" (334). Myers is particularly interested in subliminal consciousness as the source of articulate speech and art. He sees trance and hypnosis (induced by a doctor or self-induced) as ways in which the creative subject concentrates on hidden "subliminal" sensations that emerge in inspiration. Speaking about "internal audition" and the imagination of sounds in the artists, Myers says, "It is . . . the other branch of internal audition—that which involves complexity rather than intensity of imagined sounds—which offers, so to say, the richest opportunities for subliminal manifestation—the readiest vent-holes for the uprush of hidden fire" (342). Myers suggests a relationship of mutual dependency between supraliminal and subliminal consciousness:

> It is plain then that no support is given by what we know of this group to the theory which regards subliminal mentation as necessarily a sign of some morbid dissociation of psychical elements. Is there, on the other hand, anything to confirm the suggestion which I have elsewhere made that—in as much as the addition of subliminal to supraliminal mentation may often be a completion and integration rather than a fracturation or disintegration of the total individuality—we are likely sometimes to find traces of a more than common activity of the right or less used cerebral hemisphere? (355–56)

Morton Prince discusses hysteria as a disease that illustrates three levels of consciousness that each corresponds to parts of the brain.[34] Prince cites the work of Hughlings-Jackson in mapping consciousness in terms of "three levels of evolution" (87). For Prince,

> in the lowest level are to be found the most organised, the most automatic, and the least complex nervous arrangements. . . . They represent comparatively limited regions of the body. . . . In the middle stratum . . . the movements are more complex, and they represent wider regions of the body. The same parts are represented as below in the lowest level, but in a more complicated manner. They are less automatic, and the centres are less organized. . . . The highest level includes much of the sensory region and all that portion of the brain anterior to the so-called motor region. (87)

Prince understands the mind arranged in three levels that evolve "bottom-to-top" from low to middle to high; these correspond to parts of the brain and organization that are highest at the bottom and least at the top. For Prince, "sensory impressions arriving simultaneously from the eye, the ear, and various parts of the body, are primarily received and recorded as sensations in the second level" (90), and hysteria results when there is an inhibition of the highest level of the brain (95). And further: "In hysteria there is a local suppression of function; in complete hypnosis, a total suppression of function of the highest level" (95). Hypnosis artificially produces in the hysteric a "going to sleep of certain limited areas" (95) in order to effect a cure. Hypnosis makes it possible for a hysteric to perceive what the hysterical symptom had kept hidden.

While Prince focuses on the relationship between hysteria and hypnosis based on a ternary extension of dual consciousness, Pearce Bailey extends the theory of hysteria emphasizing traumatic shock.[35] Like French writers, Bailey discusses hysteria as the product of a fixed idea, though he distances himself from Charcot's notion of degeneracy as essentially linked to hysteria: "the teachings of Charcot that hysteria never develops except in persons who are hereditarily or acquiredly degenerate is very difficult to substantiate" (284).[36] For Bailey, predisposition makes the appearance of hysteria more likely, but it is not necessary. Bailey is most interested in the traumatic effects of accidents; his interest is thus in the area of acquired traumatic hysteria, not hysteria based upon degenerate weakness of any sort. For Bailey, fright arises in several of his cases, from elevator collapse, train accident, electrocution from touching exposed electric cables, trolley car accidents, and accidents with carts. Bailey's article is aimed at an overview of legal cases in which the accidents caused by the machinery of modernization in public spaces are the responsibility of private companies or representatives of the social space in which the victim lives.[37] The key to the legal and psychoanalytic issues is the relationship between physical and psychic traumatic damage. Bailey holds "that physical injury is relatively unimportant in the causation of hysteria, as the disease is essentially one of fright" (283). He argues that traumatic hysteria can be cured, particularly if immediate treatment can attend a patient suffering from shock; on the other hand "a fixed idea may disorganize the life of an individual as much as a surgical injury, and ... it may at any time take root so deep that it can never be gotten rid of" (284).

I hope to have shown in the material presented above that the second half of the nineteenth century in Europe was a place in which psychoanalysis took shape as theories of hysteria moved away from a model based on predisposition and degeneracy to a complex series of responses to traumatic shock. In moving from such a wide-angle description of doctors writing across Continental, English, and American culture to a detailed examination of one movement of a multimovement piece of music written by a single composer at a specific time and place, I imply neither one-to-one correspondences between hysteria and composer, nor between traumatic shock and his work. Rather, I want to show that psychoanalysis was present in the cultural environment in which Webern grew up, in which he was educated, and in which he composed his music.

This examination of the discourse of the hysteric is also an introduction to the last chapter of the book in which Kundry, Klingsor, and Amfortas all suffer symptoms of traumatic hysteria in *Parsifal* by Richard Wagner and Hans-Jürgen Syberberg. Amfortas's wound that will not heal, the relationship between this wound and his inability to assume his symbolic mandate, Kundry's trancelike states throughout acts 1 and 2, and Klingsor's desparate self-castration, all owe a debt to the discourse of the hysteric that pervaded central Europe at the time of the opera's composition.

I will show in the rest of this chapter that there are biographical elements in Webern's *Orchesterstücke,* Opus 6 that suggest a traumatic dimension to the work's conception and content. As I discuss the music itself, I will understand both its analytical dimension and the psychoanalytic dimension of the trauma it embodies with the help of contemporary methods of music analysis and developments in psychoanalysis that occurred after the work's composition in 1909, bringing in writings of Freud written after the experience of World War I had cast a new, harsh light upon traumatic shock, and the writings of Lacan and his followers as they "return to Freud" many years later.

Webern's *Orchestertücke,* Opus 6, no. 4, "Marcia funebre"

By the turn of the twentieth century, Vienna had seen the effects of nineteenth-century industrialization, inventions of the photographic camera, the bicycle, the movie camera, and the phonograph. Vienna was a modern city in which abstraction in the visual arts and free atonality in music sprang into being. Psychoanalysis showed that the subject was not a unified, single consciousness but rather divided between conscious and unconscious areas of the mind. This split subjectivity affected not only the discourse of psychoanalytic pathology but everyday life as well.[38] One effect in art was that unconscious forces and conscious structures occupied different logical classes. No longer was there transparent access from manifest content to latent processes, whether one was talking about a psychic formation, a linguistic utterance, a piece of music, a social formation, or a dream.[39]

What follows is a description of the musical language of one of Webern's most massive works. The *Orchesterstücke*, Opus 6, were written in 1909 for a very large, pre–World War I orchestra.[40] Webern's contemporary Alban Berg's music is often "programmatic"; Berg needed to ground his free atonality in both an extension and incorporation of chromatic tonality and the framework of a dramatic substructure. He also needed to understand and plan each work as a "program."[41] In contrast, Webern's music is usually more "absolute"; not so with the piece at hand.[42]

Webern was aware that his *Orchesterstücke*, Opus 6, represented his relationship to the death of his mother in 1906.[43] On January 13, 1913, Webern wrote to Schoenberg how the pieces seemed to him to reenact a kind of associative narrative that represents how, as if in stages, the composer registered the death of his mother:

> The first piece is to express my frame of mind when I was still in Vienna, already sensing the disaster, yet always maintaining the hope that I would find my mother still alive. It was a beautiful day; for a minute I believed quite firmly that nothing had happened. Only during the train ride to Carinthia, it was on the afternoon of the same day, did I learn the truth.

Webern goes on to ponder his unusual reaction to the funeral procession itself:

> Even today I do not understand my feelings as I walked behind the coffin to the cemetery. I only know that I walked the entire way with my head held high, as if to banish everything lowly all around. I beg you to understand me properly. I am myself trying to gain clarity about that peculiar state. I have talked to no one as yet about it. The evening after the funeral was miraculous. With my wife I went once again to the cemetery and there straightened out the wreaths and flowers on the grave. Always I had the feeling of my mother's presence. I saw the friendly smile, it was a blissful feeling that lasted moments.[44]

At the beginning of the piece, Webern writes "kaum hörbar" under each of the three parts: "barely audible." "Audible" implies a listening subject, not just an object. Someone is listening and the music to that person is "barely audible." We are invited into this work as its implied

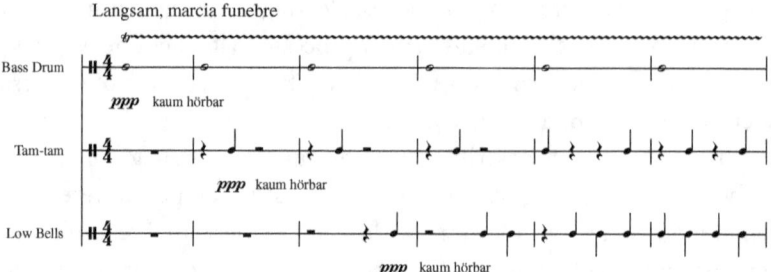

Figure 28

listener, barely able to hear its beginning.[45] The piece is in 4/4, marked "marcia funebre"—an obvious descriptive label telling the performers and anyone reading with the score that the piece is a musical representation of a funeral march. The tam-tam quarter note on the second beat of measure 2 is the first attack we can hear in the piece. Two low bells enter on the fourth beat of measure 3 (the higher of the low bells) and the fourth beat of measure 4 (the lower of the low bells). Anyone reading the score while listening to the music will know that there is no attack on the first beat of measure 2, although it sounds as if the tam-tam were articulating a downbeat here. The meter is coming into focus very slowly; the steady, marching rhythm is in place by measure 6 with the tam-tam articulating the second and fourth beats of the measure and the bells filling the measure—the higher low bell on beats 1 and 3, the lower low bell on beats 2 and 4.

Webern has composed a piece that is feathered so lightly at its outset that the threshold between silence and sound is imperceptible. No one would hear this as a traumatic breach, but this moment of the imperceptibility of the music's beginning relates profoundly to the horror of its reiterative ending. The material on hysteria and traumatic symptoms above suggests that trauma depends on repetition. There is a traumatic event, and then a subsequent event makes the earlier event manifest to consciousness, if only for a moment. The central traumatic dimension of this piece is its ending. The power of that traumatic dimension requires a hidden, earlier cause to which it subtly points. That cause is the work's opening in which sounds enter silence imperceptibly.

Pitch enters the piece in a D-natural/F-natural/F-sharp cluster played by the timpani in measure 8. D-natural will become a focal point for the work.[46] Winds enter in measure 9, as shown in Figure 29. The notes

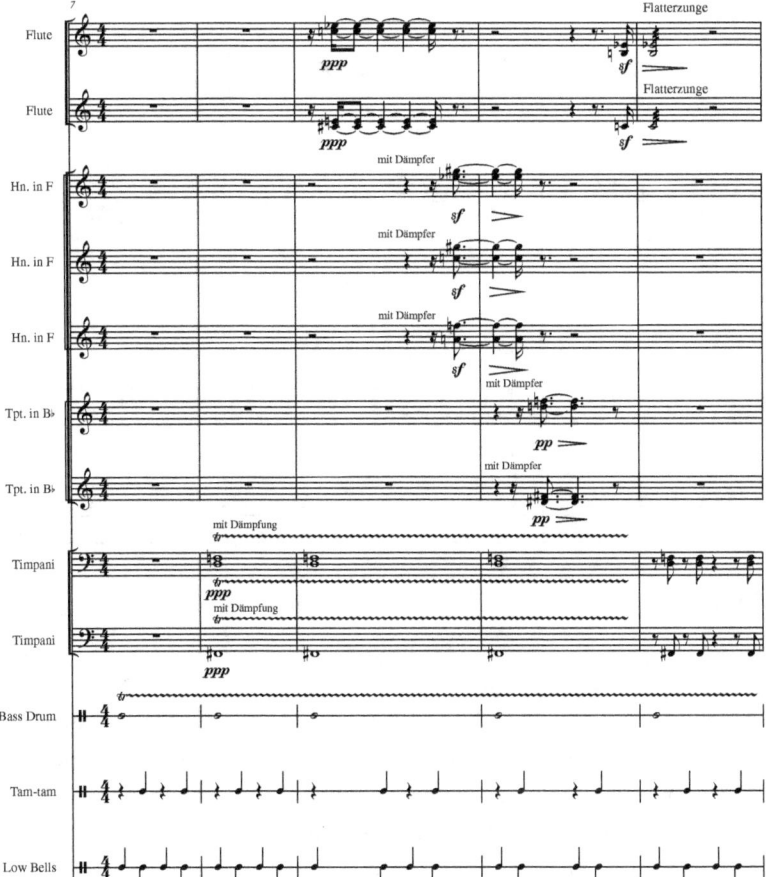

Figure 29

played by the flutes in measure 9 are c-sharp[1]/e-natural[1]/c-natural[2]/
e-flat[2]. These pitches can be thought of as the four *pitch-classes* C-natural/
C-sharp/E-flat/E-natural, which form a symmetrical collection around a
missing D-natural.[47] Webern composes a neighboring figure in the measures that follow. The flutes in measure 9 and the trumpets in measure 10
play the same pitches, with different colors: c-sharp[1]/e-natural[1]/c-natural[2]/
e-flat[2].[48] In between these groups of pitches, Webern writes a neighboring gesture in the horns, measures 9–10. Figure 30 shows the pitch content of measures 9–11 including the neighbor motions marked by an
"n" in the sketch.

This neighbor motion will resound throughout the piece, transposed
to a variety of pitch levels. The neighbor motion will also expand to a

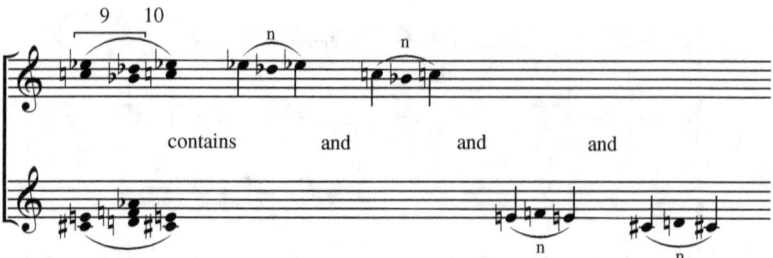

Figure 30

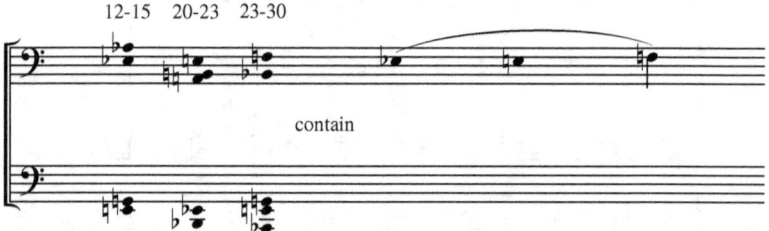

Figure 31

four-note collection leading to the stunning sonority on the last page of
the score in which the neighbor motion flattens out into a stifled, musical "scream."[49] From measure 12 to measure 30, the neighbor motions
shown above expand to a rising motion as shown in Figure 31 with the
slur connecting E-flat/E-natural/F-natural in the bass.

Measures 1–30 of the work contain sustained background collections
of pitches and solo melodies, such as the solo played by the E-flat clarinet high in its register (measures 12–15) and a solo played by the alto
flute, low in its register (measures 20–22) (not shown in the figure). The
first note of the alto flute solo is the first note in the piece to be absolutely
alone; it is therefore highly articulated by the silence around it. The note
is D-natural.

Measure 32 contains three chords. The upper notes suggest that Webern is taking pitches from the initial flute cluster and refiguring them.
The initial c-sharp^1/e-natural^1/c-natural^2/e-flat^2 becomes c-sharp^2/e-
natural^2/e-flat^2 as shown in Figure 32.

In measure 33 the brass play two chords that suggest a return to the
twin minor thirds of the opening sonority played by the flutes (c-sharp^1/
e-natural^1/c-natural^2/e-flat^2. In measure 33, the bass tuba plays a C-natural

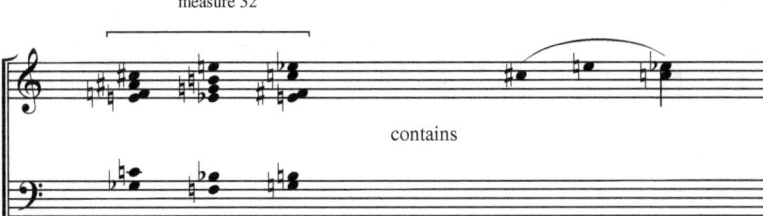

Figure 32

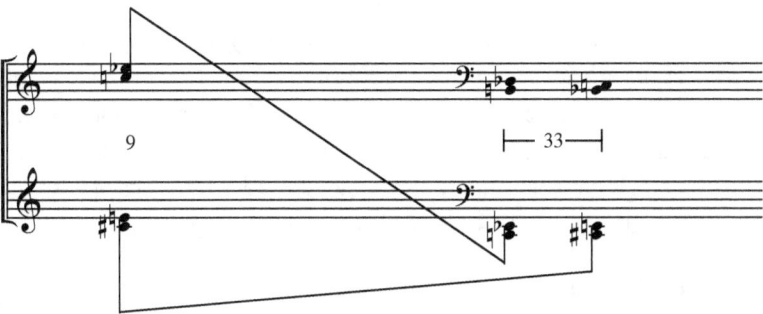

Figure 33

and above it, the fourth trombone plays a D-sharp (enharmonically equivalent to an E-flat as notated in the Figure 33). Then the bass tuba plays a C-sharp and above it, the fourth trombone plays an E-natural.

Measure 33 initiates a series of massive, vertical sonorities that culminate in the ten-note sonority of measure 39. The vertical sonorities are supported by a chromatically ascending bass line initiated by the bass tuba's C-natural in measure 33. Each note in the bass supports a third, the basic idea present in measure 9 in both the tympani trill and the flutes' twin thirds. The ascending bass suggests a heightening of affective power, and it generates "tonal" direction as well. I mentioned that D-natural is a focal point for the work. It is a focal point stripped of its tonal depth, but present as a single pitch-class whose absence marks the flutes' c-sharp[1]/e-natural[1]/c-natural[2]/e-flat[2] sonority in measure 9.

The bass line from the bass tuba's C-natural in measure 33 rises in fits and starts to the sonority in measure 39. On the downbeat of measure 39, the bass tuba plays an A-natural that supports a vertical sonority suggestive of a highly enriched augmented dominant of D, particularly strong in the bass line's approach to A-natural, through the twin half-step

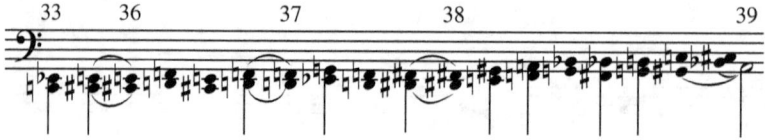

Figure 34

motion G-sharp/B-flat evocative of an augmented sixth articulation of the dominant (at the very end of measure 38).[50] Figure 34 shows the ascending bass line and thirds from measure 33 to measure 39.

The simple neighbor motion that sounds early in the piece becomes a series of superimposed neighbor motions culminating in the ten-note sonority of measure 39. Figure 35 shows these neighboring motions with slurs, in addition to the long-range voice-leading across the work that articulates its "D"-ness. The figure also shows the cross-reference of C-sharp/E-natural and C-natural/E-flat thirds from measure 9 to measure 33.

A Chord That Sticks

In measures 39–41 (the last three measures of the work), linear motion stops and a ten-note vertical sonority (the richly enhanced "augmented dominant" of D) reiterates eight times followed by a percussion cluster. Webern gives us a new sound for this ten-note collection—two piccolos playing a C-sharp (doubled by the E-flat clarinet) at the top of their registers. Allen Forte has pointed out that the pitch-class C-sharp often signifies the cross in Webern's music; this idea heightens the significance of this quite singular sonority in the work.[51] The brass are muted throughout, and although the sonority sounds quite dramatic, not all instruments are playing (no flutes, no B-flat clarinets, no bass clarinet, no bassoons). In the middle of measure 39, Webern adds the last new sonority of the piece—a suspended cymbal that is played with tympani sticks. A last iteration of the ten-note collection occurs in measure 40, and percussion crescendo through measure 41—torn off in silence after the triple forte is reached. This is the stifled, musical scream to which the entire work builds (Figure 36).

I would like to suggest that the piece of music under discussion embodies a traumatic dimension.[52] We know that Webern wrote the Opus 6 pieces in the memory of his recently deceased mother and that he experienced a strange elation at her grave. The "Marcia funebre" is of course, a genre piece; the literature contains many funeral marches—

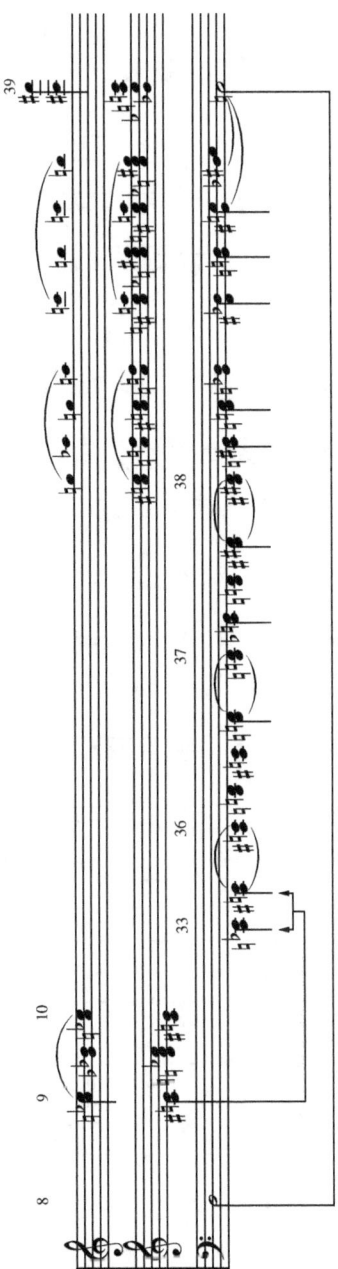

Figure 35

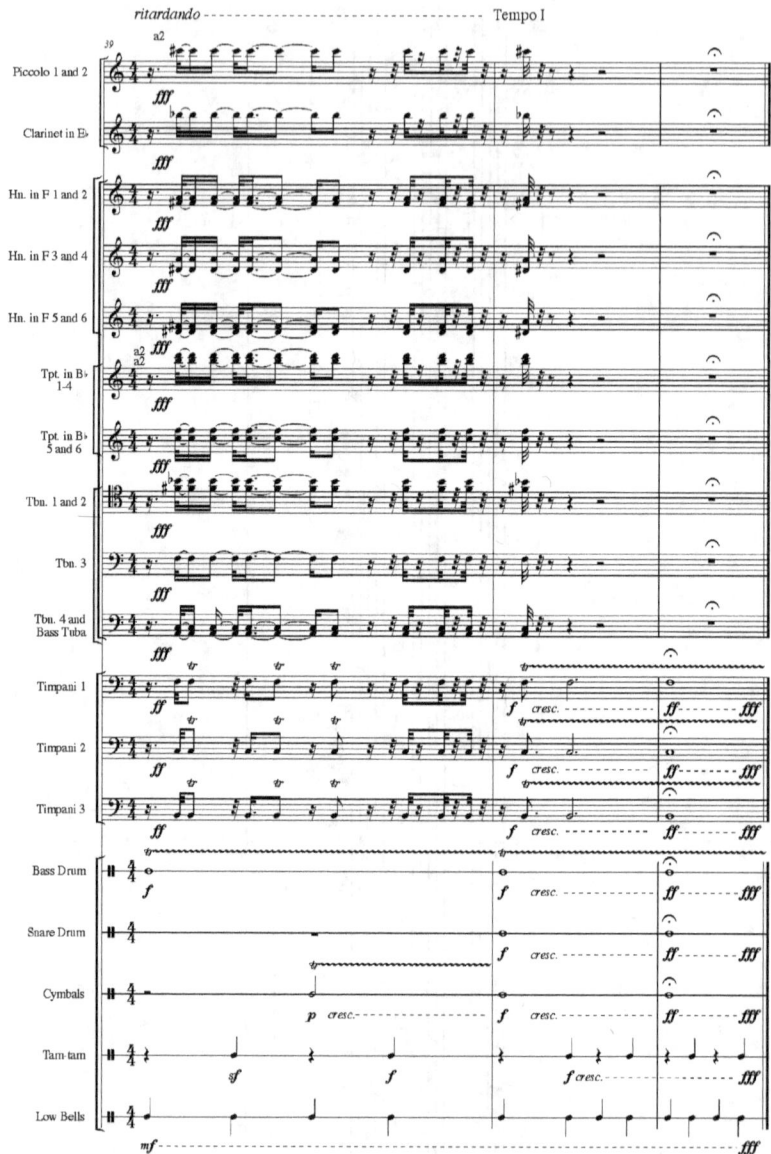

Figure 36

some explicitly connected to specific persons, some not. The pervasive-
ness of mutes is crucial in the work at hand; it is as if the entire content
of the piece were heard in an interior space blocked from open expression. And although fortissimo, not all instruments of the penultimate
cluster are playing; it is an interior scream.[53]

Of course, Webern's work is not a statement of a patient in a therapeutic exchange. The work is neither a traumatic experience nor a subsequent experience that reminds a patient of a traumatic wound; it is a highly mediated work of art. Our knowledge that Webern wrote the pieces in the memory of his mother, his "Marcia funebre" title for the movement, his letter to Schoenberg, and the cultural context of turn-of-the-twentieth-century Vienna lend support to a discussion of the piece in connection with the birth of psychoanalysis in general and the experience of traumatic shock in particular.[54] The unexpected loss of a parent is a common example of traumatic experience, along with the more historically determined factors of modernization and the industrialization of social spaces. How can we begin to understand a work of art as an embodiment of trauma? Can art be understood as a form of mediated repetition in the same logical class as memory—both in its voluntary and involuntary dimensions?

A few years after the completion of Webern's *Orchesterstücke,* Opus 6, World War I broke out.[55] In response to his examination of soldiers suffering from shell shock, Freud wrote *Beyond the Pleasure Principle* in 1920. In it, Freud outlines one of his famous distinctions:

> "Fright," "fear," and "anxiety" are improperly used as synonymous expressions; they are in fact capable of clear distinction in their relation to danger. "Anxiety" describes a particular state of expecting the danger or preparing for it, even though it may be an unknown one. "Fear" requires a definite object of which to be afraid. "Fright," however, is the name we give to the state a person gets into when he has run into danger without being prepared for it; it emphasizes the factor of surprise.[56]

Bringing Webern's piece into a conversation with subsequent theories of trauma, the death of his mother would have been the traumatic event, and the work of music would be one among presumably other ways of self-representation and embodiment of that trauma.[57] Freud discusses the death drive as an instinct to return to an inorganic state that precedes the pleasure principle; it can be brought to the fore through traumatic experiences that generate repetitive, compulsive dreams and other behaviors:

> We describe as "traumatic" any excitations from outside which are powerful enough to break through the protective shield. It seems to me that the concept of trauma necessarily implies a connection of this kind with a breach in an otherwise efficacious barrier against stimuli. Such an

event as an external trauma is bound to provoke a disturbance on a large scale in the functioning of the organism's energy and to set in motion every possible defensive measure. At the same time, the pleasure principle is for the moment put out of action. (*Beyond the Pleasure Principle* 33)

One way the subject gains active mastery over an experience of sudden loss registered passively is through representation. This empowering transformation is illustrated in Freud's famous *Fort-Da* game:

The child had a wooden reel with a piece of string tied round it. It never occurred to him to pull it along the floor behind him, for instance, and play at its being a carriage. What he did was to hold the reel by the string and very skillfully throw it over the edge of his curtained cot, so that it disappeared into it, at the same time uttering his expressive "o-o-o-o." He then pulled the reel out of the cot again by the string and hailed its reappearance with a joyful "da" ["there"]. This, then, was the complete game in itself—disappearance and return.... The interpretation of the game then becomes obvious. It was related to the child's great cultural achievement. (*Beyond the Pleasure Principle* 14)

What the *Fort-Da* game gives to the child giving up instinctual satisfaction of the mother's presence is *active*, symbolic control over an experience registered *passively* (Ibid., 15).

For Jacques Lacan, trauma coincides with the birth of psychoanalysis as the encounter with the Real: "The function of the *tuché*, of the Real as encounter—the encounter in so far as it may be missed, in so far as it is essentially the missed encounter—first presented itself in the history of psycho-analysis in a form that was in itself already enough to arouse our attention, that of the trauma."[58] As already discussed, historically speaking, trauma was inherent to discourses of hysteria in nineteenth-century Europe. Lacan is speaking of the history of the subject when he says,

trauma is conceived as having necessarily been marked by the subjectifying homeostasis that orientates the whole functioning defined by the pleasure principle. Our experience then presents us with a problem, which derives from the fact that, at the very heart of the primary processes, we see preserved the insistence of the trauma in making us aware of its existence. The trauma reappears, in effect, frequently unveiled. (*Four Fundamental Concepts*, 55)

What is it, exactly, that reappears?

Lacan revisits Freud's *Fort-Da* game and sees in it a fundamental splitting of the subject at the foundational moment of the absence of the mother:[59]

> When Freud grasps the repetition involved in the game played by his grandson, in the reiterated fort-da, he may indeed point out that the child makes up for the effect of his mother's disappearance by making himself the agent of it—but, this phenomenon is of secondary importance. Wallon stresses that the child does not immediately watch the door through which his mother has disappeared, thus indicating that he expects to see her return through it, but that his vigilance was aroused earlier, at the very point she left him, at the point she moved away from him. The ever-open gap introduced by the absence indicated remains the cause of the centrifugal tracing in which that which falls is not the other qua face in which the subject is projected, but that cotton-reel linked to itself by the thread that it holds—in which is expressed that which, of itself, detaches itself in this trial, self-mutilation on the basis of which the order of significance will be put in perspective. For the game of the cotton-reel is the subject's answer to what the mother's absence has created on the frontier of his domain—the edge of his cradle—namely a *ditch,* around which one can play at jumping. (62; Lacan's emphasis)

The ditch—an indentation, that which blocks, that into which one stumbles, that which *contains* the body as it stumbles suggests the missed encounter with the Real.

Lacan describes Freud's grandson's cotton-reel as the *objet petit a* that falls into this space as the mother's absence splits the subject:

> If it is true that the signifier is the first mark of the subject, how can we fail to recognize here—from the very fact that this game is accompanied by one of the first oppositions to appear—that it is in the object to which the opposition is applied in act, the reel, that we must designate the subject. To this object we will later give the name it bears in the Lacanian algebra—the *petit a.* (62)

To return to Webern, I would like to ask not only how psychoanalysis can describe the music but also how Webern's music embodies psychoanalysis as a missed encounter with the Real? The musical missed encounter of the Real can be heard at the edges of the work's noisy opening and conclusion. The piece opens with feathered, unpitched percussion, and during a performance the piece would *look* as if it were starting as much as it would *sound* like it were starting.[60] The voice-leading from a sounding D-natural to clusters of notes that open up around a missing D-natural all move in agonizing neighbor motions to measures 39–41 with reiterated pitches that get stuck in Lacan's "ditch" at the edge of the Real—the return of percussion at the end that can, to my ear, neither be played loud enough nor torn off with sufficient violence.[61]

CHAPTER FOUR

Left! Right! Left! Right!

Music, Bodies, Fascism

This chapter will focus, after Klaus Theweleit, on the structure of national socialist subjectivity in the texts and music of German war songs.[1] I will focus on songs of World War II and listen back to their antecedents in World War I. This chapter assumes a national socialist subject whose bodily fantasy space has always already been breached by the other and whose entire project within national socialist space is to heal such a wound. The impossibility and necessity of this task locks the national socialist subject in a lethal dimension of drive.[2]

In *Listening Subjects: Music, Psychoanalysis, Culture*, I wrote about Oi-Musik—right-wing skinhead music in Germany of the 1980s and early 1990s.[3] The disturbing genius of Oi-Musik is its thinly veiled appropriation and turn toward the right of mainstream-to-progressive music. Oi turns the blues, the music of the sixties youth movement, and punk into right-wing death metal linked to the beatings and deaths of foreigners in Germany. Throughout the years of working with this material, Oi seemed to me like the return of the repressed. I wondered whether its appropriation of mainstream-to-progressive music might have had roots in fascism.

National socialists sought to cleanse German culture of the music of the other (Jew, communist-socialist, homosexual, modern decadent),[4] appropriating vestiges of their music into their own in acts of musical cannibalism.[5] This appropriation functioned in two ways. First, there was a conscious rewriting of German music history as a cleansing of the homeland of the music of the other.[6] Second, there was an unconscious need to bind the fantasy of a new musical Germany precisely to the music most hated.[7] The musical project of national socialist Germany was so powerful because unconscious need and conscious agenda fueled a common fire.[8]

Music and Fascism

Postwar German musicologists and literary critics agreed early on that music was very important for fascism.[9] Fred K. Prieberg has written extensively on music and fascism, pointing out that the national socialists designed and put into place an enormous and complex bureaucracy to fuse the German people into a singular "Volk" through music.[10] Prieberg has also shown that, through the Hitler Youth, new singing organizations and schools were set up across Germany, in small towns as well as large urban centers.[11] All aspects of both middle- and working-class musical activities were carefully structured by the national socialists: "[this music shall serve] march singing, folk singing, hours spent at home, singing at Hitler youth squad evenings, the after-school hours, singing in camps, singing at company celebrations, at roll call and reveille, announcements, and at community festivals."[12] In describing the ideological power of the music of fascism, Johannes Hodek says, "We are talking about fulfillment [Erfüllung]. That means the process of singing and making music must stir up feelings, moods, desires that then lead to a mobilization of sensibility like an organization that was inspired from above."[13]

Monika Tibbe points out that nineteenth-century collections of folk songs were profoundly marked by censorship and ideology:

> The criteria for determining what authentic folk songs were had the effect of censorship. Herder and Goethe strove for an authentic reproduction of texts while norms from the outside increasingly rule over almost all collections of the nineteenth century. Texts that were too crude, too sensuous or political were not published or were edited. The German folk song thus increasingly became a harmless little song that referred to nature and love in naive and familiar terms.[14]

The national socialists reserved a special place for the German folk song in their project: "out of hardly any other culture other than the German has arisen such a clear and consistent concept as 'folk song.' From the beginning the folk song has borne witness to the growth and development of the German folk culture."[15] In describing the power of songs he had sung in the Hitler Youth, Hodek perceptively points out that songs he had thought of as quintessentially of his youth, were, in fact, carefully produced to construct his youth in a social context (Hodek 24).

Hodek quotes a Hitler Youth song "Mich brennts in meinen Reiseschuhn" (Figure 37):

Mich brennts in meinen Reiseschuhn
fort mit der Zeit zu schreiten

Was wollen wir agieren nun
vor so viel klugen Leuten, vor so vielen klugen Leuten?

My hiking shoes are burning
to go forth and keep up with the times

How should we act now
in front of so many smart people, in front of so many smart people?[16]

The text contains in a nutshell one of the fascists' basic ploys: to circumscribe ideological and political domination within the benign orbit of a nineteenth-century urge to hike or wander. The text contains, as well, a subtle hint of fascist anti-intellectualism: Go forth, wander, discover yourself rather than be held back by the constraints of intellectuals!

"Mich brennts in meinen Reiseschuhen" relies on the conventions of folk song: simple diatonic leaps and a melody that emphasizes scale degrees one, three, and five of the tonic G major. The fifth d-natural^2 is embellished with its upper neighbor in the penultimate measure to emphasize the descending line to tonic. The song thrives on its melodic coherence, its ease in G major, its clear final melodic descent to tonic, which, ironically, sets the unanswered question in the text. The song's meter is curious: 4/4 5/4. Most traditional German folk melodies are in 3/4 or 4/4 or perhaps a compound meter such as 6/8. Why 4/4 5/4? I suspect that the song's flexible alternation of 4/4 and 5/4 accommodates the text and gives the song a gentle tension between freedom and awkwardness.

Throughout this chapter I will argue that musicians working with the support of the national socialist propaganda bureaucracy used the strategy of taking folk songs, hymns, art songs, and ceremonial songs and altering them in the service of creating a musical fantasy of a unified, right-wing Germany:

The looming threat of an only archaic position has been overcome.
Also, the threat of art has been overcome through the realization of the

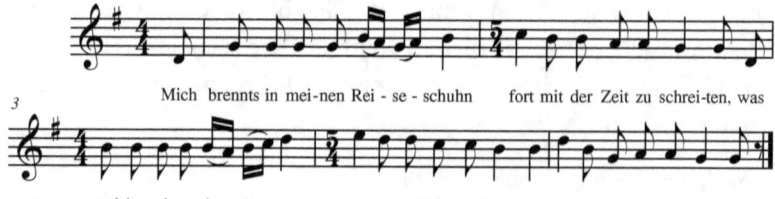

Figure 37

character and the role of folk music: we have returned to a simplicity of means and clarity of form. Thus new, screaming musical forces, which were formed by a spiritually bonded will for creation, have lead us to a deeper sense of art that does not seem as it is, but that is more than it seems.[17]

At times, the urge to give the national socialist the sense that all of German music history and musical classics are an upbeat to national socialism was subtle, as in the juxtaposition in anthologies of national socialist songs with chorales. At other times, the urge was explicit, as in articles and books that claimed that specific works and styles prefigure national socialism.[18]

In this chapter, I am not particularly interested in the role of high art music in fascism.[19] Rather I am interested in what, for lack of a better expression, must be called popular music.[20] I am interested in music that German soldiers sang to themselves and to each other in the prewar and wartime years. I am interested in anthologies of music produced by national socialists for the citizens of the Reich, from which they sang to each other, and to the community at festivals, holidays, and ceremonies. Ideology is particularly audible in this mass-produced and mass-consumed music.[21] And I am interested in how this ideology was inscribed onto the bodies of its subjects.

Music, Interpellation, and the Body

Writers of the period recalling their own experiences with music in the context of national socialism often talk about the body. According to Johannes Hodek "They [such Hitler Youth songs] sound stiff. They were sung in certain sitting or standing positions and got a hold of the lack of one's own body experience. The singing person, however, did not experience his/her lack of bodily sense, or only in a way to make this lack thereof seem natural."[22] In his article/letter to the editor of *Musik and Musikpolitik im faschistischen Deutschland,* Hans Werner Henze writes,

"As a matter of fact, my brother and I had to perform with our hands and feet the Hitler greeting every morning at breakfast and every evening going to bed as our last tenderness between parents and sons. For me the Nazi state was incarnate in my body—the body of the punitive little guy, of the weak, erroneous, intimidated, robbed of one's ideals, the slightly funny and yet feared, unpredictable fanatic."[23]

This passage reveals both the connection in fascism between the politics of the family and the politics of the state, as well as the importance of incorporation of ideology into the body.[24] The Hitler greeting, like all Althusserian hails, connects the body of the subject with the state. In the quote above, a series of male subjectivities is linked: Henze as a child, his father, his teacher, enforcers of the law, and finally Hitler.

Much has been written about Althusserian interpellation.[25] For Althusser, the hail is a performative gesture enacted in public space to locate the individual as a subject in relation to the state through a surrogate. The classic example is the policeman who shouts "hey you!" In the process of turning around to meet the gaze of the policeman, the individual inscribes him/herself as the subject of discourse ("I am that 'you'"). The Althusserian model relies on Lacan's mirror stage and its shifting forms of recognition and misrecognition.[26] Leni Riefenstahl's *Triumph des Willens* is one large-scale representation of ideological interpellation with the camera hailing its viewers as subjects of national socialism, constantly redrawing the trajectory from individual, to larger social unit, to Hitler through tracking shots, low camera positions in relation to Hitler, and "snapshots" of soldiers and citizens admiring and pledging loyalty to Hitler. Riefenstahl's camera and the radio were powerful tools that the national socialists embraced early on.[27]

Althusserian ideological interpellation works, at its core, within the visual regime of the Lacanian mirror stage and the linguistic exchange of subject/object positions as "I" converts to "you" and back again.[28] I would like for this chapter to extend the predominantly visual regime of Althusserian ideological interpellation "back" into the regime of acoustic mirroring, the sonorous envelope, and the body.[29] The quote from Henze invites us to do just that. And he is not alone.[30]

Fred Prieberg interviewed a draftsman born in 1931 who said the following about singing fascist songs as a young boy: "When I was down, I would automatically sing Nazi songs and everything was immediately snappy and straight. It was good medicine for me. Since these songs were injected into me like a drug. You know, when one has been brought up under the Nazis, then these Nazi songs stay in your brain for twenty, thirty years."[31] But how does music hail us as subjects in a pre-Althusserian form of acoustic interpellation?

In the 180-degree conversion of Althusserian, visual-linguistic interpellation there is both conscious and unconscious agency. Consciously, we tell our body to turn around and we process who is "you" and who is "I."[32] Unconsciously, we know that we are always already the subject of discourse. And Althusser includes a curious "guilt" that accompanies the subject's initial response to the call "hey you!" For Althusser, the "strange phenomenon" of "guilt feelings" has to do with whether or not the "you" is really aimed at "you" and whether or not the "you" has something on his or her conscience. For Žižek, the hail's guilty feeling is an unconscious glimpse into the shared transgression that underlies social space. For Žižek, the shared lie is more powerful as foundational ideological support of social space than a fantasy of "truth." The shared lie can take the form of the repression of those who challenge the law, the state's economic exploitation of labor, or the violence upon which all states rely to attain nationhood in the first place and sustain it against incursions. So for Žižek, when the subject turns to meet the gaze of the Other's surrogate who shouts "hey you!" the subject feels a tinge of guilt. This is interpellation prior to identification. This is interpellation being dependent upon the shared guilt of the subject with the social order that sustains him or her within the State.[33]

The vehicle for Žižek's "interpellation prior to identification" is voice not yet marked with meaning—pure sound. Sounds penetrate skin. Sounds are more threatening heard from behind since we can't see their source, since our ears have thicker hair on the smooth backs of our ears muting the sounds, and since there's a brief period of developing subjectivity in which we cannot roll over when placed on our stomachs. We can close our ears at loud sounds, but this gesture always only mutes, never cancels out sound. And at night, our subjectivity is utterly open to sounds. Sounds thus carry a profoundly imperative agency for us. Sounds enter our bodies as carriers of messages of intent from agencies benevolent, malevolent, or indifferent. Žižek's "guilt prior to interpellation" is made possible by this acoustic vulnerability.

The most powerful instrument of interpellation for the national socialists was the radio—technology that brought the voice of the surrogate of the Other directly to anyone listening to a broadcast. For Goebbels, the success of the national socialist project depended on the radio. Speaking in 1933 to national socialist officers in charge of developing radio strategies, Goebbels said, "do it well and we shall win the people; do it badly and the people in the end will run away from us."[34]

Bringing War Songs to the Front

A 1940 article in the *Neue Zeitschrift für Musik* describes the importance of music in general, and war songs in particular, for the support of national socialist politics during the war years:

> The enormous importance of marches in the lives of soldiers is by now known to everyone. Exhausted from a seemingly endless march, soldiers revive themselves as they sing a fresh song. But a soldier needs not only marches; other songs are necessary for survival [lebensnotwendig] and function for him as a release for his discouragements, his inner animal [innerer Schweinehund], his longings.[35]

The article was written by a musician reporting from the field. The author writes at length about a three-day training course he took to bring war songs to soldiers. Those attending were to be trained as song leaders ("Singleiter"). There was a main leader (the "Lehrgangsleiter") and an assistant ("Gaumusikreferent.") The main leader lectured; the assistant put the lectures into practice. On the first day, there were workshops on the structure and meanings of war songs, and the song-leaders-in-training learned several songs, supervised by the leader and his assistant. The first evening consisted of very precise instructions about how to form song evenings for exhausted troops so that a spontaneous and supportive atmosphere among the soldiers and leaders arose "organically." On the second day, the song leaders heard the songs they had been working on performed by choir with brass accompaniment. The third day summarized and brought together the content of the previous two. The author stresses the beauty, the simplicity, and the power of good war songs as distinguished from the pleasing but superficial quality of popular songs.[36]

This article shows implicitly how music functions as ideological component of national socialist politics. The connection is explicit as well. Early in the article, the author says, "Orders from above alone are never sufficient; there must always be middlemen who forge a connection between the leader ("der Führer") and the people ("Gefolgschaft.") The song leader fulfills this task best, since he belongs to the troops and can best be a beneficial influence upon them."[37]

Germany produced war songs before the national socialists gained power in 1933. There were war songs preparing the Germans for World War I, songs written in 1870 (such as "Die Wacht am Rhein" [Tibbe 21]), and songs written in the seventeenth and early nineteenth century.[38] Before examining national socialist war songs, I shall examine songs written for the Germans in World War I. These songs provide a body of practice from which the national socialists took and adapted textual and musical strategies.

German War Songs: World War I

Kriegslieder für das deutsche Volk comprised eleven volumes of songs published in 1914 and 1915.[39] The keys are simple with few accidentals and the rhythms clearly marchlike; even the songs in 6/8 and 12/8 have a duple sound (best for marching). Only the faintly liturgical "Gebet ans Volk" and "Das Marienburger Lied" are in ternary meter.[40]

"Kriegslied" presents a text from 1870 that seeks to protect the fatherland from exploitation and calls for a holy war to spill the enemy's blood (Figure 38):

> 1. Arise my people! Sword in hand! And break out from the masses! Be baptized with this fire of passion for the fatherland! The archenemy offers you insult and injury; the time has come, to war with God on our side; to war with God on our side! Onward! Onward! Onward!
> 2. Your intent and wish was to build a home in peace; and strife came down swollen with poison and envy. Fall upon them and their brood; the maliciously-spilled blood! Onward! Onward! Onward!

The song is a call to arms—a march to be sung in battle. The first half of the song is lyrical with gently rising and falling motions emphasizing the first, third, and fifth scale degrees of D major. For the second half of the song, lyricism yields to slower, aggressive half and quarter notes. The music sets the line "to war with God on our side" to the rising line a-natural^1/b-natural^1/c-sharp^2/d-natural^2 (measures 14–16). Text and music come together: the text's linkage of holy war and bloodletting are set to a musical achievement of the pitch d-natural^2 with a stepwise ascent from the fifth—a-natural^1. The bugle calls "Onward! Onward! Onward!" tie d-natural^2 to d-natural^1 and the octave span of the song is completely

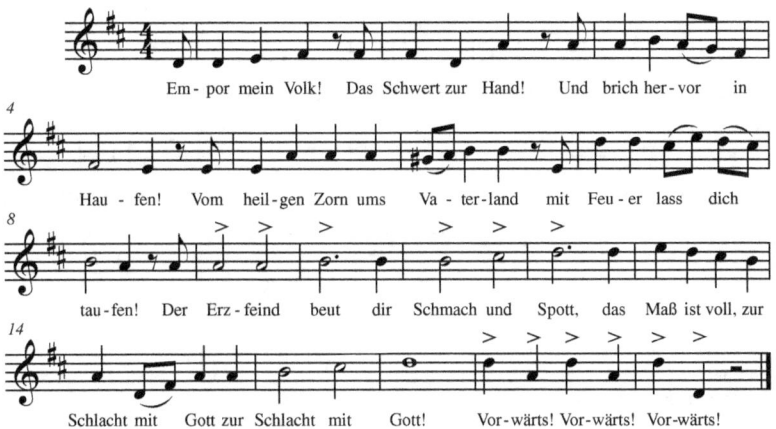

Em - por mein Volk! Das Schwert zur Hand! Und brich her - vor in

Hau - fen! Vom heil - gen Zorn ums Va - ter - land mit Feu - er lass dich

tau - fen! Der Erz - feind beut dir Schmach und Spott, das Maß ist voll, zur

Schlacht mit Gott zur Schlacht mit Gott! Vor - wärts! Vor - wärts! Vor - wärts!

Dein Haus in Frieden auszubaun, stand all dein Sinn und Wollen, da bricht den Hader er vom Zaun, von Gift und Neid geschwollen. Komm über ihn und seine Beut das frevelhaft vergossne Blut! Vorwärts!

Figure 38

resolved with the last note of the song.[41] Figure 38 includes the lyrics to the first two stanzas; the song has six stanzas and was composed in July 1870.

"Der heilige Reiter" presents a text of a holy call to war outside Christianity (Figure 39):

1. I engage in a holy war, do not ask for salary, do not ask for victory. I am a holy rider. I seek no cross and no grail and am nevertheless a thousand times more holy as fighter for my cause.
2. My heart keeps up with you, my horse. The earth trembles. Trembling sword. I am a holy rider. I know no longer what drives me on; the best thing is, the victor remains. And I seek nothing else.

The 6/8 meter suggests the ongoing pace of the narrator's horse, and the melody (while clearly located in F major) ends on the poised mediant.[42] There is a level of understated terror in the text. The first stanza asserts the narrator's holy mandate outside of Christianity; the second stanza suddenly shifts from third-person narration to a second-person form of address to the horse. And then there are two breathless lines with the repetition of "trembling." The narrator no longer knows why he is fighting. He rides on, knowing only that the victor will remain standing in the end. The strophic setting of the music guarantees that these shifts will be contained within the driving 6/8 rhythm and clear diatonic tonality of F major.

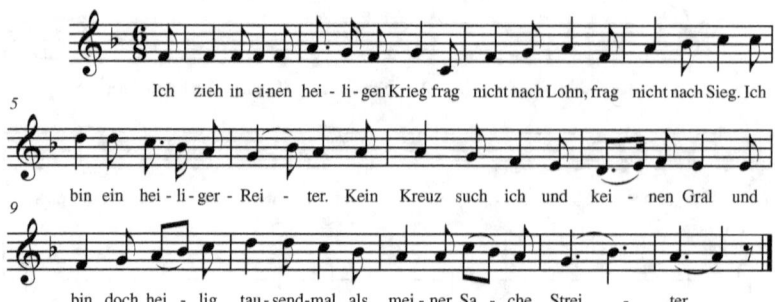

Ich zieh in einen hei - li - gen Krieg frag nicht nach Lohn, frag nicht nach Sieg. Ich

bin ein hei - li - ger - Rei - ter. Kein Kreuz such ich und kei - nen Gral und

bin doch hei - lig tau - send-mal als mei - ner Sa - che Strei - ter.

Mein Herz hällt Schritt mit dir, mein Pferd. Die Erde zittert, Zittre Schwert. Ich bin ein
heiliger Reiter. Weiß nicht mehr, was mich vorwärts treibt; der Beste ist, der Sieger bleibt.
Und ich begehr nichts weiter.

Figure 39

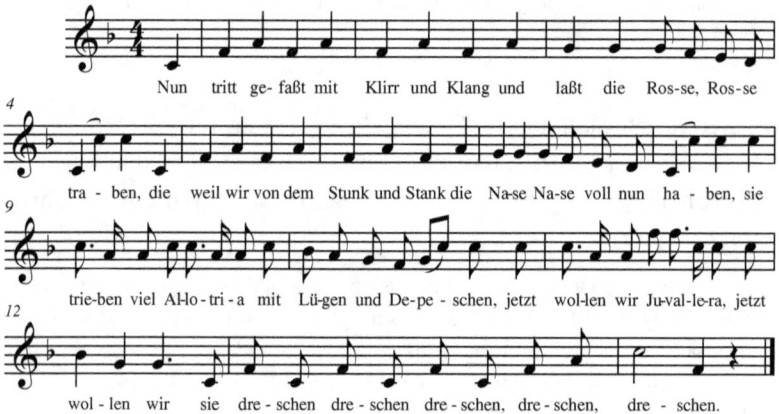

Nun tritt ge- faßt mit Klirr und Klang und laßt die Ros-se, Ros-se

tra - ben, die weil wir von dem Stunk und Stank die Na-se Na-se voll nun ha - ben, sie

trie-ben viel Al-lo-tri-a mit Lü-gen und De-pe - schen, jetzt wol-len wir Ju-val-le-ra, jetzt

wol - len wir sie dre - schen dre - schen dre - schen, dre - schen, dre - schen.

Figure 40

"Marsch! Marsch!" is a song to be sung in battle. Here is the third
stanza (Figure 40, with the words of the first stanza of the text):

> Sing the last verse quickly since bullets are already whizzing. THUD,
> the enemy got one on his hide and needs to wipe his mouth. The whole
> world looks on trembling, flipping out of their galloshes. So, majesty,
> what do you say now, you're already defeated!

The text is light-hearted and giggly in effusive confidence. The music
hammers relentlessly back and forth in tonic-mediant or tonic-dominant
motions.

The second volume of the series, *Ein Hänlein woll'n wir rupfen*, consists of reworked war songs from the sixteenth through the nineteenth

centuries.[43] Several songs in this volume deal with leaving domestic, social space for war. "Die Jäger" is a typical example that replaces affective response with childish syllables. The text is third-person narration only; here are the fourth and fifth stanzas: "4. In 1914 the troubles began, and all the maidens began to cry, the large ones and the small ones, hi-ho, hi-ho, etc. / 5. They were called to formation, called to the bloody war. To fight for the kaiser, to fight for victory." The music is a duet in absolutely placid G major emphasizing scale degrees one, three, and five in thirds and sixths.

The very next song of the volume, "Soldatenabschied," internalizes the experience. The text describes being called to service; the most telling detail in the language is the modal verb "must" that accompanies every main verb of the first stanza: "The drum has sounded, and I must go; I must follow the word of my commander; I must leave the house of my father; I must go out into the wide open world. I must protect the fatherland despite the deceitful enemy; I must leave the house of my father; I must go out into the wide open world."

"Soldatenlosung" (Figure 41, with the words of the first stanza of the text) presents a darker text; here are the second and third stanzas:

> 2. When it flashes, thunders, and pounds, the blood flows red as roses; when the blood drips from our swords, then we're happy.
> 3. Where is he? Where is my comrade? He's fallen in the battle. We Germans don't question this; we're ready for it.

The music is a duet whose A major is just as placid as "Soldatentod," with melodies that stress scale degrees one, three, and five, in thirds and sixths.

The last song in the volume stands out from the others. It is not an explicit war song. Rather its text praises, in gently sacred terms, the kingdom of God. It is a version of a chorale by J. S. Bach.[44] Having a piece connected to the Protestant church conclude the volume suggests a large-scale "amen" to the project of awakening nationalist war sentiments in the volume's listener. Bach set the melody in his chorale number 149.[45] The uppermost melody is identical in both versions, and the harmonies are roughly equivalent. Wirth has replaced Bach's fermatas with notated rhythms that keep the flow going. Wirth replaces Bach's four-part SATB texture with a piano texture notated with two tenor parts on the upper staff and two bass parts on the lower staff. Presumably, Wirth's version

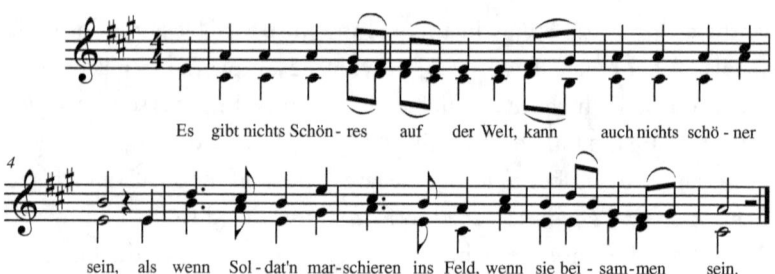

Es gibt nichts Schön- res   auf   der Welt, kann   auch nichts schö - ner

sein, als wenn Sol - dat'n mar-schieren ins Feld, wenn sie bei - sam-men   sein.

Figure 41

makes it easy for a piano to play along, doubling the voices. Bach had composed a bass line that is more rhythmically active than the upper voices; Wirth evens out the texture rhythmically, giving his version greater rhythmic uniformity.

The title of the third volume is taken from its first song, "Wohlauf Kameraden."[46] The text of "Wohlauf Kameraden" is an eight-stanza poem by Friedrich Schiller. The poem posits the soldier as absolutely isolated in his freedom in a world of corrupt enemies: here are the first two stanzas:

> 1. Arise comrade, to your horse; to your horse to the field to freedom!
> In the field, man is still valuable, his heart still carries weight. No one
> else will step in for him there! He stands there completely on his own!
> 2. Freedom has vanished from the world; one sees only lords and
> servants; deceit and tricks rule cowardly men. He who can look death
> straight in the face, this soldier alone is a free man.

Where all of the songs of the first volume are for one voice, all of the songs of the second volume are duets. Most of the songs of the third volume (including "Wohlauf Kameraden") are for solo voice.[47] The music is cast in a strophic AAB form. In the middle of the B section, a fermata announces the entry of other voices for the rest of the song. This is a unique form in the songs I have seen. The music after the fermata repeats the text the solo voice has just sung, as if the many consists of replications of solo voices, all saying the same thing. The moment will sound to the listener like an echo in which he hears his own voice returning to him in the company of others.

"Zu Strassburg auf der Schanz" is told from the point of view of a French deserter who seeks death at the hands of his German captors. The enemy soldier craves an honorable death; here are stanzas five and

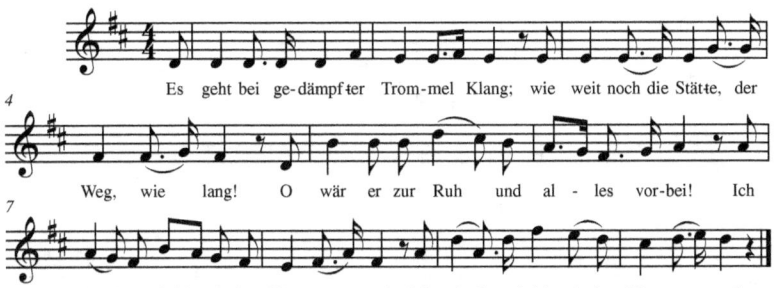

Es geht bei ge-dämpf-ter Trom-mel Klang; wie weit noch die Stät-te, der Weg, wie lang! O wär er zur Ruh und al - les vor-bei! Ich glaub es bricht mir das Herz ent - zwei, Ich - glaub es bricht mir das Herz ent - zwei.

Figure 42

six: "5. You brothers, all three of you, I beg you to shoot all at once. Don't spare my young life! Shoot so that the red blood springs from my body, I beg you! 6. O queen of heaven, take up my soul! Take it to you in heaven; dear angels forget not mine!"

"Es geht" (Figure 42, with the words of the first stanza of the text) presents a text in which a woman witnesses the execution of her beloved. Here is the fourth stanza: "4. Nine took aim and eight bullets flew past; all tremble in agony and pain, but I, I struck him straight in his heart." The song mimics the staccato beat of a snare drum. There is bitter irony in the song as the beloved's heart is at once struck by the lover's devotion and the executioners' bullets.

"Frisch auf, Soldatenblut" (Figure 43, with the words of the first stanza of the text) provides a stark contrast between text and music:

1. Arise you soldier's blood; arise in good spirits! And don't let yourself feel fear when cannons are trembling. Beat the drum nice and strong; I want to be the first!

2. The drums roll; their sound is terrible. One sees almost no ground at all from all the dying and the dead. Here lies a foot; there lies an arm; Oh! May God have mercy!

3. One falls sprayed with his own blood. He folds his hands in prayer; his time is almost up. Dear one, good night!

4. How many young brides cry bitterly! Because she has been faithfully loving, he has stayed with the battle; his path is now complete. Dear sweetie, good night!

The music has the bright bounce of a bugle call in A major, sounding first, third, and fifth scale degrees within a limited range stressing a-natural[1]. The music consists of three four-measure phrases; phrase one

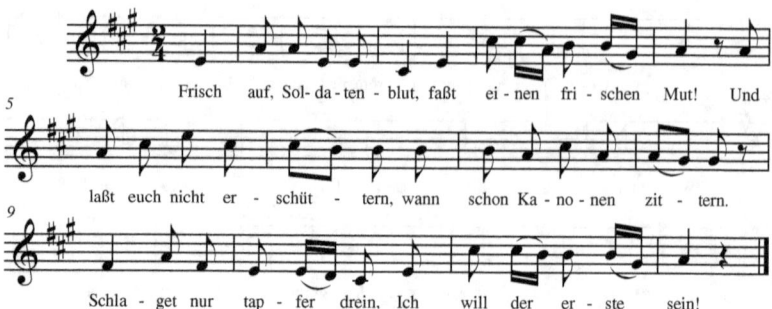

Figure 43

ends wrapping the tonic a-natural[1] in both of its neighbors—b-natural[1] and g-sharp[1] (measures 3–4); phrase two ends on an unresolved leading-tone g-sharp[1] (measure 8); phrase three ends again wrapping the tonic a-natural[1] in both of its neighbors—b-natural[1] and g-sharp[1] (measure 12). The melodies of phrases one and three close on a-natural[1], outlining a compound melody (measures 3–4 and 11–12). The top portion of the melody moves in a 3-2-1 motion down to a-natural[1] (see the c-sharp[2] sixteenth note / the b-natural[1] sixteenth note / moving down to a-natural[1]), while an implied lower voice articulates tonic from below—a-natural[1] / g-sharp[1] / a-natural[1].

The tenth volume of songs contains a very vivid account of a soldier dying—"Der sterbender Krieger" (Figure 44):

1. Far away on a green meadow lies a dying soldier who here on the field has fought honorably as a hero.
2. He heard the trumpet calling him to the dance of weapons and sees in his mind his homeland, forest and field in the brilliant sun.
3. His lips tremble gently "O, what a short path of life! I and many comrades will never again see my homeland again.
4. "If only I could shake the hands of my love one last time; I must leave the world, and I die for the fatherland.
5. "In my homeland I entrust my loved ones to God; may so much young, German blood not have flowed in vain!"
6. Evening winds blew around him, his breast is breathing hard; his limbs trembled gently and then his heart beats no longer.

A binary meter would have made this song sound like a funeral march; instead, the 3/4 meter gives it a hushed, sacred quality. The music is unique in the double quality of its 3–2–1 descending final line. The melody closes once, quickly in its higher register f-sharp[2]/e-natural[2]/

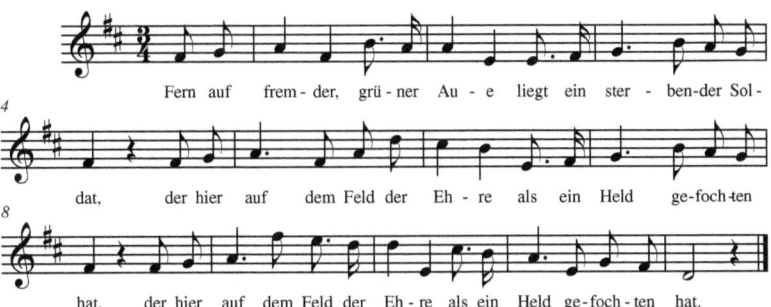

Fern auf frem - der, grü - ner Au - e liegt ein ster - ben-der Sol-

dat, der hier auf dem Feld der Eh - re als ein Held ge-foch-ten

hat, der hier auf dem Feld der Eh - re als ein Held ge-foch - ten hat.

Figure 44

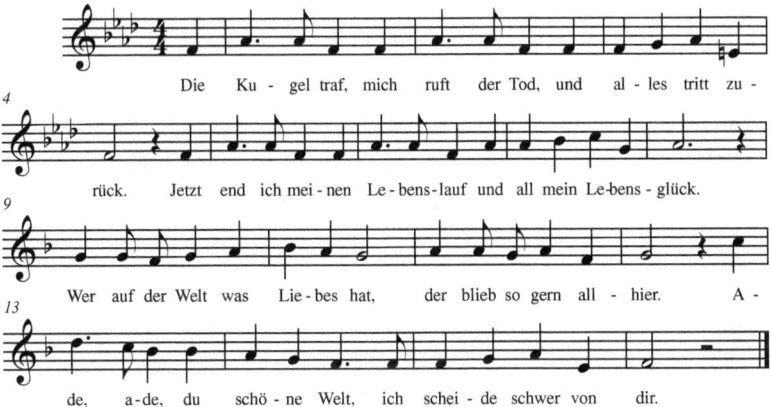

Die Ku - gel traf, mich ruft der Tod, und al - les tritt zu -

rück. Jetzt end ich mei - nen Le - bens-lauf und all mein Le-bens - glück.

Wer auf der Welt was Lie - bes hat, der blieb so gern all - hier. A -

de, a-de, du schö - ne Welt, ich schei - de schwer von dir.

Figure 45

d-natural^2 in measure 9. The earlier f-sharp^{1}s still resound however, and the last phrase of the music gently pulls the melody through e-natural^1 (measures 10–11) to its final resting point—d-natural^1 (measure 12).

"Der sterbende Soldat" from volume 9 ("Ich weiss einen Linden-baum stehen") is very unusual in the series (Figure 45, with words of the first stanza of the text). The pain of death is plentiful in the text: "The wound burns, the eye fails, everything is faint around me. I was sent so soon into battle and now I lie dying here. Farewell sunlight; I shall see you no longer." The music (by Arnold Mendelssohn) begins in F minor and shifts to F major—a Schubertian touch. The poignancy of the song resides precisely in this modal shift as the dying soldier remembers what might have been in major. The range of the song is limited to a major sixth f-natural^1/d-natural^2 (plus the e-natural^1 leading tone). Note the imagery of the soldier's heart breaking in two at once from his fatal injury and from love for his beloved.[48]

Of the remaining songs in the series, all are in major with only five exceptions.[49] There are two songs by major classical composers.[50] Most of the composers are men, but there are several songs in the series composed by women.[51] The other songs in the series set texts in ways similar to the songs discussed above. The overwhelming use of major keys in the songs in this series and the preponderance of duple division make them ideal marching songs, with an occasional song in a darker minor mode and an occasional song in triple meter. The texts of the songs discussed above prepare the listener for the death and suffering of others and for his own death and suffering. The use of major keys in such songs produces a discrepancy in them between text and music.

German War Songs: World War II

A new version of *Wohlauf Kameraden* was published as *Wohlauf Kameraden! Ein Liederbuch der jungen Mannschaft von Soldaten, Bauern, Arbeitern und Studenten* in Berlin in 1934. The dedication to the volume reads:

> Arise Comrades! A songbook of young people—soldiers, farmers, workers, and students. In cooperation with the national socialist, German student organization, the national organization of German technical and vocational education, the national association for the study of the German nation and homeland, edited by Gerhard Pallman. Bärenreiter, 1934.[52]

Listing all these administrative groupings is the bureaucratic equivalent of the structure Leni Riefenstahl captures so clearly in *Triumph des Willens,* especially in the scene in which frontal medium shots capture German soldiers calling out their home regions. The exhaustive, bureaucratic subheadings of *Wohlauf Kameraden* make it possible for each German student, worker, and farmer to find him- or herself in the book.[53]

The anthology as a medium is an ideological construct. It began in the nineteenth century as an outgrowth of the relatively recent inauguration of the masterwork in the Western canon. As soon as pieces of music achieved the status of monuments in culture, lesser pieces arranged themselves around the edges. Collections of such pieces became a common genre intended to provide pedagogical and recreational activity for the middle classes. The national socialists used this tradition of the anthology to further their project. *Wohlauf Kameraden* not only presents its performer/listener with pieces that celebrate the new Germany; the anthology also embodies the act of purification itself, avoiding the stain of decadent music.[54]

The title of the collection, *Wohlauf Kameraden*, embodies in miniature one aspect of my thesis about right-wing ideology. The editors have taken the leftist word *comrades* to refer to fascist subjects. The book is an anthology of German music that presents, as if an organic whole, a history of chorales, folk songs, national socialist war songs, and songs of workers and laborers whose texts have all been bent to the right.[55]

The book has a foreword by Frick, interior minister of the Nazis. With reference to the folk song, Frick writes:

> If this weapon, which has been proven within our own ranks, is placed in the hands of the German worker, it will fundamentally contribute to the manifestation and internal realization of the national socialist revolution. "Wohlauf Kamaraden" should be the battle cry to war in which the Hitler youth and the university and college students step up to the great task of a higher calling with the will to form a new internal unity of the nation based on the foundation of its thousand years of cultural heritage.[56]

Two things strike me as remarkable about this anthology. First, the speed with which it came out—a mere year after the national socialists attained power in 1933—and second, the gesture of re-marking the entirety of German music history, including socialist worker songs, into the ideological circle of fascism.[57] The book's sources are well documented. Brief citations at the bottom of each song suggest the apparatus of musicological scholarship. Many of the citations say "mundlich überliefert" or "aurally transmitted." This, too, is ideological, as if to add a touch of the authenticity of the aural tradition to the powerfully mediated production of national socialist ideology.[58]

Pallman's *Wohlauf Kameraden* of 1934 opens with a transposed and altered version of a song that had begun the earlier collection of the same title published in 1914. The 1914 version has eight stanzas of a text by Friedrich Schiller set to a song in B-flat major. For his 1934 work, Pallman transposes the song to a brighter A major. The 1914 version is for one voice alone; the 1934 version for two and then three voices. In the 1914 version there are eight stanzas of text; in the 1934 version, Pallman has omitted stanzas 4–7. Pallman might have wanted to edit out particularly gruesome lines such as "he digs and shovels as long as he lives and digs till he digs his own grave" from the end of stanza 4.[59] The

1914 version had a fermata in the middle of the music; Pallman deletes the fermata in favor of constant, fluid, rhythmic motion.[60]

Much of the power of *Wohlauf Kameraden* derives from juxtaposition. The songs seem loosely organized—within each section of the book they are unnumbered—but the editor seems to alternate between the archaic and the contemporary to create in the ear of the singing subject a sense of deep connection between the texts and music of Germany's past and national socialist present. To see how this works, I will examine the sixteenth and seventeenth songs of the first section "Volk und Reich": "Gelöbnis" and "Die Fahne hoch," respectively. Here is the text of "Gelöbnis":

> I swear to you, o fatherland
> with clean sword firmly in my hand
> upon the altars of the holy shrine
> to be true to you unto death.
>
> I swear to you, o freedom
> to serve you as well till my last breath
> with heart and soul, courage and blood,
> a man's best attributes.
>
> I swear I will enflame bloody hatred
> and the deepest rage
> without regard to whom and whose land
> who disgrace our German soil.
>
> You above in heaven
> who steers both suns and hearts
> you great God, o abide by my side
> that I remain true and faithful to you.

The music (Figure 46) is extraordinary in many ways. The meter is 5/2. Each line of text gets one measure of music, beginning and ending with half notes; quarter notes are in between. Each measure is a single phrase. The meter is simple and declamatory. The half notes mark off the modality of D dorian: d-natural[1]/a-natural[1] for the first phrase, a-natural[1]/d-natural[1] for the second phrase, a-natural[1]/f-natural[1] for the third phrase, and f-natural[1]/d-natural[1] for the fourth phrase.[61] Half notes are points of departure and destination. It is as if the rhythm embodied the declamatory gesture of the text's oath taking; from one half note to another, the singer pledges his or her allegiance.

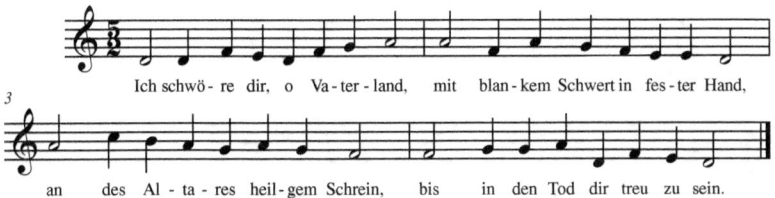

Figure 46

The archaic D dorian has no leading tone and fails to reach d-natural^2, coming very close with the c-natural^2 in the third phrase.[62] The dark, failed apex of the melody sets up the powerful descending perfect fifth dead center of the fourth phrase. The perfect fifth sets "Tod" (death). There is a religious undercurrent in this work, both in the text and music. Fred K. Prieberg has argued extensively that the national socialists carefully refigured church music in the years from 1933 to 1945. The national socialists discouraged texts that were "confessional" and pointed away from "das Volk" as source of meaning in German life. Textual alterations ranged from subtle to explicit, including the project of reading Bach and Handel as composers of the new Germany (Prieberg 344–75).[63]

"Gelöbnis" is followed by a song that has become infamous, the "Horst-Wessel Lied," published in *Wohlauf Kameraden* as "Die Fahne hoch":

Raise the flag, the troops in tight formation!
The SA is marching in calm, steady formation.
Comrades who were shot as reactionaries,
they march as ghosts with our formations.

Clear the street for the brown battalion!
Clear the street for the storm troop leader,
millions are already gazing with hope at the swastika.
The day for freedom and bread has come.

The attack alarm has sounded for the last time:
we all stand ready for the fight.
Soon Hitler's flag will flutter above all streets,
the servitude will last only a little longer.

Raise the flag, the troops in tight formation!
The SA is marching in calm, steady formation.
Comrades who were shot as reactionaries,
they march as ghosts with our formations.

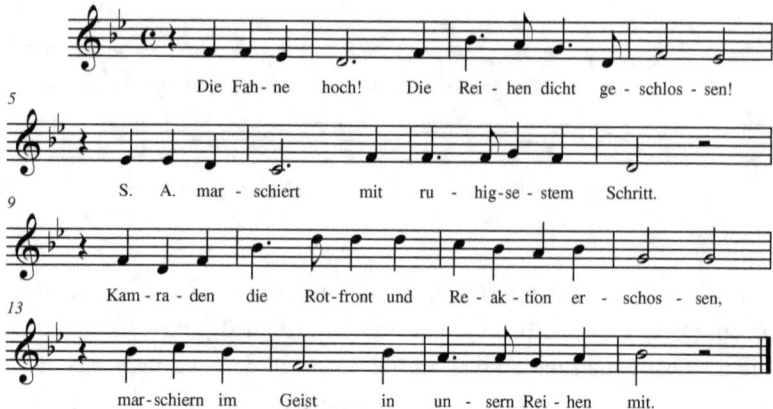

Die Fah - ne   hoch!   Die   Rei - hen dicht   ge - schlos - sen!

S.   A.   mar - schiert   mit   ru - hig-se - stem   Schritt.

Kam - ra - den   die   Rot-front und   Re - ak - tion er - schos - sen,

mar - schiern im   Geist   in   un - sern Rei - hen   mit.

Figure 47

Like "Gelöbnis," "Die Fahne hoch" (Figure 47) gives each line of text a phrase of music.[64] Unlike "Gelöbnis," "Die Fahne hoch" is in fully realized, modern B-flat major, complete with leading tone a-natural[1] and the bright and powerful third scale degree d-natural[2] (the note that the previous song had failed to reach) in the third phrase. More importantly, "Die Fahne hoch" rhythmically resolves the irregular 5/2 of "Gelöbnis." "Die Fahne hoch" is in clear 4/4, the meter of the text's calm SA formations. This is a marching motion of complete confidence and expansive certainty. Each phrase begins with a quarter rest in which the singer can comfortably take in breath for the next phrase. And while a dark, descending third ends "Gelöbnis," a bright, ascending third concludes "Die Fahne hoch."[65]

"Spruch" is quite similar to "Gelöbnis." The text is from Ernst Leibel; the setting from Walther Henkel in 1929:

And the fist will be weak from bruises,
we believe in our eternal goals
and incite the red-hot fire.
And hope deep in hard humiliation
that Germany's sun shall rise again.

The haggling foreigners became guilty;
we have suffered long enough, patiently in God's eyes.
But now it has come to an end!
God gives the insolent, malicious power of money
back into our hands.

Then let us build upon spirit and love!
The chaff is separated and the red kernels
remain in our strainer.
To work! To work! The vein
sows it blessingly in the fields.

Writing in 1944, Richard Eichenauer speaks of "bäuerlich" as a state of mind of national socialist "Bodenfestigkeit," of being rooted in time and space as opposed to the nomadic "hin und her" of Jews and Gypsies.[66] For Eichenauer the "Bodenfestigkeit" of national socialist ideology is reflected in the simple acts of farming, of working with the seasons, as reflected in the text of "Spruch" (Figure 48).[67] The national socialists skillfully blended politics and nature in their music anthologies. *Musika-lische Feiergestaltung* was published in 1938; it is an annotated bibliog-raphy of music with brief essays aimed at giving teachers and music leaders throughout the country a guide to what music to sing for specific occasions. The cycle of seasons is stressed throughout with key festivities, including the "Tag der Machtergriefung" (January 30), blended seam-lessly into a series of seasonal celebrations.[68]

The text alludes to Germany's post–World War I economic woes in conventional anti-Semitic discourse. The text focuses on reclaiming the land in idealized agricultural imagery. The five-line stanza gives the text a heavy, labored quality. The music, like "Gelöbnis," is in a combination of meters: 3/2 and 2/2—a pacing but awkward meter. Each line of text gets a phrase, each beginning with an upbeat. Like "Gelöbnis," each phrase reaches out. Rhythmically there is an upbeat, a measure of 3/2 or 2/2 followed either by repeated notes or two half notes. "Spruch" is in D dorian without leading tone The range is an octave from d-natural^1 to d-natural^2 (with an upper neighbor e-natural^2 extending the octave to a ninth). The archaic modality is articulated by the endings of the three phrases. The first phrase ends with ascending g-natural^1 / a-natural^1 slur followed by a half-note a-natural^1 in measure 2. The second phrase closes on two half notes: b-natural^1/a-natural^1 in measure 6. The third phrase brings the entire song down to the modal point of origin with e-natural^1 moving to d-natural^1 in measure 10.

The next song in *Wohlauf Kameraden*, "Deutsches Weihelied,"[69] moves the modality of D dorian into the tonal D minor:

We raise our hands in deep, bitter misery.
Lord God send us a leader

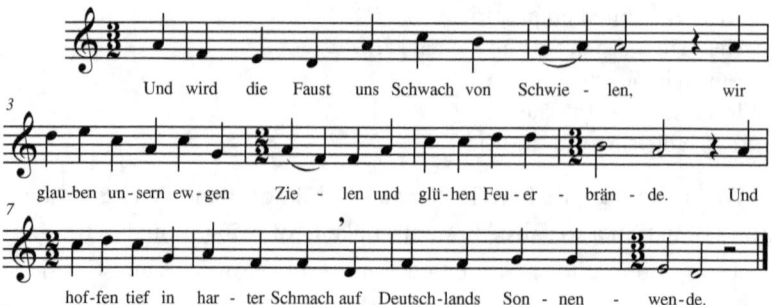

Und wird die Faust uns Schwach von Schwie - len, wir

glau-ben un-sern ew-gen Zie - len und glü-hen Feu-er - brän - de. Und

hof-fen tief in har - ter Schmach auf Deutsch-lands Son - nen - wen-de.

Figure 48

who will turn around our sorrows,
with powerful command
with powerful command.

Awake for us, the hero
who has mercy on his people;
the people that has been weighed down by darkness,
sold and betrayed,
and are in the hands of our enemy.

Awake for us the hero,
who is strong in times of need,
who will stir his Germany powerfully,
who leads your Germany with belief
into the red of the morning sun.

We bless our arms and weapons,
our heads, and heart, and hand!
Do not let your light, people
of the earth and my mother's land,
be ruined.

This text, from 1919, brings to the surface the anthology's strategy of
stirring post–World War I outrage at reparations. The image of Germany marching, renewed, into the red sun of morning condenses the
move of making a glimpse to the east represent rebirth (simultaneously
of the new day and the new German nation) as well as a right-wing
appropriation of left-wing workers' imagery. The text's urge is for prayer,
however, not revolution. The text associates the national socialist response
to Germany's post–World War I humiliation with the Pfingsten religious holiday. And the title of the song, "Deutsches Weihelied," connects
the work to songs of blessing and devotion (Figure 49).

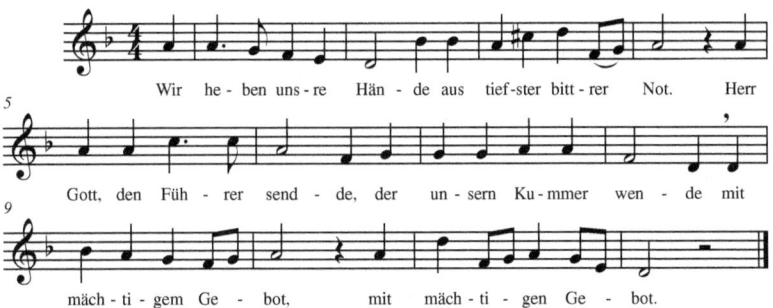

Wir he - ben uns - re Hän - de aus tief-ster bitt - rer Not. Herr

Gott, den Füh - rer send - de, der un - sern Ku - mmer wen - de mit

mäch - ti - gem Ge - bot, mit mäch - ti - gen Ge - bot.

Figure 49

This song takes the laconic, awkward D dorian of "Spruch" and brings it into the diatonic tonality of D minor. "Deutsches Weihelied" has three phrases. Each phrase is split into two subphrases. The first subphrase moves from a-natural[1] down to d-natural[1] through the third f-natural[1]/e-natural[1]/d-natural[1] (measures 1–2). The second subphrase introduces the leading tone of the now decidedly diatonic D minor and pauses at its conclusion on a-natural[1] (measure 4). Both subphrases of the next phrase outline F major (measures 4–6 and 6–8). The third phrase (measures 8–12) brings us back to D minor with the first subphrase (measures 8–10) ending on the f-natural[1]/g-natural[1]/a-natural[1] rising motion. After the horn-call perfect fourth from a-natural[1] to d-natural[2], the same rising motion is repeated, and the song ends on d-natural[1].

The next song continues to work with the D dorian / D minor modal/tonal binary. "Morgenruf" (Figure 50) has, according to the song's documentation, a complex history. The text is Schenkendorf (1813); the music from Heinrich Schütz (1628); the version at hand by Ernst Sommer:

Arise from the earth, you who are slumbering!
The horses whinny the good morning to us.
The lovely weapons are shimmering
so brightly in the red of the morning sun;
one dreams of victory wreaths and of death.

You splendid God, in grace
look down from the blue tent above!
You yourself brought us here
to this field of weapons.
Let us have the day
and give us victory;
the Christian flags are fluttering,
the war, dear Lord, is yours.

A morning shall come,
a morning mild and clear;
the devout are waiting expectantly
the company of angels gazes at them.
Soon he shines like a mantle
upon each German man;
O day of fullness, break forth,
you day of freedom, break forth!

Then resounding from all the towers
and resounding in every chest,
and quiet after the storm
and love and high spirits!
All paths resound
then cries of victory,
and we the loyal soldiers
we were also there!

The conflation of religion and war is condensed in the phrases "Engel Schar" and "Christenbanner." "Engel" and "Christ" are Christian images; "Schar" and "Banner" are military images. The music is a hybrid of modality and diatonic tonality. The first phrase (measures 1–4) suggests D minor with the ascending line b-natural^1/c-sharp^2/d-natural^2. The rest of the piece sounds like D dorian with C-naturals and B-flats.[70]

"Das Lied vom neuen Reich" (Figure 51) is explicit national socialist propaganda. The text is by Hermann Claudius 1933; the music by Konrad Ameln:

We want a strong, united empire
for which our fathers fell.
That's why we march, you and I,
and hundreds of thousands, too,
and our flags unfurl.

We want a strong, united empire
for us and our descendents.
That's why we march, you and I,
and hundreds of thousands, too.
And for this, we wish to die!

We want a strong, united empire
full of high spirits.
That's why we march, you and I
and hundreds of thousands, too.
And our flags blow.

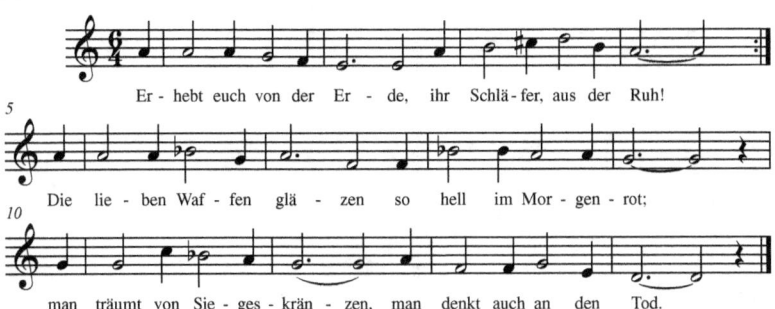

Er - hebt euch von der Er - de, ihr Schlä- fer, aus der Ruh!

Die lie - ben Waf - fen glä - zen so hell im Mor - gen - rot;

man träumt von Sie - ges - krän - zen, man denkt auch an den Tod.

Figure 50

We want a strong, united empire
of our own German blood.
That's why we march, you and I,
and hundreds of thousands, too.
Help, O Lord, our courage.

There is one vocal phrase for each line of the text—an uneven five-line form. The song is in D dorian. While the vocal line reaches d-natural^2 (measures 3, 5, and 8) and sounds bright, the lower register sounds dark, poised on e-natural^1 at the end of the song.

One of the clearest examples of musical appropriation occurs in the *three* versions of the socialist worker song "Brüder zur Sonne zur Freiheit" in *Wohlauf Kameraden* (1934). The Russian revolutionary Leonid P. Radin wrote the text in 1897. "Arbeiterlied" bears the closest resemblance to the original. It contains a different second and third stanza that connect the worker of the first two stanzas with a national socialist worker of the new third stanza, as follows:[71]

Break the yoke of tyranny!
Its sowing must sprout!
Then fly the flag of the swastika
over the nation of workers!

See Figure 52 for "Arbeiterlied" with the added third strophe.

Monika Tibbe points out that the imagery and political orientation of the original leftist text was vague and hidden because the text and song were written in prison. The words had to be coded (Tibbe 39). It is precisely into this vague text that the national socialist interpolation of a new stanza can be placed.

Both other versions set text to this music exactly, with no change of tonality or articulation. Since this is a well-known song in its socialist

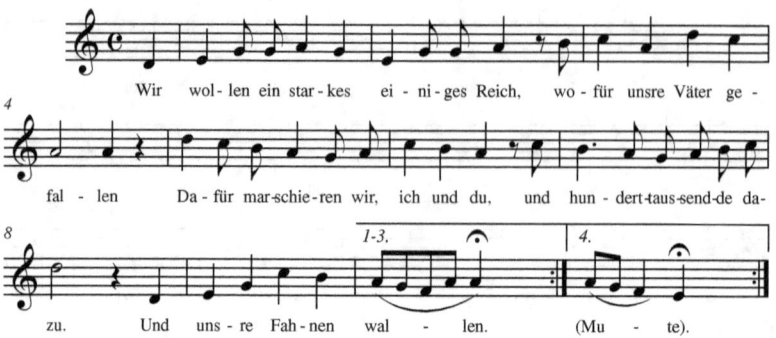

Figure 51

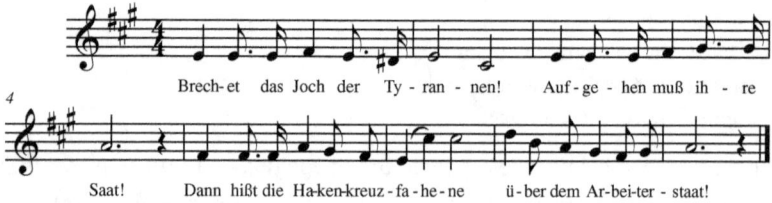

Figure 52

original, and since Pallman included three rewritings of it in *Wohlauf Kameraden* (1934), I shall offer translations of the other two versions in their entirety. "Brüder formiert die Kollonen" occurs early in the volume and concludes the first section, entitled "Volk und Reich."

1. Brothers, form columns!
Listen to the cries of thousands!
Germany, my Germany, we are coming
Coming to liberate you!

2. Hear what the dead are saying!
Working Germany is in need.
We unfurl our flags in storms
Blood-red and black as death.

3. Brothers, let's make an end of this.
Tear yourselves loose from your chains.
Germany, great Germany,
We are coming to make you unified and large once again.

4. Brothers form into columns.
Make an end to distress.
Germany, my Germany
We are coming with bread and freedom for you!

The other version of the song occurs right after the only work in the volume ascribed to a great composer: "Arbeiter tretet ein," with music by Ludwig van Beethoven. "Arbeiter, tretet ein" is in F minor. The song is based on Beethoven's three-part canon "Abbe Stadler," originally in G minor.[72]

The song that follows reworks the melody of "Brüder zur Sonne, zur Freiheit" one more time, in A major. Pallman is skillful throughout the anthology, linking songs in a gentle series of modal and tonal configurations. Having a piece in F minor be followed by a piece in A major sounds very bold, and it is an unusual harmonic opposition in the volume. F minor and A major are distant, chromatic mediants. "Brüder in Zechen und Gruben" has the same pitch structure as "Arbeiterlied" shown above. To this music, the following text is grafted:

1. Brothers in the mines and pits
Brothers behind the plow
Out of the factories and inns and offices
Follow the procession of the banner!

2. Hitler is our leader
He hasn't been tainted by the gold
Of Jewish thrones that
Roll at his feet!

3. The day of revenge is near!
One day we'll be free.
Working Germany awaken,
Break your chains in two!

4. Then let the banner fly,
So our enemies will see it, too!
We will always be victorious
As long as we stick together.

5. Load the empty rifles!
Load them with powder and lead.
Shoot the betrayers of the fatherland!
Down with Jewish tyranny!

6. Remain true to Hitler
True to the death!
Hitler will lead us
Once and for all from this distress.

Jews are only mentioned explicitly twice in this anthology—once in "Volk ans Gewehr" (to be discussed at the end of this chapter) and here in "Brüder in Zechen und Gruben." The anti-Semitism in "Brüder in Zechen und Gruben" is particularly virulent, an extraordinary act of musical aggression for anyone with the socialist song in his or her ears.

There are several songs in *Wohlauf Kameraden* that set texts describing a soldier's death to simple, clear, diatonic harmonies. These songs depend on a simple and severe contrast between text and music. "Der Trommelbube" is an example:

1. We march along the street with calm, steady step
and the flag flutters above us.

2. The drummer boy marches at the front drumming well,
the boy has no idea, as love has no idea, who will be taken.

3. He drums many into blood and grave,
and yet each loves this happy drummer boy.

4. Maybe it will be me tomorrow who will die in blood,
the boy has no idea, as love has no idea, who will be taken.

There is a powerful disavowal of an affective response to death in this text. The happy drummer boy marches on in the dimension of drive, oblivious to the death around him. The implied narrator ponders the possibility of his own death; yet he, and all other implied subjects in the text, love the drummer boy nevertheless (Figure 53).[73]

The music is in clear G major, moving from g-natural^1 (measure 1), to b-natural^1 (measures 2 and 5), to d-natural^2 (measure 6)—a clear arpeggiation of the triad of G major. The piece ends on b-natural^1 suggesting continuous motion, the implication of a first-inversion G major triad making the song resonate at its conclusion.

"Der Trommelbube" is very much like "Von allen den Kameraden" (Figure 54, with the words of the first stanza of the text):

1. Among all of our comrades
no one was as good and so true
as our little trumpeter
inspired by the joy of Hitler.

2. We sat so happily together
one stormy night,
and he made us happy
with his songs of freedom.

3. Then during his happy song
an enemy's bullet

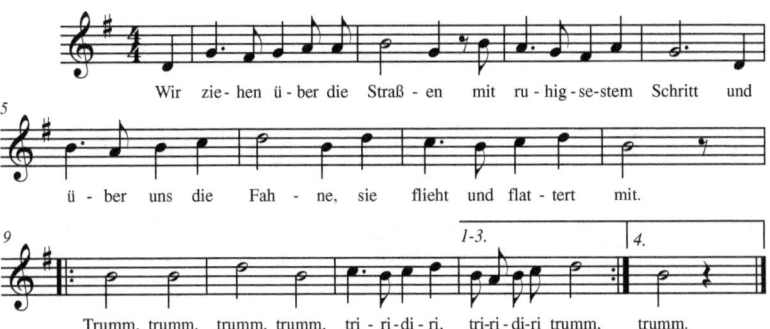

Wir zie- hen ü - ber die Straß - en mit ru - hig - se-stem Schritt und

ü - ber uns die Fah - ne, sie flieht und flat - tert mit.

1-3. *4.*

Trumm, trumm, trumm, trumm, tri - ri - di - ri, tri-ri - di-ri trumm, trumm.

Figure 53

struck him down
with a wistful smile on his face.

4. We took shovels and spades
and dug a grave for him.
And those who liked him the best
lay him down to rest.

5. Sleep well you little trumpeter,
we all liked you;
sleep well you little trumpeter
inspired by the joy of Hitler.[74]

The music is in a clear and unremarkable C major. "Der Trommelbube" and "Von allen den Kameraden" are both songs in which fantasies of dying are set in very bright, diatonic harmonies.[75] There is, in both cases, a crass discrepancy between lyrics dark with ominous forebodings of death and very bright, diatonic music. This is a music of disavowal— profoundly psychotic at its edges.[76] As well, the songs give to the subject singing them a self-pitying fantasy projection of what it would be like to have comrades mourn one's own death.[77]

We have listened to several songs of *Wohlauf Kameraden* that typify national socialist strategies for creating a musical vehicle of interpellation. Some songs rely subtly on appropriation of Jewish elements (as does "Volk ans Gewehr," to be discussed below); other songs take music and openly substitute new, national socialist texts (i.e., "Lied der alten Garde," not discussed here). Some songs turn a worker's song to the right (three versions of "Brüder zur Sonne zur Freiheit"). Some songs use bright, diatonic harmonies to disavow affective responses ("Der Trommelbube"

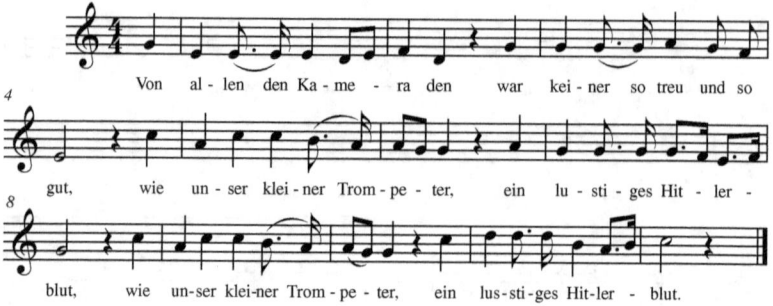

Figure 54

and "Von allen den Kameraden"). Several songs evoke a dark, pretonal modality to evoke, simultaneously, a purer German past and a burden to be overcome ("Das Lied vom neuen Reich"). Other songs move in pairs back and forth between tonal and modal musical materials ("Gelöbnis" and "Die fahne Hoch"). Such binary motions create at once an evocation of a pretonal world of German purity (better than the national socialist "present") and a triumphant rebirth of the German spirit (better than the dark, modal "past").

One of the main differences between *Wohlauf Kameraden* (1914) and *Wohlauf Kameraden* (1934) is that, in the world of the latter collection, the enemy is both without and within German social space.[78] As a result, the binary oppositions upon which national socialist aggression are based are much more complex than those that underwrite the German songs of World War I. The psychoanalytic structure of sadism can help us understand subject formations based upon complex (mis)identifications of the enemy within and the enemy without.

Music as Sadism

Masochism and sadism and were first coined as psychoanalytic terms in 1893 by Richard Freiherr von Krafft-Ebing, with reference to the lives of the Marquis de Sade and Baron von Sacher-Masoch, respectively.[79] Sigmund Freud discussed sadism and masochism as the two poles of pleasure resulting from inflicting pain on the other (sadism) and inflicting pain on the self (masochism). For Freud, the violent component of sexuality produces, in extreme versions, the perversions of sadism and masochism. For Freud, sadism is primary; masochism, secondary.[80]

At the end of his lecture "The Deconstruction of the Drive," Lacan says, how can one say, just like that, as Freud goes on to do, that exhibitionism is the contrary of voyeurism, or that masochism is the contrary of sadism? He posits this simply for grammatical reasons, for reasons concerning the inversion of the subject and the object, as if the grammatical object and subject were real functions. It is easy to show that this is not the case, and we have only to refer to our structure of language for this deduction to become impossible. But what, by means of this game, he conveys to us about the essence of the drive is what, next time, I will define for you as the trace of the act.[81]

For Lacan, the sadist is more interested in the gaze of the Other than an other he abuses. Let us consider the voyeur as an illustration. Lacan situates the articulation of the voyeur's subject position with a look at an other imbricated withing the symbolic and inscrutable gaze of the Other in whose service the entire scenario takes place.[82] When Lacan says that sadism "is a question of *Herrschaft*, of *Bewältigung*,"[83] he means mastery of an other in the service of the Other.

Let us imagine how this works with Lacan's well-known broken circle of drive. At the tiny horizontal bar that suggests a starting point, the drive moves toward its object counterclockwise, aiming at the other imbricated within the symbolic gaze of the Other. If brute cruelty were at stake, an act of violence would close the circle. But these war songs suggest in their proliferation, their strophic structures, their reworkings of a small number of images, motives, and calls to arms, the dimension of drive.

If you write a computer program as a series of if-then statements and variables, the program will run once and stop. In the old days of slow computers, a programmer could see the singular event in a flawed program and fix it; now since computers are so fast, a singular run through a program occurs so quickly it is hard to distinguish what has happened from what hasn't. But with the addition of a "repeat loop," the program will run over and over again, with a sense of digital "presence" simulated by reiterated "nows" at the speed of the processor. So what is the sadist's repeat loop? What keeps the sadist from exhausting his energy in a single expenditure of pain?

The sadist's other can never feel enough pain since what the sadist really wants resides in the symbolic space of the Other—always at an inscrutable remove from the imaginary oscillations of (mis)identifications moving back and forth between the self and the other.[84]

"Volk ans Gewehr" and Sadism

"Volk ans Gewehr" is the fourth song in *Wohlauf Kameraden*. It was written by Arno Pardun, composer of several songs in the anthology. It was dedicated to Goebbels and, according to Theodor Adorno, was "in the desolate air of Berlin in 1932 and 1933."[85] According to Hodek, "Volk ans Gewehr" was one of the most often sung SS songs of the fascist years (Hodek 31). Leni Riefenstahl included the song in the soundtrack of her 1934 classic *Triumph des Willens*:[86]

1. See in the east the red of morning?
A sign of freedom of the sun!
We'll stick together, in life as in death,
whatever comes our way!

Why do we still doubt?
Stop quarrelling,
There's still German blood in our veins
The people to arms! The people to arms!

2. Many years passed.
The people betrayed and oppressed.
Traitors and Jews profited;
they had legions of victims.

A leader arose from the people,
restored belief and hope
to the people of Germany.
The people to arms! The people to arms!

3. Germans arise and stand in line for battle;
we march ahead to victory!
Work shall be free and we want to be free
and courageous and bold.

We ball up our fists and will dare
there's no turning back now
and no one can back out.
The people to arms! The people to arms!

4. Young and old, man for man,
embrace the flag of the swastika.
Whether townsman, or farmer, or worker,
they swing the sword and the hammer.

For Hitler, for freedom, for work, and bread.
Awaken Germany!

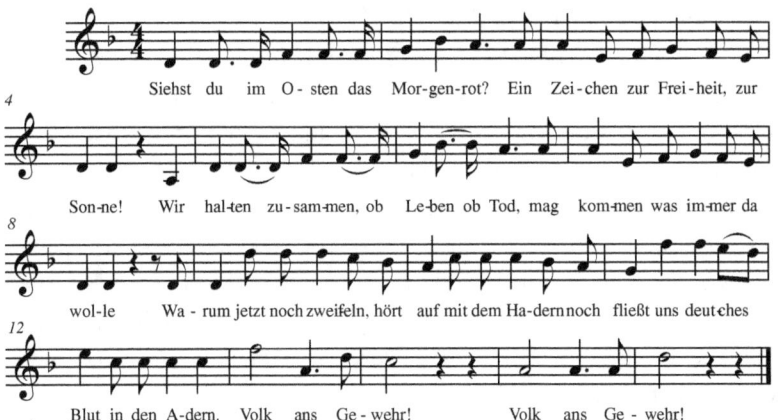

Siehst du im O - sten das Mor-gen-rot? Ein Zei - chen zur Frei - heit, zur

Son-ne! Wir hal-ten zu - sam-men, ob Le-ben ob Tod, mag kom-men was im-mer da

wol-le Wa - rum jetzt noch zweifeln, hört auf mit dem Ha-dern noch fließt uns deut-ches

Blut in den A-dern. Volk ans Ge - wehr! Volk ans Ge - wehr!

Figure 55

An end to distress.
The people to arms! The people to arms!

The song appropriates the music of the other in an act of barely disguised musical cannibalism (Figure 55). The music that sets the first stanza sounds like a Jewish melody.[87] The dotted rhythm, the gently rising melody in D dorian rises to the fifth, inflected with the flatted sixth, B-flat, before falling again back to D-natural. The repeated melody sounds gentler with the a-natural in measure 4 that is an upbeat to measure 5. One could hear the melody in D minor, but for me the song is more modal than tonal with the absence of the leading-tone C-sharp.[88]

The setting of the second stanza opens up suddenly with the octave leap from d-natural[1] to d-natural[2] (measure 9). This leap signifies for me a gesture of mastery that eradicates the melancholy of the first stanza. And more pointedly, the octave leap musically replaces the music of the other with a move to the masculine, contemporary, German F major. The octave leap is followed by a minor seventh that is very hard to sing, setting the words "uns deutsche." The g-natural[1] to f-natural[2] seventh (measure 11) strains the voice and threatens to tear apart the unison texture of male voices.[89] This minor seventh did not need to happen. The melody is descending from g-natural[1], and the song could have continued its descent; it would, in fact, have been more singable that way.[90]

The musical setting of the first iteration of the phrase "Volk ans Gewehr" describes the descending perfect-fourth f-natural[2] (downbeat of measure 13) to c-natural[2] (downbeat of measure 14) outlining F major

in a tonic to dominant motion. The musical setting of the second iteration of "Volk ans Gewehr" returns suddenly to D dorian, with the hail-
like ascending perfect-fourth a-natural[1] to d-natural[2] (measures 15–16).
F major suggests the impossibly perfect, purged body of the male, fascist
subject ("noch fließt uns deutsches Blut in den Adern").[91]

Before the settings of the line "Volk ans Gewehr," the note values are
sixteenth notes, dotted eighth notes, quarter notes, and dotted quarter
notes in the song. The first "Volk" (measure 13) repeats the song's climactic f-natural[2] held for two full beats; after two beats of rest, the next "Volk"
and the syllable "-wehr" (of the word "Gewehr") also get half notes
(measures 15–16).

The song is strophic—the same music is set to each stanza. This is a
highly conventional structure in religious, folk, and art music. In this
song, however, the strophic setting qualitatively contributes to the song's
structure. Over and over again, the music embodies the music of the
other in D dorian followed by a leap to f-natural[2] in F major. The music
stiffens then collapses and as men and women fill and empty their bodies
and the bodies of those around them with sound.[92]

The phrase "Volk ans Gewehr" occurs at the ends of stanzas 2, 4, 6,
and 8. Understanding these occurrences of the phrase as repetition might
lead to a state of military readiness, as in "people to arms (repeated),
and once you're ready, attack!" On another level, the phrase "people to
arms" suggests a desire for readiness that is always already too late. Thus
no amount of military readiness will ever sufficiently protect the state,
since it is always already infected by the other. In this sense, occurrences
of the phrase "the people to arms" are reiterative—saying the same thing
over and over again.[93]

In the late nineteenth, early twentieth century, traumatic neuroses began
to emerge in Europe and America as the result of industrialization and
its capacity to produce severe accidents. The trauma of highly mechanized war supported many of the war songs that prepared German soldiers for World War I. Several of these songs explicitly represent dismemberment, especially "Frisch auf, Soldatenblut" discussed above.[94]
The songs from *Wohlauf Kameraden* (1934), however, have no such
explicit representations of dismemberment.

While the World War I songs contain works written by women,
Wohlauf Kameraden (1934) contains no songs by women, reflecting the

gender politics of the national socialists that held that women belong at home raising children or in a social position clearly subordinated to male authority figures.[95] Like their antecedents, the songs of *Wohlauf Kameraden* (1934) reach far back into German history for textual and musical sources. Unlike their antecedents, the songs of the later *Wohlauf Kameraden* use a wide variety of meters to simulate spoken language, evocative of German theater of the 1920s, and skillfully oscillate between tonal and modal musical materials.[96]

Both the earlier and the later *Wohlauf Kameraden* contain songs whose texts suggest a connection between war and love beyond imagery of the sacrifice of domestic love for love of country or thinking of one's beloved at the moment of falling in the field. In particular, "Es geht" from *Wohlauf Kameraden* (1914) and "Der Trommelbube" from *Wohlauf Kameraden* (1934) connect love and war. To think of a bullet piercing a soldier's heart as love that breaks his heart ("Es geht") and to think of the appearance of death in war as the appearance of love in peacetime ("Der Trommelbube") suggest that these are less *war* songs than *love* songs: love of country, love of family, love of comrades, love of adventure, love of independence, and love of one's beloved at a distance.

CHAPTER FIVE

Closing the Wound

Parsifal *by Richard Wagner and Hans-Jürgen Syberberg*

This chapter explores representations of alterity in nineteenth- and twentieth-century Germany in Richard Wagner's opera *Parsifal* (1882) and Hans-Jürgen Syberberg's film *Parsifal* (1982). Having discussed the origins of the libretto, I will examine a wide variety of nineteenth-century writings (including Wagner's) on the Jewish question. I will then explore the role of Wagner's music in general and *Parsifal* in particular as ideological support for the project of national socialism. In moving along the trajectory anti-Semitism to Wagner to national socialism, I would like to avoid the trap of black-and-white claims of deterministic cause and effect. I will suggest that the varied and broadly disseminated discourse of nineteenth-century anti-Semitism underwrites a pathological dimension of Wagner's opera. I will also suggest that this dimension of Wagner's opera, in turn, underwrites the pathological ideology of purging psychic and social space of the other in national socialism. I will ground these ideas in details of the libretto and music, focusing on Amfortas's wound and the crucial moment of its closing in act 3. The chapter and book close with a rereading of *Parsifal* by the German filmmaker Hans-Jürgen Syberberg.

Richard Wagner and the Libretto for *Parsifal*

Chrétien de Troyes wrote *Perceval, ou Conte de Graal,* between 1180 and 1190; Wolfram von Eschenbach wrote *Parzival* at the beginning of the thirteenth century, based on the earlier material.[1] *Parzival* contains twenty-five thousand verses, and approximately eighty manuscripts of the work have survived in various stages of fragmentation (Wapnewski 13).[2] According to Ulrich Müller, a revival of interest in national epics was particularly strong in the late eighteenth and early nineteenth centuries in European countries that lacked national identities—Germany in particular: "The story of Siegfried, the Nibelungs, and the Burgundians, published in full in 1782 for the first time by the Swiss Christoph Heinrich Myller, gradually became something like a German national myth" (Müller 245). Wagner worked on the libretto for *Parsifal* from 1845 to 1877.[3] He read Eschenbach's epic in 1845 and began reading various accounts of the Grail myth in the same year.[4] In April 1857, Wagner was inspired to dramatize in music the Grail myth in connection with the beauty of Good Friday, and work on the libretto began in earnest (Holland 26–27). A summary of the action follows.

Act 1

In a medieval forest near the castle of Monsalvat, Gurnemanz, knight of the Grail, awakens two boys. Two knights arrive to prepare a morning bath for their king, Amfortas, who suffers from a wound in the side that cannot heal.[5] Kundry, an ageless woman, rushes in with balsam for Amfortas brought from Arabia. The king then enters and accepts the gift. Gurnemanz laments Amfortas's wound and tells its story. Klingsor, in a desperate attempt to gain acceptance by the Knights of the Grail, had castrated himself only to be rejected once and for all by the Knights. In response to this failure, he created a castle and garden of magic in which he charges Kundry with the seduction and destruction of the Knights of the Grail. Klingsor lures Amfortas into his trap, and while Amfortas lies in Kundry's arms, having succumbed to her seduction, Klingsor snatches his holy spear and stabs him in the side.

The Knights of the Grail seek redemption through a pure fool ("Der reine Tor") made wise through compassion ("durch Mitleid wissend"). Suddenly a swan falls to the ground, struck by an arrow. The Knights find Parsifal—a boy who had killed the swan for fun. Gurnemanz instills in Parsifal a sense of guilt for shooting the creature who had given the king a ray of hope. Parsifal flings away his bow and arrows in shame. Kundry tells the story of Parsifal's past. After Parsifal's father, Gamuret, had died in battle, his mother, Herzeleide, reared Parsifal in the forest, far from the world of men and weapons, but now she too is dead. As the

Knights carry Amfortas away, Gurnemanz leads Parsifal to the Grail ceremony to see if he is the one to redeem the Knights of the Grail.

As the ceremony is prepared, the voice of the king's father, the aged
Titurel, asks Amfortas if he is in a position to perform his office ("Mein
Sohn Amfortas, bist du am Amt?" [Amfortas, my son, are you in your
place?]); Amfortas hesitates in prolonged silence. Titurel orders the uncovering of the Grail. Gurnemanz asks Parsifal what he saw. In response
to Parsifal's silence, Gurnemanz tells Parsifal to leave and to hunt not
swans but geese.

Act 2

Klingsor awakens Kundry and charges her with the seduction of Parsifal. Having secured Amfortas's spear, he now seeks to inherit the Grail
by destroying Parsifal, whom he recognizes as the order's salvation.
Kundry, hoping for redemption, protests in vain. In Klingsor's magic
garden, flower maidens beg for Parsifal's embrace. Kundry enters and
touches Parsifal with tender memories of his childhood and mother.
Their lips touch ("der Liebe ersten Kuss") and Parsifal recoils, first mis-
taking his reaction for a sympathetic identification with Amfortas and
then as an expression of his own awakened sexual desire. Kundry continues to try and seduce Parsifal by telling him of her curse at having
laughed at "him" (Christ on the cross). Parsifal assures her that redemption will come to her, too, if she leads him to Amfortas. She refuses and
calls Klingsor, already weakened because of Parsifal's refusal of Kundry's
double seduction. Parsifal takes the spear and departs.

Act 3

A long time has passed between acts 2 and 3. The now-aged Gurnemanz
finds the corpselike Kundry in a thicket. As he revives her, a knight in
armor approaches in silence. Gurnemanz recognizes Parsifal and the
spear. Gurnemanz removes Parsifal's armor, and Kundry washes his feet,
drying them with her hair. In return, he baptizes her, then celebrates the
beauty of the spring fields. Distant bells announce the funeral of Titurel.
They walk toward the castle. No longer able to uncover the Grail, Amfortas begs the Knights to end his ongoing pain with death, but Parsifal
touches him with the spear, healing the wound. The ceremony has been
accomplished and Kundry falls dead ("entseelt").

Eschenbach and Wagner

Wagner made major changes to Eschenbach. According to Holland, the climax of Eschenbach's epic occurs at the work's exact midpoint: Parzival's transformation from a path of sin to a path of redemption in the extended discussion with Trevrizent. In Wagner, on the other hand, the magic of Good Friday is latent in act 2 and leads to the manifest culmination of the work in act 3.[6] Wagner has made Parsifal as passive as possible throughout his revisions of Eschenbach's epic; even moments in which Parsifal slays enemies in Wagner's opera occur offstage.[7] Holland points out that Eschenbach's climax is discursive—a dialogue between Parzival and Trevrizent; Wagner's is darkly erotic (Holland 29). Wagner wants Parsifal to represent a hero who responds to an inner calling rather than an external, active, heroic quest.

In both Eschenbach and Wagner, the hero is named by a woman, but to very different effect. In Eschenbach, Parzival learns of his name from his cousin; in Wagner, Kundry tells him his name as a move in the complex plan of seduction. She wants to have been under his skin when she tries to seduce him in act 2 (Holland 30). Eschenbach's Parzival is married, while Wagner's Parsifal remains chaste for the crucial Grail ceremony in act 3. For Holland, Parsifal's chastity is crucially linked to his destiny as he who will heal Amfortas's wound (Holland 28–29).[8] While Eschenbach's Parzival learns of the death of his mother as he begins his transformation from a path of sin to the path of redemption, in Wagner, Parsifal learns of the death of his mother from the mother-figure/seductress Kundry. At precisely the moment she tells Parsifal that his mother is dead, she has already begun to take advantage of her position with the still-innocent boy.

For Eschenbach, the posing of the question "Was fehlt dir?" ends the suffering of Amfortas. For Wagner, the spear and the Grail are integrated as Parsifal touches the wound with the spear that caused it, closing Amfortas's wound, reestablishing the circle of the Knights of the Grail, emptying Kundry of her last glimmer of life, and concluding the opera. Amfortas's suffering and his yearning for death, Klingsor's agony at his self-castration and rejection from the social space of the Knights, Parsifal's identification with Amfortas's wound and his renunciation of seduction suggest associations among sexuality, spirituality, sacrifice, death, and immortality for Wagner.

It is well known that Wagner was reading Schopenhauer's *The World as Will and Idea* during the *Parsifal* years. Wagner's reading of Schopenhauer is highly mediated and selective. Schopenhauer distinguishes between the affirmation of the will to live and the denial of the will to live. For Schopenhauer, the affirmation of the will to live is to fall into life, to live in the body, to embrace sexuality, and to live beyond oneself through procreation. Schopenhauer sees the denial of the will to live as a higher level of being, related to Christian sacrifice and Buddhist renunciation; one renounces sexuality and corporal sensation; one accepts death as absolute.[9] For example:

> Finally, if death comes, which breaks up the phenomenon of this will, the essence of such will having long since expired through free denial of itself except for the feeble residue which appears as the vitality of this body, then it is most welcome, and is cheerfully accepted as a longed-for deliverance. It is not merely the phenomenon, as in the case of others, that comes to an end with death, but the inner being itself that is abolished; this had a feeble existence merely in the phenomenon. This last slender bond is now severed; for him who ends thus, the world has at the same time ended.[10]

Richard Wagner's *Parsifal*

William Kindermann points out that, although we know that Wagner first expressed interest in the Parsifal story in 1845 and finished work on the libretto in 1877, the development of the music is less certain.[11] According to Kindermann, the first documented sketch for *Parsifal* was written in February 1876; this material became the "Komm! Holder Knabe" music from act 2.[12] Intensive work on the opera occurred between the end of summer 1877 and January 1882 (Kindermann, "Entstehung 1," 70–71). The Prelude to *Parsifal* was premiered in Bayreuth on December 25, 1878, with Wagner conducting.[13] The premiere of the entire opera took place on July 26, 1882, in Bayreuth with Hermann Levi conducting.[14]

The following analytical remarks on the opera will focus upon major thirds that descend by half step across the opera. Kindermann discusses Wagner's discovery of this musical idea as follows: "On the 26th of December [1877] Cosima wrote: 'Yesterday afternoon while I was still in the room, Richard delighted in discovering a major third from F-sharp/A-sharp that moved to F-natural/A-natural that had come to him.'"[15]

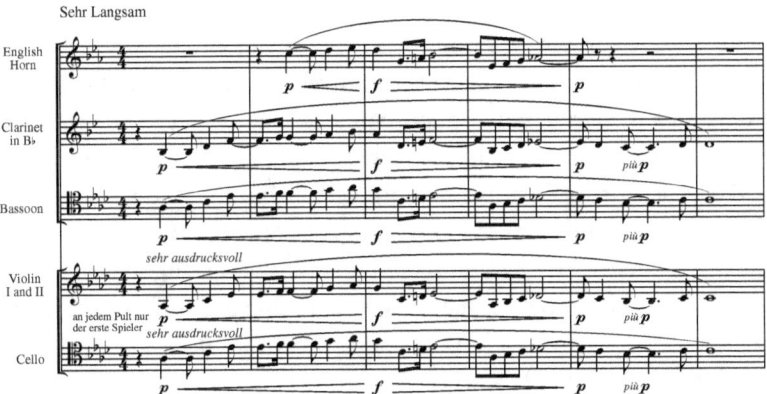

Figure 56

Major thirds that descend by half step pervade the opera. There are, how-ever, two crucial and linked moments at which a major third *ascends* by half step, once as Parsifal takes the spear from Klingsor in act 2 and once when Parsifal touches the spear to (heal) Amfortas's wound in act 3.[16]

The falling major third idea is not present explicitly in the *Vorspiel* of the opera; it derives, instead, from the half-step A-flat/G-natural stressed by the opening melody. The score shows how subtly Wagner orchestrates this opening melody. Notice first the delicate balance between winds and strings; the string component of the texture is thin, with celli and only one violin per stand playing.[17] This melody is doubled by the first clarinet and bassoon, and the English horn enters right on the F-natural on the second beat of measure 2—an exquisitely subtle way to strengthen the winds as the entire texture emphasizes the A-flat/G-natural half step (see the upbeat to, and the down beat of measure 3 in Figure 56). Kinder-mann points out Wagner's emphasis on the A-flat/G-natural half step and the way the opening melody prefigures in miniature the large-scale tonal pairing of A-flat and C.[18] The *Vorspiel* does not prefigure all the musical materials of the opera, though it does get the half-step A-flat/G-natural under our skin so that when we hear the Grail music at the end of act 1, it sounds as if we knew it already.

Kindermann hears the A-flat/G-natural half step as a representation of Amfortas's pain: "'The pain of Amfortas is suggested in measure three with the turn to C minor—a gesture strengthened by rhythmic context and the crescendo."[19] All transpositions of the opening melody that occur in the *Vorspiel* necessarily suggest a pair of keys, linked by the half-step falling motion. Kindermann points out that at the end of the opera the double-tonic complex is resolved as A-flat major emerges as the single, final key of resolution—the musical correlate of the redemption of the Knights of the Grail. For Kindermann, the final A-flat major chord of the opera "takes the place of the dissonant, descending half step, which had been a source of tension from the very beginning."[20] On a large scale the evacuation of the double-tonic complex at the end of the opera is the musical correlate of the libretto's imperative of cleansing social space of alterity. I will argue below that another correlate of the libretto's imperative is the transformation of a major third that *descends* to a major third that *ascends* in the work.

The Transformation Music

The major third descending a half step does not make an explicit appearance until the Transformation Music connecting Gurnemanz's narrative, the arrival of Kundry and Parsifal, and the exposition of Amfortas's plight with the Grail ceremony and the troubled relationship between Titurel, the aged king, and his son, Amfortas—the wounded king. The Transformation Music begins after Kundry's "sinking away" as Gurnemanz leads Parsifal to witness the ceremony of the Grail. The music has three climactic moments at which a major third descends in searing intensity: measures 1123–24, 1134–35, and 1137–38. Measures 1123–24 are shown in Figure 57.

In these measures, the major third that descends a half step can be heard for the first time in a powerfully orchestrated progression in D-flat minor (a key to be associated later in act 1 with Amfortas's crisis of investiture).[21] The major third that descends a half step is explicitly linked in this passage to the A-flat/G-natural half step of the very first musical idea in the work, as discussed above. In measure 1123, the major-third F-flat/<u>A-flat</u> in the entire wind and brass section (except the trombones and bass tuba), moves to E-flat/<u>G-natural</u>, continuing down an additional half step to D-natural/F-sharp in measure 1124. That major third descends to C-sharp/E-sharp, melting into the triplets at the end of the measure. The initial A-flat/G-natural half step of measures 2–3 of the *Vorspiel* is thus reharmonized here (note underlined pitch-classes above). A-flat is the fifth scale degree of D-flat minor; A-flat moves to G-natural, here the leading tone of the dominant of the dominant. Rather than *ascending* to A-flat, this leading tone *descends* to F-sharp. This descend-

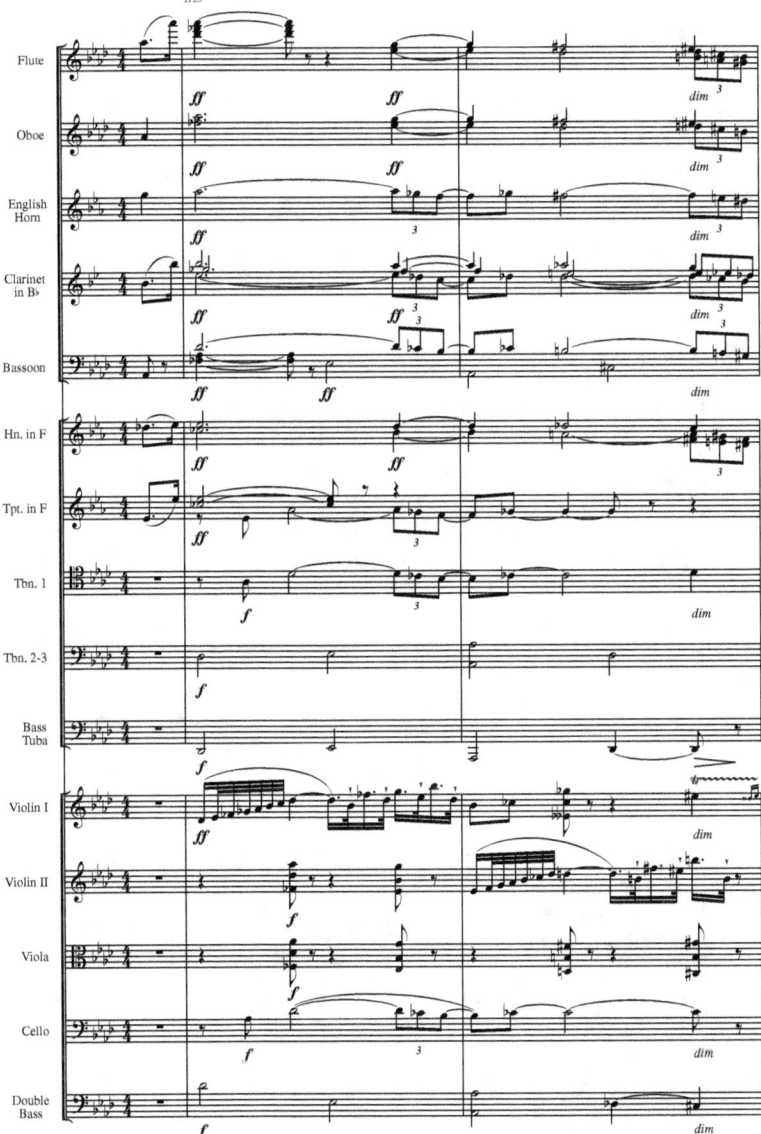

Figure 57

ing half step motion (A-flat/G-natural/F-sharp and its transpositions)
gives the Transformation Music its poignancy.[22]

A major third descends by a half step again in measures 1134–35; this
progression is in D minor—a half step higher than measures 1123–24.[23]
A major third descends by a half step one last time in measures 1137–38

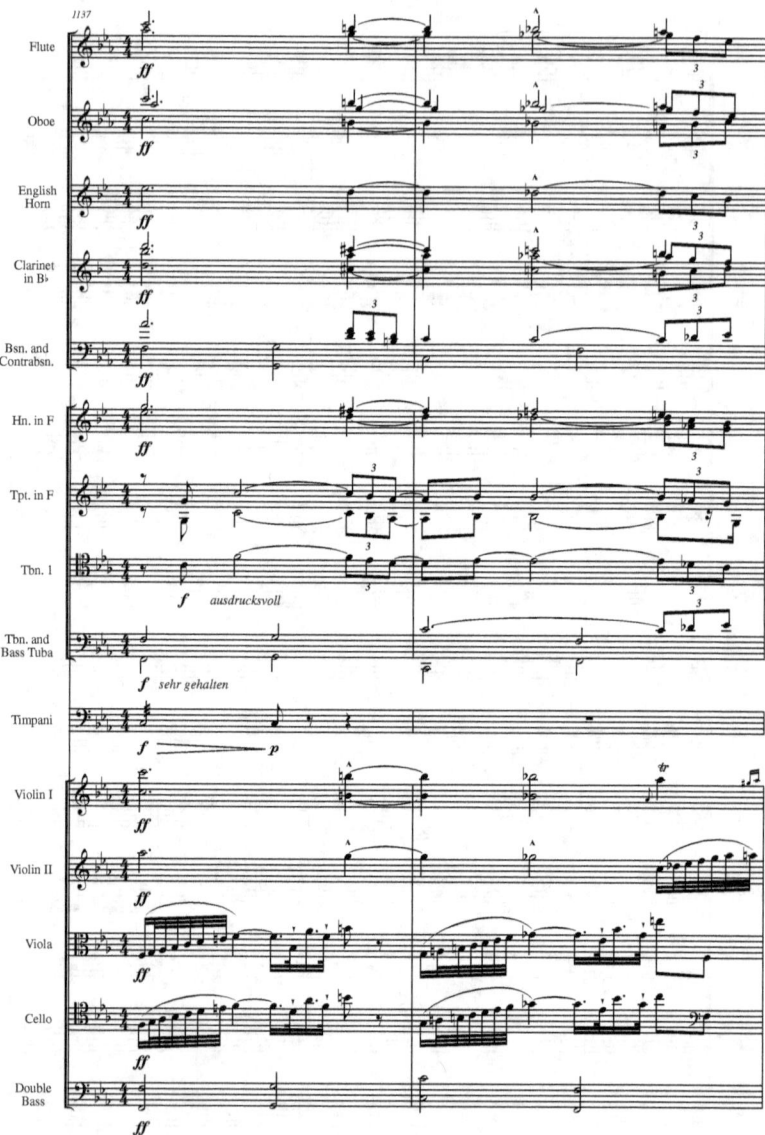

Figure 58

of the Transformation Music (Figure 58). This progression in F minor again gives us an A-flat/G-natural/G-flat melodic descending line, not as a top line but as an *inner voice* underneath a C-natural/B-natural/ B-flat line. The major thirds are **A-flat/C-natural** (measure 1137); G-natural/B-natural (measures 1137–38); G-flat/B-flat (measure 1138).

The underlined pitches represent the A-flat/G-natural half step. The boldface pitches represent the major third on the downbeat of measure 1137, a clear reference to the double tonic complex that governs the entire act. Figure 59 presents a voice-leading graph from measure 1123 to the downbeat of measure 1127 of the Transformation Music.

The graph shows the major thirds f-flat^2/a-flat^2 (measure 1123), e-flat^2/ g-natural^2 (measures 1123–24), d-natural^2/f-sharp^2 (measure 1124), c-sharp^2/e-sharp^2 (measure 1124) that descend in half steps at this first climactic gesture of the Transformation Music. Notice the diatonic underpinnings of the highly chromatic surface of the piece. Beneath the stately diatonic progressions lies a stepwise descent of a tritone: A-flat minor/G-sharp minor, F-sharp minor, E minor, D minor. The D minor of measure 1127 is an expressive variant of the D-flat minor sonority with which the passage began in measure 1123. The passage is then all about a minor "D" sonority, first D-flat minor, then D minor. The passage thus moves far and remains static at the same time—a musical correlate for Gurnemanz's words to Parsifal as the Transformation Music opens: "Du siehst mein Sohn, zum Raum wird hier die Zeit" [You see, my son, time here becomes space].

The Grail Ceremony and Amfortas's Crisis of Investiture

The Grail scene sets the opening melody of the *Vorspiel* to the line "Nehmit hin meinen Leib, nehmet hin mein Blut" [Take this my body; take my blood]. In this scene, Parsifal witnesses the failure of Amfortas to assume his symbolic mandate (uncovering the Grail and leading the Grail celebration); this is the central crisis of investiture around which the entire drama circulates. David Lewin suggests that "it is not the pain of the physical wound which Amfortas finds unbearable, and it is not the healing of the wound which the drama makes obligatory. Rather, it is Amfortas's inability to perform his office which he finds unbearable, and it is the relieving of Amfortas from that duty which is the obligatory event."[24] In the well-known passage from measures 1246–49, Titurel asks Amfortas, "Mein Sohn, Amfortas, bist du am Amt?" In measure 1245, the entire orchestra has a fermata over a whole-note rest; everyone is silent (Figure 60).

The investiture is condensed in one brief question. Titurel asks Amfortas not only if he will uncover the Grail but if he is in a position to do so. Of this question, Žižek writes, "Contrary to the misleading

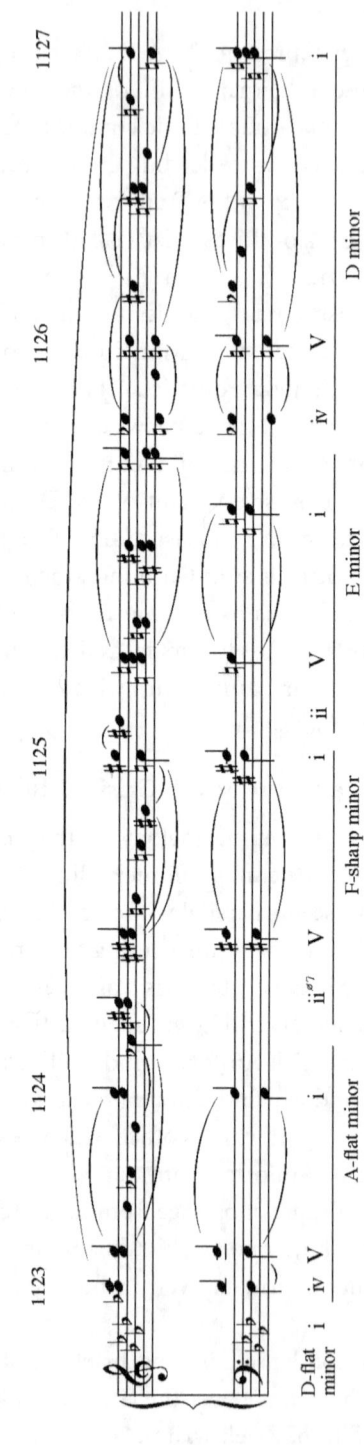

Figure 59

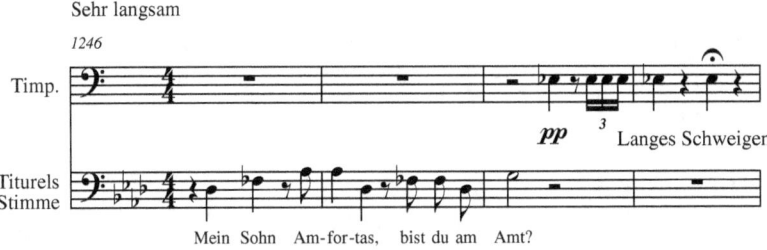

Figure 60

appearances, it is not Amfortas's succumbing to Kundry's advances that sets in motion the catastrophe but Amfortas's horrifying superego father Titurel's excessive attachment to the Grail."[25]

Titurel sings in D-flat minor—a key heard prominently in the Transformation Music. Recall that the D-flat minor progression (i–V/V) of measure 1123 harmonized an A-flat/G motion (the A-flat was the fifth scale degree of D-flat minor; the G-natural the third scale degree of a V of V). In measures 1246–49, Titurel's imperative-as-question outlines the D-flat minor triad; *A-flat* (downbeat of measure 1247) moves to *G-natural* (downbeat of measure 1248).[26] Thus across the entire act, Wagner links the A-flat/G-natural half step explicitly to Titurel and the demand he places on his son to assume his symbolic mandate.

Instead of saying "yes" or "no," Amfortas suffers, crying "Wehe" [alas] in measure 1259 (not shown in the figure). In this measure, Wagner has the major third descending by a half step at the original pitch level he discovered in 1877: G-flat/B-flat that moves down to F-natural/A-natural (plus an additional descent to F-flat/A-flat in measure 1260).

After the Grail ceremony, Gurnemanz asks Parsifal what he saw (measures 1638–39). The dramatic parallel between the previous question and the resulting silence is striking. On one level Gurnemanz is to Parsifal as Titurel is to Amfortas; both Amfortas and Parsifal suffer questions of the other in silence.[27] Wagner's music embodies neither a "yes" nor a "no" to Gurnemanz's question. The first violins play a familiar melody of descending half steps—f-natural[1]/e-natural[1]/e-flat[1] (measures 1639–41); these pitches would have been harmonized in major thirds either above or below in music associated with Amfortas's failure to assume his mandate. This music "almost" registers the major third that descends in half steps. The f-natural[1] is harmonized by a perfect fifth below—b-flat; e-natural[1] is harmonized by a-natural below; e-flat[1] is harmonized by b-natural, producing the enharmonic equivalent of a major third. This passage is a witty embodiment of Parsifal having not quite registered what he saw. Gurnemanz angrily dismisses him and act 1 ends.

Act 2

In act 2, Wagner connects Amfortas's suffering to its source, Klingsor and Kundry, an embodiment of his will. In measures 236–39, the full orchestra plays, fortissimo, a massive descent of *seven* major thirds (lower notes italicized to suggest the descent from G-natural to C-sharp): *G-natural*/B-natural, *F-sharp*/A-sharp, *F-natural*/A-natural, *E-natural*/G-sharp, *E-flat*/G-natural, *D-natural*/F-sharp to *C-sharp*/E-sharp (moving as a dominant to F-sharp minor). This chain of descending major thirds embodies Klingsor's "furchtbare Not"—an excruciating evocation of the longings of a self-castrated man rejected by the Knights of the Grail.

There are three occurrences of the major third that descends in half steps associated with Kundry's music: from measures 186–87, in which she associates her desire "Sehnen! Sehnen" [Yearning! Yearning!] to her curse; measures 281–82, also in reference to her curse that causes all to fall ("meinem Fluche mit mir alle verfallen" [all fall victim to my curse]); and measures 284–85, in which she wishes to sleep ("O ewiger Schlaf, einziges Heil" [Oh endless sleep, only release]). Kundry is a vessel for the will of others—Klingsor, primarily, but Gurnemanz as well. When she receives her mandate from a male other (as in the beginning of act 2), she resists and suffers. Kundry evokes the "second state" of consciousness described by the French theorists of hysteria. She is under the spell of Klingsor throughout acts 1 and 2. Once the spell has been broken at the end of act 2, the real Kundry emerges as an empty vessel. There is a long-range "cross-fade" that occurs across act 3: while Parsifal returns with the spear to heal the king and restore health to social space, Kundry withers and dies.[28]

After the scene of the flower maidens in which young women pique Parsifal's curiosity, Parsifal begins to remember his "calling" (he will soon refer to it as "meine Sendung") in another very witty musical representation of "almost remembering." In measures 952–53, Parsifal asks himself "Ha! Was alles vergass ich wohl noch?" [Ha! What else have I forgotten?]. In measures 953–54, the first flute and the first horn play the descending line a-flat[1], g-natural[1], g-flat[1], f-natural[1]. The suffering (what would have been Parsifal's fully realized memory) would have harmonized this descending line with either a major third above, or a major third below these pitches. Instead, Wagner has the second violin *invert* the idea. Rather than writing c-natural[2], b-natural[1] (or c-flat[2]), b-flat[1], a-natural[1] *above*, Wagner writes this line *below*, creating a chain of not major thirds but *minor sixths*. There is a rhythmic component to the almostness of the music from measure 953 to measure 954 as well. The falling major thirds have descended throughout the opera *together*; in measures 953–54 they do not. This both is and is not the major third descending by half step suggestive of suffering throughout the opera.

The kiss between Kundry and Parsifal is the psychological center of the opera. David Lewin points out how the moment of the kiss in act 2 is the "seam" in the opera that enables Wagner to move from the diatonic world of Montsalvat through the chromaticism of Klingsor's realm and back again to the diatonic world of Montsalvat. For Lewin "Kundry has just cadenced in the local key of C-flat, and vocal cadence on the word 'Kuss' in m. 983 is notated as a C-flat; thereupon Wagner begins notating the orchestra in B, making the notational shift at that key word. Here we are at the very crux of the enharmonic shift involving C-flat and B in Act II, and hence in the opera as a whole."[29]

Parsifal does not so much reject her kiss as reject the sexual consummation that might have followed. Parsifal's rejection takes place in two crucial stages. First, he (mis)identifies with Amfortas, imagining his bleeding wound and empathetically suffering with him; second, Parsifal realizes that his pain is not one of identification with Amfortas but a sign of his own awakened sexual desire. Wagner sets the moment of recognition as an apotheosis of this major third idea (Figure 61).

The major third D-flat/F-natural descends to C-natural/E natural in measure 1010; E-flat/G-natural descends to D-natural/F-sharp in measure 1011; F-natural/A-natural descends to E-natural/G-sharp in measure 1012; G-natural/B-natural descends to F-sharp/A-sharp in measure 1013. The progression culminates not in a descending motion but to a single major third— A flat/C-natural on the word "Jammervollste!" [most pitiable] (measures 1014–15).

The major third descending in half-steps sounds in its familiar form a few measures later (not shown in Figure 61) as Parsifal feels the wound bleeding within himself ("Die Wunde sah ich bluten, nun blutet sie in

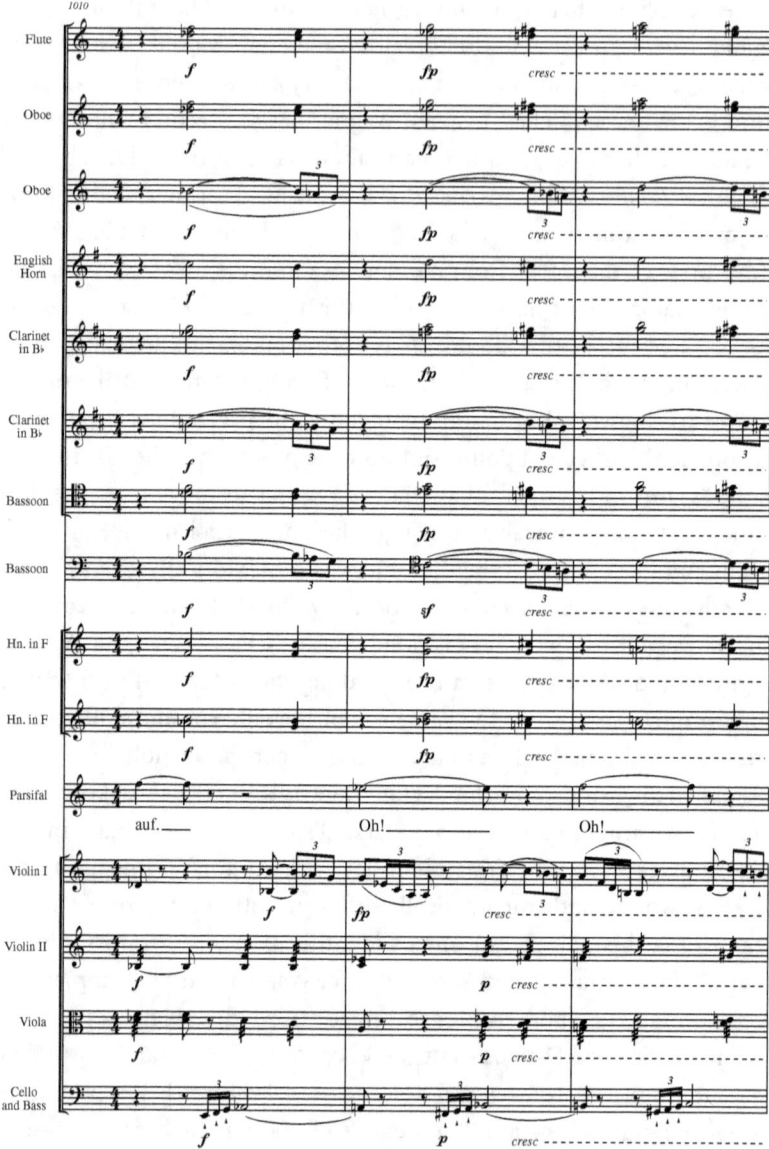

Figure 61

mir! Hier! Hier!") in measures 1020–22 (*A-flat*/C-natural, *G-natural*/
B-natural, *G-flat*/B-flat, *F-natural*/A-natural).

Parsifal then realizes that he has not identified with Amfortas's wound
but feels the birth of sexual desire in himself: "Nein! nicht die Wunde ist
es. Fliesse ihr Blut in Strömen dahin! Hier! Hier, im Herzen der Brand!"

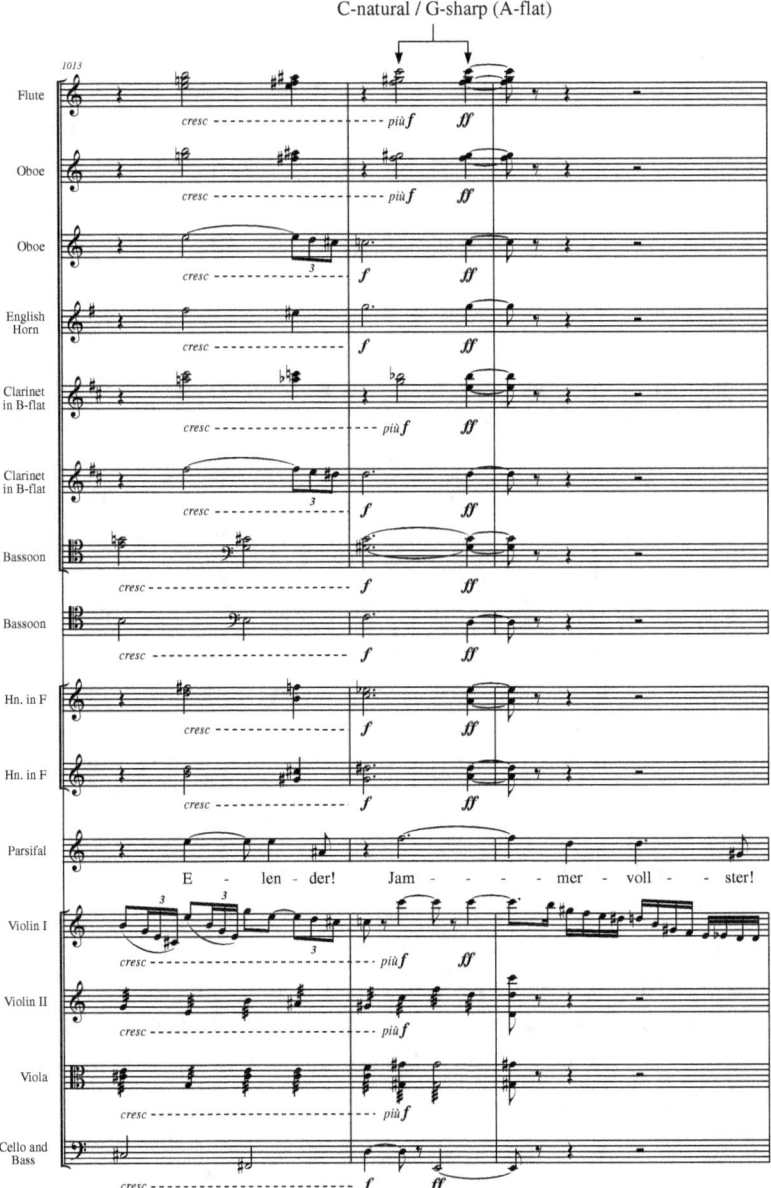

[No, no! It is not the wound. Flow in streams, my blood, from it. Here! Here in my heart is the flame!]. Wagner sets Parsifal's full recognition of his pain as a sign of his own awakened sexual desire in measures 1037–39. In these measures, a single major third D-natural/F-sharp descends to D-flat/F-natural to the text "Qual der Liebe!" [Torment of love].

Parsifal's refusal of Kundry's seduction does not end with his first refusal. His first refusal was predicated on a (mis)recognition of his pain as
one of identification with Amfortas. This misrecognition makes Kundry's
second seduction structurally necessary. Klingsor and his seductress
Kundry utterly fail, and in a brilliant wash of D major, Parsifal takes the
spear from Klingsor (to be discussed below). Klingsor's castle crumbles;
the flower garden turns to a wilderness; Parsifal exits; Kundry collapses;
the act ends.

Act 3

A major third *ascends* as Parsifal touches Amfortas's wound with the
spear that had originally caused the wound. This moment is the apotheosis of the libretto and the music. In Figure 62, see the bracket
with arrows over measures 1035–36 showing the major third C-sharp/
E-sharp ascend in the flutes, oboes, and second violins to D-natural/
F-sharp.[30] There are three large-scale cross-references at work here.
First, Parsifal sings g-sharp[1], a-natural[1] to the words "sie schlug" across
the bar line from measure 1034 to 1035. In act 1, Amfortas had sung
g-sharp, a-natural to the words "schliesse die Wunde" (measure 1399)
with the first violins echoing the half step in measures 1399–1400 (Figure 63). Second, the D major harmony heard in measure 1036 of Figure 62 is the key that had emerged at precisely the moment Parsifal took
the spear from Klingsor in act 2 (Figure 64). Klingsor is about to throw
his spear at Parsifal. As Klingsor sings "Meisters," his c-sharp[1] supports
f-natural[1] and f-natural[2] (the enharmonic equivalent of e-sharp[1] and
e-sharp[2]) in the winds (prolonged through a lower neighbor e-flat[1] and
e-flat[2]) for the first three beats of measure 1492. On the downbeat of
measure 1493, this c-sharp[1]/f-natural[1] major third (hearing f-natural[1] as
e-sharp[1]) rises to the d-natural[1]/f-sharp[1] major third, extended dramatically by the harp glissando in D major. Wagner creates an enormous
cross-reference in the work, connecting the moment Parsifal regains the
spear (act 2, measures 1492–93 set to D-flat/F-natural ascending to
D-natural/F-sharp) with the moment that Parsifal touches Amfortas's
wound with the spear that had opened it (act 3, measures 1035–36 set to
C-sharp/E-sharp [the enharmonic equivalents of D-flat/F-natural] moving to D-natural/F-sharp). Redemption takes place in two stages in the
music. First Parsifal actually takes the spear from Klingsor, and then he
symbolically touches it to Amfortas's wound, cleansing social space of

the other. I will return to this point after an examination of pathology in the opera.

And finally, the major third C-sharp/E-sharp that *ascends* to D-natural/F-sharp (act 3, measures 1035–36) resolves Parsifal's own suffering; he had sung the major third D-natural/F-sharp *descending* to D-flat/F-natural in act 2, measures 1037–39 to the text "Qual der Liebe." The *ascending* gesture in act 3 is a musical embodiment of "Erlösung dem Erlöser" [Our redeemer redeemed]. In touching the spear to the wound that had caused it, in bringing redemption to the Knights of the Grail, Parsifal has also redeemed himself.

Music and Pathology

I am examining Wagner's libretto and opera from the point of view of a pathological fantasy of purging psychic and social space of the other. But where exactly is this pathological dimension? Is it in the very project of fantasy formation in the text of Wagner's libretto? Is it in the anti-Semitism that had underwritten, explicitly or implicitly, the discourse of the Jewish Question in Germany and other European states since the Enlightenment? Is it in the pitches of the opera? If so, how can a pitch or interval be pathological?[31]

Pitches or intervals are not necessarily pathological, just as pitches and intervals are not necessarily healthy. Pitches, intervals, and the entire inventory of musical materials at the disposal of a composer can be more or less healthy or pathological depending on the conditions under which music circulates in social spaces, in historical circumstances, associated with words in a libretto, a dramatic action, stage directions, discourses of criticism, psychoanalysis, and historical writings.

Purging psychic and social space of the other in Wagner's *Parsifal* is embodied in the twin moments of redemption set to major third C-sharp/E-sharp (D-flat/F-natural) ascending to D-natural/F-sharp at the moment Parsifal regains the spear and the moment at which he touches it to Amfortas's wound. There is certainly nothing inherently pathological about this rising motion of a major third. I will now explore how alterity functions in the context of the work's cultural context.

Wagner and the Jewish Question

Jacob Katz points out that, after centuries of persecution, Jews began to be incorporated (emancipated) into German life in the late eighteenth

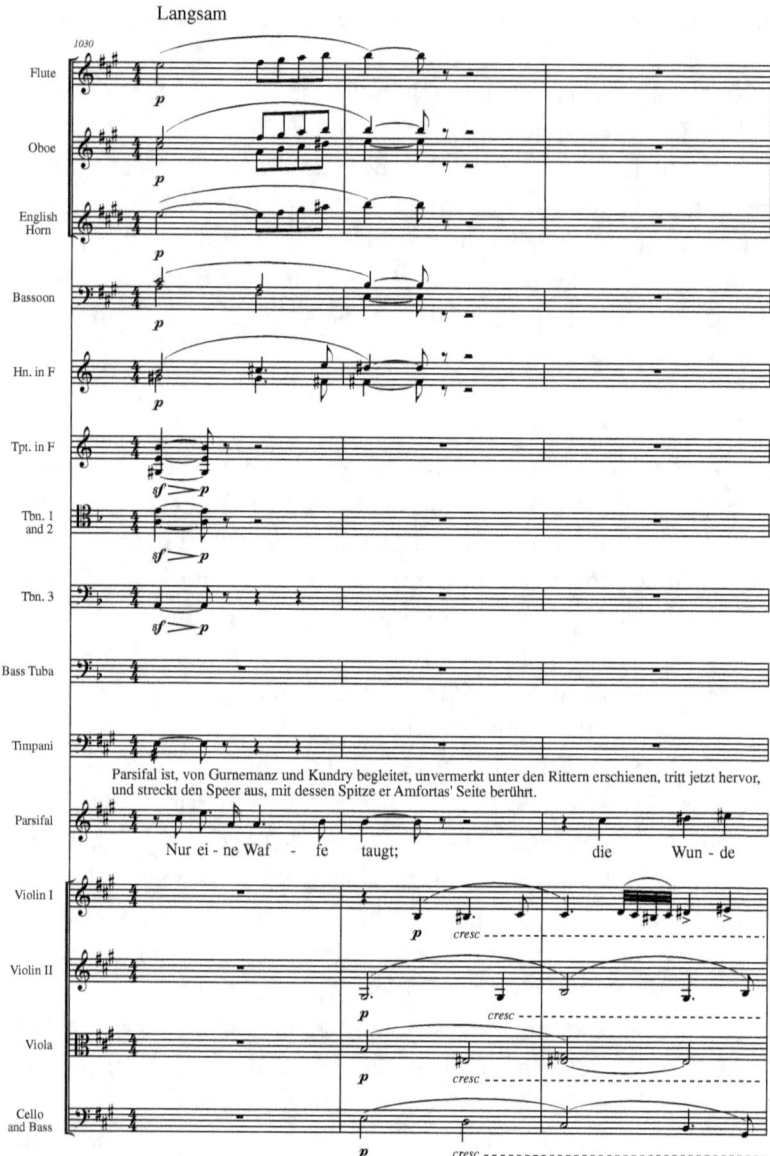

Figure 62

century as an outgrowth of the Enlightenment, particularly in France and Germany.[32] In Germany, the process of incorporation was encouraged by Joseph II's Edict of Tolerance in the 1780s; Jews were accorded half-rights of naturalization in Prussia and Bavaria in 1812–13, although contact between Jews and non-Jews was still discouraged (Katz 8). The

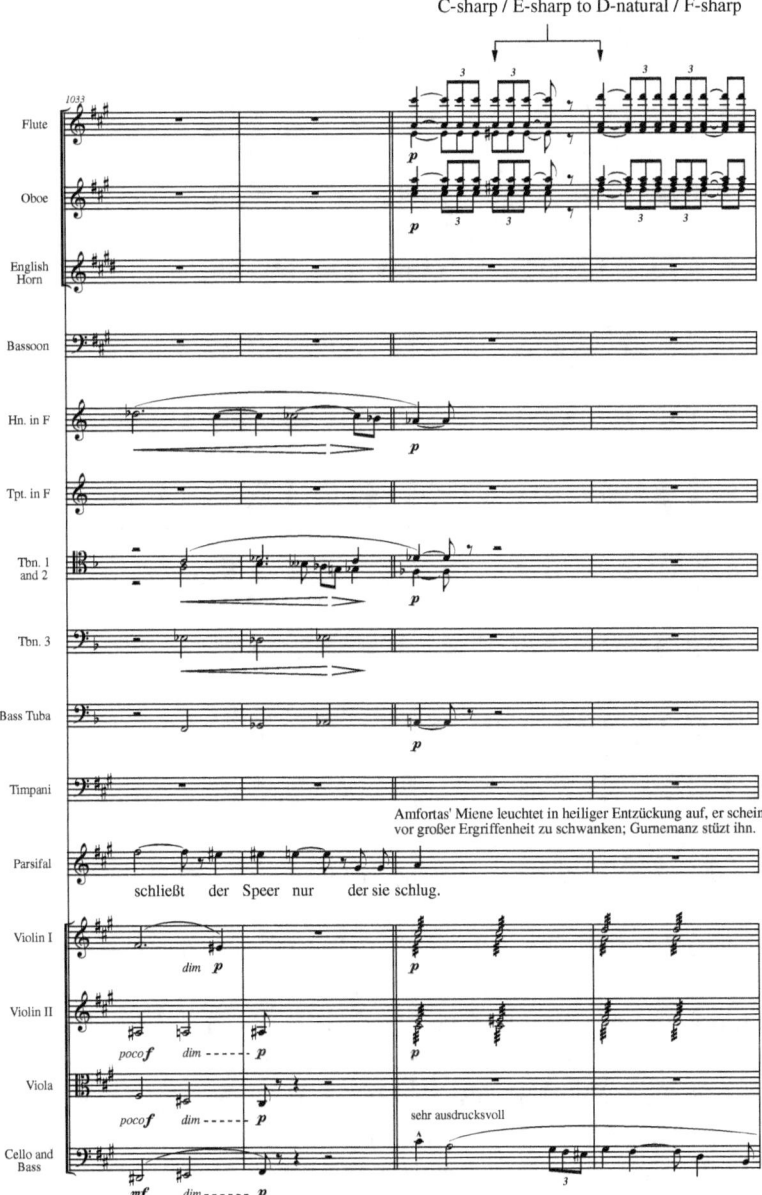

so-called Hep-Hep riots of 1819 embodied a public reaction to this lib-
eralization (Katz 9).

While public policy exhibited a degree of enlightened tolerance, German Romantic writers were laying the groundwork for discussions of
the Jewish Question in coming decades. In his article on the languages

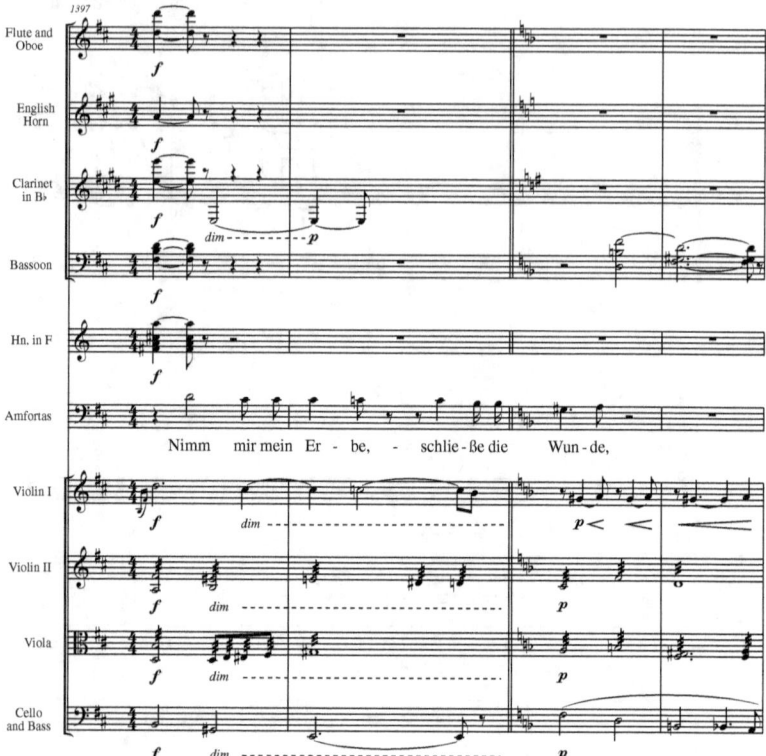

Figure 63

of India, Friedrich Schlegel asserted that languages are not equal in their expressive capabilities. For Schlegel, only those languages that derive from Hindi and Greek are capable of serious thought and refined expression.[33] Schelling offered a geographical complement to Schlegel. For Schelling, nature and mythology mutually reflect one another as finite and infinite; people who live in desolate parts of the world are incapable of myth beyond the level of tales of adventure.[34] For Fichte, Jews should be sent to a sovereign country of their own: "to give them civil rights [Bürgerrechte], for that I can only imagine cutting off all their heads in the night and replacing them with new ones that contain not a single Jewish idea. In order to protect ourselves against them, I see no other means but to conquer their holy land and to send them all there."[35]

Three writings of the 1840s addressed the Jewish Question with particular force: Bruno Bauer's *Die Judenfrage* (1843), Karl Marx's *Die Judenfrage* (1844), and Heinrich Laube's *Streunsee* (1847). Bauer argues that

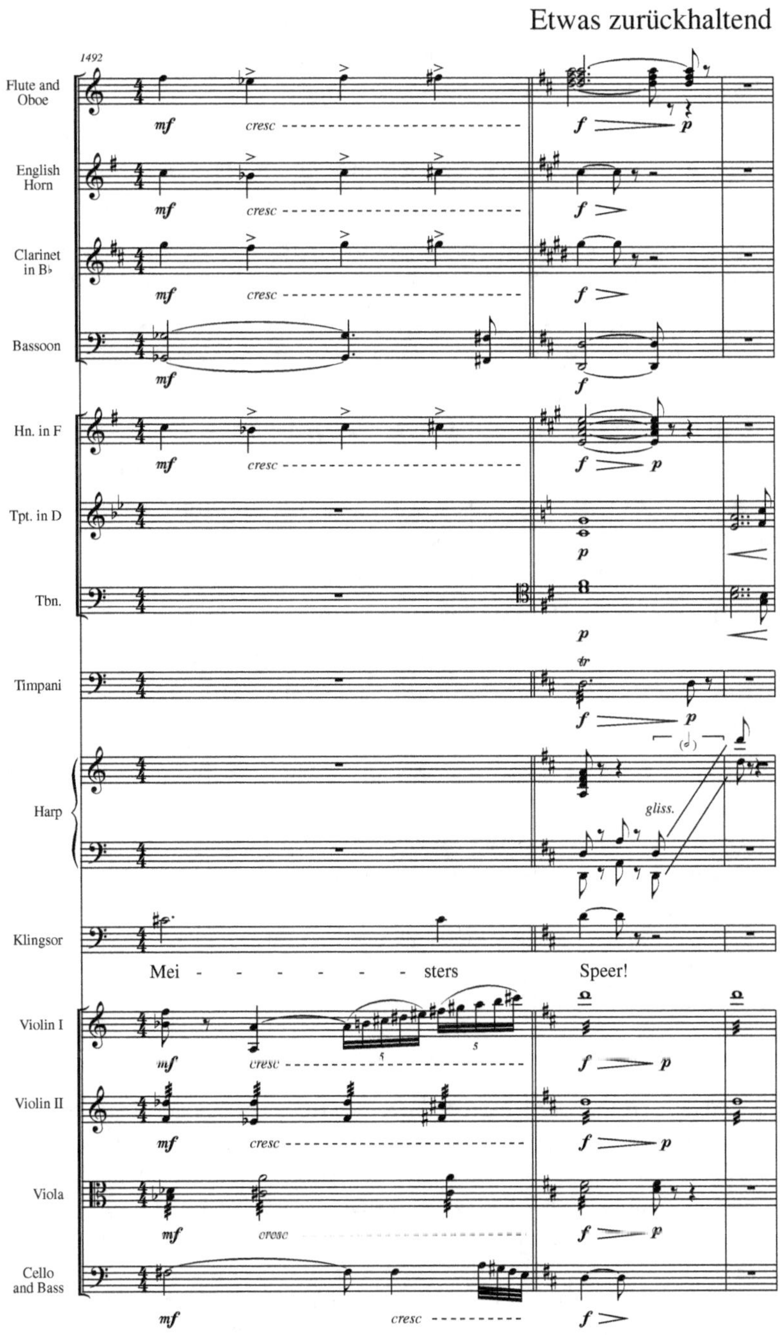

Etwas zurückhaltend

Figure 64

"Jews and Christians can consider each other and treat each other as *men* [Bauer's emphasis] only when they have given up the special nature which separates them and enjoins them to 'eternal segregation' when they acknowledge the common nature of man and consider humanity as their true nature."[36] Bauer argues throughout *Die Judenfrage* that the essence of Judaism is its otherness in relationship to history, art, reason, and Christianity.[37] Furthermore, "Not only the Jews, but we, also, want to be emancipated. Only because nobody was free, because privilege was the ruling power, the Jews could not have freedom either. We all were surrounded by barriers; the Jewish quarter is right next to the police-supervised quarters where all of us are registered" (Bauer 63).

Karl Marx responds to Bauer in his *Die Judenfrage* (1844).[38] For Marx, the Jewish Question always relates to the nation in which it arises; in Germany the question is religious, since in the mid-nineteenth century there was no nation "Germany"; in France, the question is constitutional; in America, according to Marx, the Jewish Question is at its most secular (Marx 50). Marx locates the emancipation of Christian and Jew alike not simply in moving beyond religious difference but in the formation of a new relationship between individual and state:

> Political emancipation is the reduction of man on the one hand to a member of civil society, an egoistic and independent individual, on the other hand to a citizen, a moral person. The actual individual man must take the abstract citizen back into himself and, as an individual man in his empirical life, in his individual work and individual relationships become a species-being; man must recognize his own forces as social forces, organize them, and thus no longer separate social forces from himself in the form of political forces. Only when this has been achieved will human emancipation be completed. (Marx 64)

Heinrich Laube sees the Jewish question as follows:

> Not being emancipated leaves them with a feeling of being beleaguered, and he who is beleaguered remains the enemy, instinctively defending himself with all possible weapons, but also in this case that which is most natural to them—a nationality that is most alien to us. Thus we see in Jews that which is fundamentally contrary to us. All the innermost maxims of life that we seemingly oppose a hundredfold will be held upright in the character of Jews, through our partial defense. We are either barbarians and must drive out the Jews until the last one has left, or we must incorporate them.[39]

Dieter Borchmeyer points out that there are two forms of anti-Semitism in nineteenth-century discourse: traditional and modern anti-Semitism. Borchmeyer explains the distinction: "whereas traditional antagonism towards the Jews was directed against the policy of integrating the religious and social practices of a minority into the rest of society, modern anti-Semitism takes as its starting point the fact that the basic solution to the Jewish Question, the granting of equal political and social rights to the Jews, is already a part of history."[40]

Richard Wagner[41] expressed himself in print for the first time on the Jewish Question in 1850. "Das Judentum in der Musik,"[42] was printed in *Die neue Zeitschrift für Musik,* a slim journal published initially under the stewardship of Robert Schumann. Each issue featured one long article followed by shorter announcements and miniature essays of interest. In 1850, most of the main articles were on symphonies of Beethoven, Schumann, or issues relating to opera, symphonic music, and chamber music. The issue published on September 3, 1850, featured the first part of an essay entitled "Das Judentum in der Musik" signed by "K. Freigedank," who Wagner acknowledged in 1869 to be himself. Part two of the essay was published three days later, on September 6. The appearance of these two issues featuring Wagner's essay was a powerful contribution to anti-Semitic discourse in German musical and cultural life of the nineteenth century. Wagner writes of Jews in connection with money, appearances, and cultural contribution.[43]

Of the Jew and money, Wagner writes, "According to the present constitution of this world, the Jew in truth is already more than emancipate: he rules, and will rule, so long as money remains the power before which all our doings and our dealings lose their force" (Ellis 81).[44] Of the Jew and appearances, Wagner writes,

> The first thing that strikes our ear as quite outlandish and unpleasant, in the Jew's production of the voice-sounds, is a creaking, squeaking, buzzing snuffle: add thereto an employment of words in a sense quite foreign to our nation's tongue, and an arbitrary twisting of the structure of our phrases—and this mode of speaking acquires at once the character of an intolerably jumbled blabber; so that when we hear this Jewish talk, our attention dwells involuntarily on its repulsive *how,* rather than on any meaning of its intrinsic *what.* (Ellis 85)[45]

Of Jews and culture, Wagner writes,

So long as the separate art of music had a real organic life-need in it, down to the epochs of Mozart and Beethoven, there was nowhere to be found a Jew composer: it was impossible for an element entirely foreign to that living organism to take part in the formative stages of that life. Only when a body's inner death is manifest, do outside elements win the power of lodgment in it—merely to destroy it. Then indeed that body's flesh dissolves into a swarming colony of insect-life. (Ellis 99)[46]

Of the music of Mendelssohn, Wagner writes,

To professional critics, who haply have reached a like consciousness with ourselves hereon, it may be left to prove by specimens of Mendelssohn's art-products our statement of this indubitably certain thing; by way of illustrating our general impression, let us here be content with the fact that, in hearing a tone-piece of this composer's we have only been able to feel engrossed where nothing beyond our more or less amusement-craving Phantasy was roused through the presentment, stringing-together and entanglement of the most elegant, the smoothest and most polished figures—as in the kaleidoscope's changeful play of form and color—but never where those figures were meant to take the shape of deep and stalwart feelings of the human heart. (Ellis 94)[47]

And finally: "Without once looking back, take ye your part in this regenerative work of deliverance through self-annulment; then are we one and un-disevered! But bethink ye, that one only thing can redeem you from the burden of your curse; the redemption of Ahasuerus—*Going Under!*" (Ellis 100).[48] Ahasver, or Ahasverus, stands for the wandering Jew "who was supposedly present on the day they crucified Jesus and mocked him on his way to Golgotha; in return, the redeemer condemned him to wander the face of the earth, forsaken and unhappy, until he returned to usher in the Final Judgement and the end of the world."[49]

There is a curious sense of enlightened discourse running throughout "Das Judentum in der Musik." Borchmeyer understands a discrepancy in nineteenth-century liberal politics between arguing for the assimilation of the Other as an abstraction and arguing for the assimilation of others as concrete, actual individual subjects. Borchmeyer argues that "Das Judentum in der Musik" is informed by a critique of this binary opposition. Accordingly, "he [Wagner] seeks to criticize the liberal movement and its attitude toward the Jewish question not as an outsider but apparently from within, as a participant who has contributed toward the emancipation of the Jews" (Borchmeyer 169). Thus Wagner argues that he has fought for the liberation of the Jew writ large but that the actual Jew has turned out to be repugnant. According to Borchmeyer, "Wagner exhausts the whole xenophobic arsenal of traditional anti-Jewish feeling, not in order to define, in rational terms, the catalogue of prejudices, stereotyped images, and antipathetic emotions and thus to overcome them in a spirit of enlightened humanism, but rather to invest them with greater legitimacy" (171).[50]

Three other sources are important contributions to this record: the essays "Erkenne Dich" and "Heldenthum und Christentum," both published in the *Bayreuther Blätter* in 1881, and a letter written to Ludwig II in November 1881.[51] In this letter, Wagner says, "that I view the Jew as the natural-born enemy of pure humanity in all its nobility: that namely we Germans shall be destroyed by them is certain, and perhaps I am the last German who has known how to sustain himself as an artist against the Judaism that already controls everything."[52]

Wagner, the Jewish Question, and Hitler

One of the strongest and most articulate arguments *against* making a connection between Wagner's writings and national socialist politics is presented by Borchmeyer toward the end of the article quoted above. Writing in response to claims that the last, famous sentence of "Das Judentum in der Musik" invites genocide, Borchmeyer says,

> To quote this final sentence out of context and to read into it the idea of genocide . . . is completely misleading. . . . The question is not simply one of self-destruction—the voluntary nature of which excludes any thought of physical liquidation—but one of rebirth and redemption through this act of (self-) destruction, an act . . . of a symbolic nature, intended to bring about a mystic transformation of the whole of mankind. (Borchmeyer 174)

For Borchmeyer, Wagner's call to Ahasuerus to destroy himself harkens not forward to genocide but *back* to representations in early nineteenth-century poetry of *Weltschmerz*, and a broad semantic field of wanderers alienated from social space (Borchmeyer 174–75).

In theorizing relations between Wagner and later genocidal policies of the national socialists, a distinction must be made between the prose of "Das Judentum in der Musik" and Wagner's musical compositions. I will discuss below a tenuous relationship between the publication of "Das Judentum in der Musik" and the rise of national socialist anti-Semitic policies. In terms of Wagner's music in general, and *Parsifal* in particular,

I am more interested in *latent* rather than *manifest* elements of anti-Semitism. On the level of manifest content, Borchmeyer is right; in his art, Wagner in no way can be found guilty of causing the national socialist genocide or even being one of its many material causes. On the other hand, Wagner, in both the libretto and music of *Parsifal*, has created an idea of a nation of tainted subjects who restore to their nation a state of purity predicated upon the purging of social space of the other. I believe that this fantasy has a pathological dimension in the context of nineteenth-century anti-Semitism and the emergence of the German nation-state in 1870.

And that purging is in no way voluntary in the opera. The destruction of Klingsor's castle is violent, even apocalyptic, at the end of act 2. And Kundry's "redemption" is predicated on the evacuation of her last vestiges of subjectivity toward the end of act 2 as well—hardly a voluntary act of (self-)destruction that will lead to the salvation of mankind as a whole. Parsifal's passivity throughout Wagner's opera is a cover for the necessary activity upon which the opera and the redemption of the Knights is predicated. Parsifal kills the swan, he goes to Klingsor's castle, he takes back the spear from Klingsor, he returns to the Knights, he redeems the Knights. He actively purges social space of the other.

Direct connections between Wagner and Hitler are complex and highly problematic. From the point of view of Wagner's influence on Hitler, there are (a) a tenuous chain of events that connect the publication of "Das Judentum in der Musik" to national socialist policies; (b) direct, personal relations between Hitler and the Wagner family who inherited and mediated the Wagner myth for German culture of the late nineteenth, early twentieth century; (c) performances of Wagner's works that inspired Hitler; and (d) anti-Semitic writings that influenced Hitler and other national socialist officials.

Here is an account of a tenuous relationship between the publication of "Das Judentum in der Musik" and national socialist anti-Semitism. According to Borchmeyer, Wagner was reading anti-Semitic works with great interest in the 1880s (Borchmeyer 167). In particular, Wagner was sympathetic to the views of Adolf Stoecker, founder of the Christian Social Movement in 1880, "a body which two years later spawned the Berlin Movement, the cell from which grew all the anti-Semitic parties that sprang up in Germany over the course of the following decades, culminating in the National-Socialist Worker's Party, founded in 1919"

(Borchmeyer 167). Borchmeyer points out that Cosima mentions in a diary entry that she had read Stoecker and discussed the Jewish Question with Richard: "I [Cosima] read a very good speech by the preacher Stoecker about the Jews. R. is in favor of expelling them entirely. We laugh to think that it really seems as if his article on the Jews marked the beginning of this struggle."[53] It would be wrong in many ways to overinvest these statements with deterministic causality. A widely prevalent German and European anti-Semitism of the nineteenth century (and much earlier) lent support to the national socialist project. Also, Cosima and Richard are congratulating themselves in a perhaps exaggerated way for the actions of others; as Borchmeyer points out, Wagner was reluctant to get publicly involved in anti-Semitic campaigns toward the end of his life for at least two reasons. For one, he needed to allow the Jewish Levi to conduct the premiere of *Parsifal*, and, according to Borchmeyer, he was becoming less and less interested in conventional religions in general, favoring instead a *Parsifal*-like fantasy of the redemption of all races (Borchmeyer 168).

In terms of direct connections between Hitler and the Wagner family, Hitler visited Wahnfried in 1923 — a visit of crucial importance for his political career.[54] In *Confessions of Frau Wagner*, Winifred speaks at great length of Hitler's yearly visits to Bayreuth once the national socialists gained power. During all of these visits, Hitler stayed at Wahnfried and entertained guests, including Dr. Goebbels and his wife and a wide array of national socialist funtionaries.[55] According to his friend August Kubizek, Hitler and Kubizek saw a performance of *Rienzi* in Linz during the winter of 1905; Hitler is alleged to have told Winifred Wagner, in reference to the *Rienzi* performance, "In jeder Stunde begann es" [It began at that time] (quoted in Vaget 181). Peter Viereck reports that, according to Goebbels, Hitler saw *Die Meistersinger* more than a hundred times during his lifetime (Viereck 16).

According to Vaget, Hitler read and was deeply influenced by two anti-Semitic works: Josef Engel de Sinoja's *Antisemitismus in der Musik*[56] and Houston Stuart Chamberlain's *Grundlagen des neunzehnten Jahrhunderts*.[57] Gottfried Wagner claims that the work of Gobineau is also an important link between the music of Richard Wagner and the policies of Hitler.[58] And there is one very vivid and very precise connection between *Parsifal* and Hilter's attitudes toward the other: "All of us are suffering from the ailment of mixed, corrupted blood. How can we purify ourselves and make atonement? Note that compassion, through which man gains enlightenment, is only for the corrupted man at issue with himself. And that this compassion knows only one treatment—the leaving of the sick person to die."[59] That Hitler understood *Parsifal* as a vehicle for national socialist policy does not mean that *Parsifal* underwrites national socialism. It does mean, however, that there are attributes of Wagner's libretto and his opera that offer felicitous symbolic support for totalitarian politics.

Parsifal, Pathology, Social Space

There are characters in Parsifal who signify as Jewish. Klingsor is the only character in the opera to refer to money and its power over people, and his self-castration suggests a hysterical dimension often associated with Jews.[60] According to Borchmeyer, "the only one of Wagner's characters to be associated with a Jewish figure in the work itself is Kundry in *Parsifal,* whom Wagner himself interprets as a female counterpart to the wandering Jew" (Borchmeyer 184).[61] Cosima reports in a dairy entry from May 17, 1879, "R. told me that Kundry was his most original female character; when he realized that the servant of the Grail was the same woman who seduced Amfortas, he said, everything fell into place, and after that, however many years might elapse, he knew how it would turn out" (*Diaries* 2:310).[62] Combining the servant of the Grail and Amfortas's seductress into a single person guarantees a pathological dimension of Kundry's alterity as it relates to the community of the Knights of the Grail. She is always already inside the community as other when the opera begins.

The deaths of Klingsor and Kundry can be seen as the conditions under which a certain kind of Christian redemption occurs by the end of the opera. Such a reading might associate Amfortas's wound with the wound of Christ; Parsifal is a redeemer who fights the Antichrist Klingsor, defeats him, and on Good Friday, redeems the community in a holy act of sacrifice and grace. The redemption of the opera is predicated on finding and eradicating in redemption the other at the fringes of social space. But what about traces of alterity always already *within* social space?

Žižek described the Jew as that other that seems to be *without* but is a placeholder for a disavowed dissatisfaction *within*:

The anti-Semitic Jew...bears witness to the fact that the ideological desire which sustains anti-Semitism is inconsistent, 'self-contradictory.'... In order to maintain this desire, a specific object must be invented which gives body to, externalizes, the cause of the non-satisfaction of this desire (the Jew who is responsible for social disintegration). The lack of positive ontological consistency in this figure of the Jew is proved by the fact that the true relationship of causality is inverted with regard to the way things appear within the anti-Semitic ideological space: it is not the Jew who prevents Society from existing...; rather, it is the social antagonism which is primordial, and the figure of the Jew comes second as a fetish which materializes this hindrance.[63]

Thus *Parsifal* circulates angrily around a disavowed dissatisfaction that is always already within social space. In his book *On the Psychotheology of Everyday Life*, Eric L. Santner reads Freud and Rosensweig against each other to discover what it means to live in a community in modern social space. At the core of much of Santner's discussion is a sense that living in the world requires coming to terms with a certain strangeness both within oneself and within one's neighbor: "In the Freudian-Rosenzweigian view I will be elaborating here, the biblical traditions inaugurate a form of life structured precisely around an openness to the alterity, the uncanny strangeness, of the Other as the very locus of a universality-in-becoming."[64] This uncanny strangeness can take the form of an odd manner of speech in a friend, the sound of a foreign language to which one has no access, the irreplaceable twitch of a lover's eye. These are all examples of what is more in that person than themselves, and much current psychoanalytic thought suggests that subject formations in a wide variety of registers collect around such residual, gritlike bits of alterity.[65] For Santner, "the crucial point in all of this is that it is precisely when we, in the singularity of our own out-of-jointedness, open to this 'hindered' dimension—the internal alienness—of the Other that we pass from one logic of being-together to another, that we shift from the register of the global to that of the universal which remains as such a universal-in-becoming" (Santner 7).

The founding moment that produces the crisis at the heart of *Parsifal* is Titurel's imperative-as-question to Amfortas: "Mein Sohn, Amfortas, bist du am Amt?" On a surface plot level, Titurel asks the question before the Grail ceremony so that Parsifal can witness Amfortas's silence-as-failure and assume (in Amfortas's place) the symbolic mandate of "he who will regain the lost spear of the Grail" and perform the office that his symbolic father cannot. But Amfortas has already failed and the energy of his failure builds to the breaking point. His wound that bleeds whenever the Grail is revealed is too much for him. His wound is the "too-much-ness" of his blocked response to his (failed) investiture. Santner discusses a failure of symbolic investiture in precisely these terms. In what could be a gloss to Titurel's imperative-as-question, Santner says,

> Both of these terms—"discharge" and "excitation"—are . . . particularly hybrid in nature, belonging to a semantic field of energetics as well as of intersubjective events and meanings. An excitation is a kind of pure stress, a pressure or tension in the body demanding some form of release. But in a more literal sense, an *ex-citation* denotes a summons, a calling out, and so a form of address or interpellation. The same, of course, goes for "discharge." Not only do we speak of discharging excess energy but also of discharging one's duties and responsibilities, that which one has been *charged* with doing." (31; Santner's emphasis)

Amfortas's wound is a traumatic symptom of his ongoing failure of investiture, and it comes in the progress of the opera to stand for a more general degenerative state of the Knights of the Grail, with the Knights, one by one, falling into the zombie-like arms of Kundry at Klingsor's command. Titurel and Klingsor are two voices of a furious call.

Parsifal refuses Kundry's twin seduction as mother/lover. The moment of Parsifal's sexual awakening produces in him the moment of his disavowal of sexuality; Kundry's kiss and first seduction produce the former; her second seduction and its devastating discourse of confession produce the latter. Parsifal's disavowal of sexuality is a more elegant version of Klingsor's self-castration. It enables him to take Klingsor's spear as it hovers in the air over his head and to return to the Knights of the Grail, touch Amfortas's wound, healing it, and to perform the ceremony purging all traces of alterity from the Knights of the Grail. Here is the work's pathological dimension, in its large-scale project of redemption not as cleansing social space of the other but as a rewinding of the clock of time as if alterity had not yet appeared—to a kind of Eden before Eden. Žižek points out that *Parsifal* functions not unlike so many science fiction films of the current era in which disaster is averted by returning to a position in the past and changing the course of events so it never happens. The moment of Parsifal touching the wound with the spear that had caused it is a dramaturgical hitting of the "rewind" button.[66]

At the end of *Parsifal* there is no alterity within the Grail community. The characters most richly endowed with alterity have been necessarily killed (Klingsor and Kundry); the character stained by alterity (Amfortas) has been healed and then left to die. Titurel's cruel demand has multiplied into the menacing Knights of the Grail as a whole who call for the ceremony to be performed with ominous singularity—"zum lezten Mal!"[67]

Santner has a provocative way of describing the energy of demand in the call of the Other: "We are, in a crucial sense, placed in the space of relationality not by way of intentional acts but rather by a kind of *unconscious transmission* that is neither enlivening nor simply deadening but rather, if I might put it that way, undeadening; it provokes in us an internal alienness that has a peculiar sort of vitality and yet *belongs to no form of life*" (36; Santner's emphasis). This is precisely what happens to Parsifal across the entire opera. His silence to Amfortas after the Grail ceremony in act 1 is symptomatic. On the one hand, the reality of what lies ahead has simply not yet sunk into the boy. On the other hand, he will become a kind of zombie himself—Kundry's good twin—as he follows the path of his "Sendung." The response to the call of investiture is Parsifal as "undead" life.

This call, of course, has no internal consistency, no necessary content. Santner explains the binary between the empty container–ness of the call and its content as follows:

> The universe of Kafka's protagonists is, in other words, animated by a message that penetrates, even frames, intentional life, a message that in some sense *causes life to matter*, but not in the form of a belief, thought, or meaning; what is at stake is a form of expressivity—"interpellation without identification"—that, in the absence of any propositional content, nonetheless gets under our skin and has some sort of (hindered) revelatory force, has, as Scholem puts it, *validity without meaning*. (38–39; Santner's emphases)[68]

The simplest form of "validity without meaning" is the fact that the Law *is*. Wagner gives great resonance to the brute fact of Titurel's demand through the half-step A-flat/G-natural that musically supports his demand "Mein Sohn Amfortas, bist-du am Amt?" at the Grail ceremony in act 1. The closing of the wound represented in the music as shown above suggests a musical and dramatic fantasy of redemption as succumbing to the demand of the Other.

The redemption of the community of the Knights of the Grail takes place in two stages—literal and symbolic. Figure 64 shows the moment in act 2 when Parsifal takes the spear from Klingsor (the initial stage of redemption that is external). Figure 62 shows the moment in act 3 when Parsifal touches Amfortas's wound with the sword, allowing it to close (the symbolic stage of internalized redemption). The psychoanalytic literature contains many examples of "living between two deaths"—one literal, one symbolic. Wagner has written an opera in which the main characters are living between two stages of redemption—an act taking back an instrument of vitality once stolen by the other (Parsifal regaining the spear from Klingsor in act 2), and a symbolic internalization of that action (Parsifal allowing Amfortas's wound to close redeeming the community of the Knights of the Grail in act 3).

I am suggesting that Wagner has composed *Parsifal* as a negation of what Santner describes as a Judeo-Christian ability to live in social space coming to terms both with the strangeness within and the strangeness without. I have moved from an overview of the Jewish Question in Germany in general, to Wagner in particular, to open theoretical space for Santner's approach to community. *Parsifal* does not call for a renewal of the Aryan race in Germany, but it sets the stage, as it were, for such a renewal by creating a fantasy of redemption based on the total purging of social space of the other.

Parsifal, Syberberg, Puppets

Filmmaker Hans-Jürgen Syberberg was born in 1935 in the former GDR; he moved to the West in 1953, having begun his career filming rehearsals and performances of the Brecht plays *Mother Courage, The Mother,* and *Urfaust.*[69] His films are either extensions of cinéma verité, straight documentaries, or monologues.[70] They are highly mediated, interior collages of a wide variety of images, artificial props, puppets, objects and replicated objects, dummies, and dolls, often brought together by a single emblem.[71]

In his "Letter from Bayreuth" dated July 1882, Eduard Hanslick made the following remark about *Parsifal:* "The further the plot progresses, the more arbitrary, mystical, and symbolical it becomes. We human beings finally lose all sense of identification with these occurrences bound up in holy miracles and with these abnormal super- and sub-beings who move as if dangled from celestial marionette strings" (Hanslick 194). Hanslick's embedded metaphor of puppetry in his remarks is suggestive. Indeed, the characters of *Parsifal* are less characters with clear-cut, internally consistent motivations, than types, symbols, "puppets." Hans-Jürgen Syberberg often uses puppets in his films, and his choice to film *Parsifal* is fortuitous, given his penchant for very traditional forms of animation. The following discussion of Syberberg will take puppetry as its starting point, taking another pass, as it were, at *Parsifal* from the perspective of Syberberg's imagery.

Syberberg's film contains Wagner's opera presented in its entirety. Syberberg adds material to the beginning and ending of the work, and he dramatizes the *Vorspiel* to acts 1, 2, and 3. He adds a brief transition from the end of act 2 to the beginning of act 3; Easter bells prefigure the magic of Good Friday. In Syberberg's *Vorspiel* to act 1, puppets enact the seduction of Amfortas by Kundry, Klingsor's theft of the spear, the wounding of Amfortas, Titurel's lament, and Parsifal's killing of the swan. It is a cinematic story within a story, reinforcing Gurnemanz's narration in act 1.

Staged animation pervades this film. Not only are there puppets in the *Vorspiel*, the stage itself is a gigantic death mask of Wagner. Some of the characters in the film respond to others as animations of forces external to them. Some of the characters in the film exert force over others as animated objects. And finally Amfortas's wound is itself a crucial object of animation.[72]

The Vorspiel

The film opens with a rewritten version of measures 165–79 of act 2, in which Kundry awakens to the call of Klingsor: "Ach! Ach! Tiefe Nacht, Wahnsinn . . . Oh! Wut . . . Ach! Jammer! Schlaf- Schlaf . . . tiefer Schlaf . . . Tod!"[73] A few details of Wagner's orchestration remain, but the passage used for the beginning of the film has the Easter bells of the Grail ceremony accompany Kundry's words as she awakens.[74] To the music in A-flat major from measures 1–19, we see shots of a ruined temple and photos emblematic of German history floating in water. To the music in C minor from measures 20–38, we see a red-feathered arrow enter the ground and Parsifal as a very young boy with his mother (Kundry) in a white dress with stars of David. Parsifal gazes at his near future as Parsifal I (boy) and Parsifal II (girl) approach sitting side by side in a carriage.

Parsifal is a triad of neuter, male, and female components lingering for a moment before splitting into sexual difference.

To the music of measures 39–77, we see Parsifal as a very small boy watching the puppet show that tells the story of Amfortas's wound. The artifice of puppetry is readily apparent in traditional forms of the art. For Frank Proschan, the split of voice and action typical of many puppetry traditions is a source not of alienation for the audience but of identification. Proschan understands puppets as far more than simple figurines moved by hands:

> Dancers who wear masks, bards who use scroll-paintings or dolls to illustrate their narrations, children who create dramatic scenes in doll-play, worshipers who bear icons in a religious procession, and storytellers who trace images in snow or sand all manifest the urge to give life to nonliving things, as they animate objects in dramatic performances and use material images as surrogates for human actors. (Proschan 3)[75]

The artifice is on the surface of the film with visible rods moving the puppets.

The puppets in Syberberg's film are mute; in some ways the music speaks for them as they speak for the music. As mutes, and as generalized types, they suggest Icons as much as puppets. Kay Turner makes the distinction as follows: "The Icon, at least in the western Roman Catholic tradition, is most often a mute, motionless statue or painting that nevertheless is imbued with life by being looked at and spoken to by a believer."[76] Turner addresses an inherent dynamic of projection in witnessing an Icon: "Nothing so crucially distinguishes these performing objects [between puppet and Icon] as the fact that Icons are brought to life by people who speak to them because they believe in them, while puppets are enlivened by themselves being given the power of speech through the mediating puppet master" (Turner 317).

Syberberg's film opens with nested structures of identification—us watching Syberberg watching a performance of a child playing Parsifal watching puppets that stand for characters with whom he will interact after he undergoes sexual differentiation. In the puppet show that Parsifal watches, Kundry is dressed as not a seductress but a bride. With a kiss and embrace, she and Amfortas come together, allowing Klingsor the opportunity to take the spear and wound the vulnerable king. This interpretation of the story raises the stakes on the mechanism of seduction central to the opera. The puppet show suggests that it is not through sexual intercourse that Amfortas falls to Kundry but simply a kiss. And it is with a kiss in act 2 that Kundry will seduce Parsifal.

To the music of measures 78–114, we see one of the most crucial "performing objects" of the film—Amfortas's wound, several puppets of Wagner (including one of Wagner nailing into an ear with blood spurting out and another of Wagner on the cross), and Parsifal I and II intertwined.[77] As the final dominant seventh chord of the *Vorspiel* sounds, Parsifal I splits off from Parsifal II, who continues to sleep. She shall awaken and take her place besides Parsifal I in act 2 in the scene of Kundry's seductions to be discussed below.

Amfortas's wound is a unique "performing object" in Syberberg's film.[78] It changes in every scene it appears. As a performing object with no internal consistency from moment to moment, it is the purest form of Icon—one in which meaning is projected at every moment, changing the object each time it is seen.[79]

Act I

While it is commonplace to synchronize music to visuals in films of operas, the procedure is taken to its logical endpoint by Syberberg: all vocal parts (even those for characters who sing their own parts) are synchronized to action. While the synchronization is skillfully achieved, the artifice is visible on the surface of the film at all times. Singing bodies visibly channel energy to the throat, chest, and head in a way that speaking actors do not. Just as Syberberg does not hide the rods controlling his puppets, so, too, he shows the space between the gestures of enunciation and the actual music. There is very little sense of space "outside"; most of the film has a sense of interiority.[80] It is one grand puppet show.

To the music of act 1, measures 993–1036, we see Gurnemanz leading Parsifal around the features of Wagner's face, through a passageway draped with flags from German history, into the inner sanctum in which the Grail ceremony will take place. The Transformation Music is preceded by the famous line of Gurnemanz to Parsifal "Du siehst, mein Sohn, zum Raum wird hier die Zeit." Syberberg represents the transformation of time into space in two ways. First he has the action move through the mask and into the inside of Wagner's head—a dramatic correlate for the dynamic of internalization driving the entire opera and film. Second, and more crucially, Syberberg arranges the flags in reverse chronological order, moving early past a flag of the swastika back into

Germany's distant past. This reverse chronological order is crucial for Syberberg's intervention in the Parsifal myth. For Syberberg, Parsifal's mission is at once to move forward in diachronic time (to regain the spear from Klingsor, to assume his symbolic mandate at the Grail ceremony, to execute his office where his symbolic father had failed) and, crucially, to regress back in time to a period before culture was stained by the alterity-writ-large called modernism. In Syberberg's representation of the Transformation Music, we see time becoming space in precisely this way.

The Grail Ceremony

To the music of Titurel's imperative-as-question "Mein Sohn Amfortas, bist du am Amt?" (act 1, measures 1131–36), we see Titurel in an underground grave/cave as he sings. This is the most interior space of the film (an interior [Titurel's grave/cave] inside an interior [inside Wagner's head] inside an interior [the diegetic space of the film]). Wagner's stage direction clearly suggests a disembodied voice of Titurel rising from the depths as if from a grave.[81]

As Syberberg shows us Titurel in his grave/cave, we see and hear— water. The film is excruciatingly silent. We see the seam always before our eyes between gestures as if singing from *within* the body and singing synchronized from *without*. We hear water twice in the film: in act 1 in Titurel's grave/cave and in act 3 as Parsifal passes a water fountain on the way to the Grail ceremony. Thus through this one diegetic sound, Syberberg marks a large-scale cross-referential link for us between Titurel's demand in act 1 and its execution in act 3. And since there is so little diegetic sound in the film, it is extraordinarily emphasized.[82]

The voice that calls another to act is a metaphorical puppet rod connecting master to the object of his will. As Kundry falls asleep in act 1, we sense that she is being called back to Klingsor, which is confirmed at the outset of act 2.

Act II

For Parsifal's turn away from Kundry after their kiss in act 2, Syberberg has Parsifal II (an adolescent girl) "join" Parsifal I (an adolescent boy)— an extraordinarily puppetlike gesture—making "Parsifal" into a pair of characters. Syberberg introduces us in the *Vorspiel* to act 1 to Parsifal as two young adolescents sitting side by side in a carriage—the object of the

gaze of Parsifal as a young child. "Parsifal" is thus a complex of identifications at once male, female, and neuter, little bits of subjectivity that
correspond to all three genders of the German language (*der, die, das*).

In act 2, measures 983–1040, we see Kundry in her first attempt at se-
ducing Parsifal I, with a doll embodying Parsifal as a young baby. Kundry
and Parsifal I kiss, and Parsifal turns away from a consummation of the
seduction, as we have seen above. As we saw in Wagner's opera, Parsifal
I's "Nein" is crucial as he realizes that his pain is not one of identification
but of his own awakened sexuality. As her first seduction fails, Kundry's
face falls into her hands—a gesture of falling asleep that Syberberg had
shown us in the *Vorspiel* to act 1. At the moment of Parsifal I's correction
of his experience (not simply an identification with Amfortas's wound
but an awakening of his own sexual desire), Syberberg has Parsifal II
awaken and walk up to Parsifal I in a side-by-sideness evocative of the
two Parsifals sitting side by side in the carriage in the *Vorspiel*.

Kundry's second seduction focuses on Parsifal II as Parsifal I with-
draws into the dark. This seduction fails utterly, and Kundry calls upon
Klingsor, who collapses, having already lost his symbolic power, and the
spear falls. Parsifal I holds the spear and utters the last words of the act
to Kundry. Syberberg adds two things to the end of act 2: (1) we hear the
Easter bells, and (2) we see the zombie-like Kundry of the very beginning of the film raising her head from the crystal ball. At the beginning
of the film, her face *descends* upon the ball; at the end of act 2, it *ascends*.
As Klingsor dies at the end of act 2, "she" awakens, but what remains is
not a character with internal consistency. She has just the faintest outlines of subjectivity. This becomes clear in act 3 where she utters only a
few words, witnesses the Grail ceremony, and dies, redeemed.

Syberberg's intervention into the moment of Parsifal's turning away
from Kundry's kiss radically redraws the lines of sexual difference of
Wagner's opera. How are we to understand this moment of the two Parsifals? Syberberg maintains Parsifal I as a character (he turns to Kundry
at the end of act 2 and says the words "Du weisst wo du mich finden
kannst" [You know were you can find me again]).[83] Since both Parsifals
abide in the rest of the film, it cannot simply be a question of a transformation of one gender into another. Syberberg films the moment of
the awakening of Parsifal II as a (re)unification of complements, lost as
Parsifal I awakens at the end of the *Vorspiel* to act 1. How though are we
to understand this (re)unification of complements, who have awakened

at different times, in terms of Parsifal's revision of his response to Kundry's kiss? What does Parsifal I's turn away from sexuality have to do with this (re)unification?

Parsifal II could have rejected Kundry's second seduction, regained the spear, and executed the Grail ceremony, bringing redemption to the Knights of the Grail. Her diachronic quest would have been completed and fully realized. By having Parsifal II awaken at the moment of Parsifal I's recognition of his sexual desire, Syberberg achieves both a diachronic representation of Parsifal's quest, and a regressive fantasy of Parsifal turning away from his sexual awakening, moving back to a time and place during which / at which the two elements of sexual difference embraced each other side by side in a perfect union. Syberberg achieves a large-scale transformation of time becoming space by combining the forward-moving diachronic trajectory of quest with a backward rewinding of the tape to a moment before sexual difference. In Syberberg's words: "Now the child in the film is no longer a child but a representation of the belief in the final unification of ancient and opposing worlds—an illuminating and mutually reflecting entity of innocence, which just seems possible in this phase of childhood before its division into conscious sexual difference."[84] This is the fantasy of perfection with which the film will end, of reaching forward to outer redemption in social space, and moving backward to inner redemption in psychic space.

Act 3

From the beginning of act 3 to measure 1061, we see Parsifal II as we hear the same voice that had sung Parsifal I's music throughout the film. We had seen Syberberg articulate the alterity of voice throughout his film with synchronization throughout of all voices we hear to all the actors we see. In Parsifal II, this split of voice and subject is particularly evident. This is the most puppetlike character in the film, with the male tenor's voice thrown onto the female body of Parsifal II.

We saw in the opera that much time had elapsed since the end of act 2 and the beginning of act 3. As she arrives at the beginning of act 3, Parsifal II is mute and unresponsive. This muteness is a function of her exhaustion at her ordeal and the long journey without direction that led her from Klingsor's realm back to the Knights of the Grail. Parsifal II's muteness also suggests that she is still just a vessel for the voice of the

Other. She still needs to hear the call of the Other, to bear witness, to perform the office of the Grail. As she is recognized, and as the spear is recognized by Gurnemanz, Parsifal II is animated, anointed, and made king.

Both Parsifal and Kundry are "called" throughout the film. Kundry is called by Gurnemanz as well as Klingsor. She is a puppet reduced to a doll in act 3. She reiterates the word "dienen" to a perfect authentic cadence in D minor in measures 136–37 and is mute for the rest of the work. Parsifal is a very different puppet. Into Parsifal the voice of the Other penetrates. Into Kundry the voice of the Other *cannot* penetrate; she can only be redeemed in death. The voice of the Other sticks only to those vessels that are pure; to those that are impure, it slides off and is silent. Parsifal has shards of a history but a pure character. Kundry has *only* shards of a history and no character. She can serve for ill or for good. And, as the wandering Jew in the final words of Wagner's "Das Judentum in der Musik," she can die.

To the music of act 3, measures 1030–35 and the words "Nur eine Waffe taugt; die Wunde schliesst der Speer nur, der sie schlug" [But one weapon serves: only the spear that smote you can heal your wound] at which Parsifal heals Amfortas's wound, we see Parsifal II on top of a hill with Amfortas and the Knights below. Wagner's stage directions say that Parsifal's spear touches Amfortas's wound in measure 1035. Syberberg has Parsifal II sing at a physical remove from Amfortas and his wound. Speaking, calling, naming are far more crucial in the opera and film than the performance of actions. And it is in the spirit of Eschenbach's *Parzifal* that an act of speech heals the king in Syberberg. Parsifal II heals the wound and proclaims that he/she will perform the "Amt"—the highly charged word that had designated the office Titurel had asked/demanded of Amfortas in act 1.

To the music of act 3, measures 1061–64, we see Parsifal I sing the line "Den heiligen Speer, ich bring' ihn euch zurück" [I bring back to you the holy spear!], suggesting an association of Parsifal I with speech-as-action and Parsifal II with reflection. It is crucially important, however, that the goal of the redemption brought by "Parsifal" is the redemption of the community of the Knights of the Grail and not simply the redemption of Amfortas—thus the second-person plural pronoun.

To the music act 3, measures 1067–88, we see Parsifal I (with the spear) and Parsifal II (with the cross) side by side singing *together* the lines: "O! Welchen Wunder's höchtes Glück! Der deine Wunde durfte schliessen, ihm seh ich heil'ges Blut entfliessen in Sehnsucht nach dem verwandten Quelle, der dort fliesst in des Gralles Welle. Nicht soll der mehr verschlossen sein: Enhüllet den Gral, öffnet den Schrein!" [O supreme joy at this miracle! This that could heal your wound I see pouring with holy blood yearning for that kindred fount which flows and wells within the Grail. No more shall it be hidden: uncover the Grail, open the shrine]. These are the last words spoken by Parsifal or any other character in the film (except choirs of knights).

This is the apotheosis of the film's representation of Parsifal's transformation and quest. He/she/they have redeemed Kundry, Amfortas, the community of the Knights of the Grail. And he/she/they have achieved a regression to their mute side-by-sideness of the *Vorspiel* to act 1. Parsifal I and II embrace, and the film ends with a shot of the zombie-like Kundry raising her head above a crystal ball, closing her eyes, and then slowly lowering her head.

Syberberg, Film, Aesthetics: A Conclusion

Thomas Elsaesser discusses historical forces at work in late nineteenth-century Germany between Bavaria and King Ludwig II's self-conscious and luxuriant decadence, and Bismark's Prussianism that will subsume regional interests into the new nation-state Germany (119–20). For Elsaesser, this is a binary that runs beneath Syberberg's films, particularly his two films about Ludwig II. Elsaesser points out that the terms of this binary opposition are *connected*; decadent, luxuriant myth-making turns into the material support for capitalist exploitation, as a thriving tourist industry became attached to Ludwig's castles after his death (120–21). Accordingly, Elsaesser discovers in Syberberg two histories: a mythic history in which characters, fetishized objects, resonate metaphorically with supreme beings and utopian fantasies, and a materialist history in which art participates in the circulation of capital (123). Wagner's *Parsifal* contains both elements of Elsaesser's binary: it is myth-making in its puppetlike characters who represent as in a morality play forces of good, evil, and redemption, and it simultaneously provides the symbolic support for an object of exchange value. Under the direction of his Jewish conductor Hermann Levi, *Parsifal* becomes another of King Ludwig II's expensive fantasies.

Syberberg's aesthetic is kitsch: the ear that bleeds, dolls of various "Wagners," puppets, postcards floating in the waters of history, Amfortas's wound. For Elsaesser,

> Nothing is more saturated with the past than kitsch, whose passing it perpetually regrets and laments. Kitsch is the gesture that embraces what once was product of a living tradition, covering the gap between past and present which only historical understanding could otherwise rescue with a desperately fake aura. (Elsaesser 115)[85]

For all of Syberberg's polemics against film and the marketplace, Elsaesser points out that Syberberg's films are products of the culture of the Federal Republic of Germany, with its heavily subsidized opera and film industry (Elsaesser 108–9). Syberberg would like to withdraw as far as possible from the marketplace of exchange, as his numerous interviews and writings make very clear.[86] And yet he has chosen a medium of expression that is completely dependent on major funding and the major vehicle of mass culture in the West in the postwar years.[87]

In her essay on *Hitler—Ein Film aus Deutschland*, Susan Sontag suggests that Syberberg is both a surrealist and a symbolist:[88] "In Syberberg's meditation on history in a sound studio, events are visualized (with the aid of Surrealist conventions) while remaining in a deeper sense invisible (the Symbolist idea)."[89] Surrealism makes the unconscious visible through an openness to chance, condensation, displacement, quotation, fragmentation, lack of astonishment, ellipsis, lavish elaboration, and pastiche. Surrealism uncovers, shows, reveals. For Sontag, "There is nothing arbitrary or aleatoric about his décor, no throw-away images or objects without emotional weight; indeed, certain relics and images in Syberberg's film have the force of personal talismans. Everything means, everything speaks" (147). Sontag is right when she points out that a key element of surrealism is alien to Syberberg—a playfulness and openness to chance and absurdity (147). Syberberg's surrealism slows down without chance and play.[90] Slowness is important for Syberberg's film technique and aesthetic.[91] His camera is mostly static; he creates most of his motion through very slow zooming in and out and a careful attention to the rule of thirds in his compositions. In *Parsifal*, stage smoke swirls in many scenes, suggesting motion in slowly shifting configurations of characters.[92]

For Sontag, Syberberg is also a symbolist: "The Symbolists found the invisible stage. Events were to be withdrawn from reality, so to speak, and restaged in the ideal theater of the mind. And Wagner's fantasy of the invisible stage was fulfilled more literally in that immaterial stage, cinema" (Sontag 157). Thus the plethora of puppetlike objects, puppeteer-like agencies, stage smoke, in fact the entirely interior quality of space in *Parsifal*. For Sontag, "The Symbolist narrative is always a posthumous affair" (Sontag 159). Sontag's language is suggestive of a classic nineteenth-century German text on puppets: Kleist's "Über das Marionettenthe-ater." This work is a fragment of a dialogue in which the author as narrator speaks with a dancer who appreciates the art of puppetry. The quaint, understated, and naive nature of the narrator is a foil for the subtle and evocative musings of the dancer. The dancer speaks of puppets embodying grace in their evocation of paradise before the Fall and in their freedom from gravity. For Kleist's dancer, puppets embody pure spirit in their weightlessness and exposed manipulation of strings and rods. Kleist's dancer sees puppets looking for a back door to paradise after the Fall.[93]

Syberberg looks through *Parsifal* back at the ruins of German culture.[94] The imagery and technique are caught between the visibility of surrealism and the invisibility of symbolism. Syberberg gathers his visual energy precisely at this "catch" as he removes himself as far as possible from the external world of exchange.[95] There is something nonrepeatable about his aesthetic, something that cannot be elaborated, something singular—like turning a pocket inside out so that you can imagine objects that are no longer there, at the odd vulnerability of seams.[96]

Notes

Preface

1. Slavoj Žižek, *Looking Awry* (Cambridge, Mass.: MIT Press, 1991), 3. Subsequent references to this and all other cited works will appear in the text.

2. An anamorphotic image is one that appears distorted when viewed straight ahead; the image becomes clear when viewed through a lens, a particular perspective, or a mirror. Lacan also discusses objects in nature that can only be observed obliquely: "If you wish to see a star of the fifth or sixth size, do not look straight at it—this is known as the Arago phenomenon. You will be able to see it only if you fix your eye to one side" (Jacques Lacan, *The Four Fundamental Concepts of Psycho-Analysis,* ed. Jacques-Alain Miller, trans. Alan Sheridan [New York: Norton, 1981], 102).

3. Lydia Goehr, *The Imaginary Museum of Musical Works: An Essay in the Philosophy of Music* (Oxford: Clarendon Press, 1992), 108.

4. Michel Foucault, *The Archaeology of Knowledge,* trans. A. M. Sheridan Smith (New York: Pantheon Books, 1972), 166. For a discussion of the modern prison as panopticon, see *Surveiller et punir* (Paris: Gallimard, 1975); in English as *Discipline and Punish,* trans. Alan Sheridan (New York: Knopf, 1995). For a discussion of the humanities, see *Les mots et les choses* (Paris: Gallimard, 1966); in English as *The Order of Things* (New York: Knopf, 1994). For a discussion of the modern hospital, see *Naissance de la clinique* (Paris: Presses Universitaires de France, 1963); in English as *The Birth of the Clinic,* trans. A. M. Sheridan Smith (New York: Random House, 1994).

5. See Harold Bloom, *The Anxiety of Influence* (New York: Oxford University Press, 1997). In his Preface to the second edition, Bloom distances himself from psychoanalysis, although his work is profoundly underwritten by an Oedipal interpretation of the relations of poets with powerful antecedents.

6. Walter Benjamin, *Illuminations,* ed. Hannah Arendt, trans. Harry Zohn (New York: Schocken Books, 1968), 257–58.

1. The Rise of the Conductor and the Missing One

1. The phrase "the missing one" might remind readers of psychoanalytic criticism and art that represent various kinds of castrated subjects, missing fathers,

signifiers that are empty. In the movie *Apartment Zero* the number of the main character's apartment (it used to be "10" but is "0" because of the "missing 1") stands for a missing paternal signifier at the heart of his symbolic identity. I argue throughout this chapter that music in the late eighteenth century begins to loose its singular, material "center" (music's "1"), revealing a void at the heart of the modern musical masterpiece. Into this void (music's "0") steps the conductor.

2. I found no evidence to suggest that a conductor, a concertmaster, or a Kapellmeister in late eighteenth- or early nineteenth-century Germany was a woman, although women have entered the conducting profession in the twentieth and twenty-first centuries. I use the pronouns "he" and "him" throughout this chapter because the conductors, concertmasters, and Kapellmeisters in the time period under discussion were likely all men.

3. The double direction of the eighteenth century is well documented. See in particular Elliott Washington Galkin, "The Theory and Practice of Orchestral Conducting Since 1752" (PhD diss., Cornell University, 1960), and Georg Schünemann, *Geschichte des Dirigierens* (Leipzig, Germany: Breitkopf and Härtel, 1913). See also José Antonio Bowen, "The Conductor and the Score: The Relationship between Interpreter and Text in the Generation of Mendelssohn, Berlioz, and Wagner" (PhD diss., Stanford University, 1993), and David Woolridge, *Conductor's World* (New York: Prager, 1970).

4. Music from the ancient Greeks to the present has had "conductors" of various sorts. In his study of the conductor, Elliott Galkin suggests that modern conducting can be divided into two periods: the formative years of 1752–1844 and 1845 to the present. Berlioz's *L'Art du chef d'orchestre* appeared in 1844. The present study will focus on Galkin's formative era of modern conducting, with particular attention paid to the emergence of the single conductor of the late eighteenth, early nineteenth century who gradually separates himself from the role of keyboard artist filling gaps in the orchestral texture and the role of first chair, first violin as time beater. See Galkin 13.

5. Even the singularity of the conductor emerges in fits and starts in the early nineteenth century. It is one thing to show how the two (sometimes three) conductors of the eighteenth century converge into a single conductor in the early nineteenth century; it is another to draw a clear distinction between this new conductor and his concertmaster, who remains important even today. The concertmaster who tunes the orchestra to A440 is a relic of the premodern, single conductor whose presence still underwrites modern orchestral practice.

6. This is the task in a nutshell of criticism that seeks to understand cultural artifacts as at once products of historical specificity and psychic formations. This is the Möbius strip of modernity: on one side of the piece of paper upon which the modern subject is inscribed there is *psychoanalysis*; on the other side is *history*. For a particularly clear and helpful discussion of the Möbius strip, see Dylan Evans, *Dictionary of Lacanian Psychoanalysis* (London: Routledge, 1996), 116.

7. For the sake of simplicity and clarity, for the rest of this chapter "Germany" will refer to the collection of German-speaking countries that became the nation-state Germany in 1870.

8. Two social factors contributed to the emergence of the professional single conductor with which we have become familiar since the early to mid-nineteenth century: public concert societies and conservatories. The public concert societies

solved many problems common in eighteenth-century orchestral performances by, for the first time, providing orchestras their own place of performance. Concert halls such as the Gewandhaus in Leipzig was (like the modern museum for painting) a place devoted to a single cultural artifact—instrumental music. The rise of the middle class also provided an audience for musical consumption that would continue to grow throughout the nineteenth and twentieth centuries. The emergence of music conservatories in the late eighteenth century provided the basis not only of the modern music school but a place where performance practice and composition could develop side by side. Galkin refers to nine conservatories that became crucial for music in the period: Paris (established 1795), Milan (1808), Naples (1808), Prague (1811), Vienna (1817), London (1822), Brussels (1832), Leipzig (1843), and Munich (1846) (Galkin 319–20).

9. See, in particular, Georg Schünemann, *Geschichte des Dirigierens*, chapter 6. Unless otherwise noted, translations into English throughout the book are by the author.

10. See note 32 below for a suggestion by a writer in *Die Allgemeine Musikalische Zeitung* that musicians abandon the traditional long shelves upon which rows of music had been placed, in favor of more narrow, individual boards that would let the sound of orchestra project better into the hall.

11. There is no single time or place at which this concept appeared, but you can sense it in several articles in *Die Allgemeine Musikalische Zeitung (AMZ)* published in Leipzig in the late eighteenth century, to pick one example. It is particularly in reference to Mozart that the notion of the great genius emerges. According to *AMZ* authors, Haydn is the disciplined master; his music lends itself to the performance practice of the eighteenth century; Mozart and occasionally Beethoven write music that is informed by an inner necessity inherently at odds with conditions of performance.

12. For a thorough discussion of these social phenomena, see Galkin 319–28. For a discussion of the emergence of the notion of music as performance of a fixed, permanent "work," see Bowen, 8. Bowen also discusses the new notion of a canon emerging in the early nineteenth century. For a thorough discussion of issues of the emergence of the canon in Western culture, see Richard Leppert and Susan McClary, eds., *Music and Society* (New York: Cambridge University Press, 1987).

Lydia Goehr discusses the work as a piece of music that contributes to an ongoing canon of musical masterpieces, housed in archives and libraries and performed in that new institution of late eighteenth-century–early nineteenth-century social space—the modern concert conducted by the single, virtuoso conductor. See Lydia Goehr, *The Imaginary Museum of Musical Works: An Essay in the Philosophy of Music* (Oxford: Clarendon Press, 1992), chapter 4.

13. The Lacanian mirror phase is a crucial component of current psychoanalytic accounts of representations of subject formation in works of cinema, art, and recent music. In a nutshell, the mirror phase is about mutually exclusive binary oppositions of plenitude and lack connecting a developing subject with a fantasy projection of an ideal self reflected back to him/her from the world. See Jacques Lacan, "The Mirror Stage" in *Écrits*, trans. Alan Sheridan (New York: W. W. Norton, 1977), 1–7. See also Kaja Silverman, *The Subject of Semiotics* (New York: Oxford University Press, 1983), 157–62.

An antecedent, acoustic mirror phase has been described by Didier Anzieu in *Le peau-moi* (Paris: Bordas, 1985), in English as *The Skin Ego*, trans. Chris Turner (New

Haven, Conn.: Yale University Press, 1989). See also Kaja Silverman, *The Acoustic Mirror* (Bloomington: Indiana University Press, 1988). The acoustic mirror phase suggests that we discover our bodies in social space as a complex process of identifications and separations articulated by touch, smell, and voice projected outward and introjected inward, into and out of our bodies at our skin.

14. The opaque curtain is like a screen upon which the expectation of identification is projected from the darkened spaces of the concert hall.

15. The 180-degree conversion is an adaptation of Althusser's famous thesis on ideological interpellation. According to Althusser, when someone turns to meet the gaze of a policeman who has shouted "hey you!" that person becomes a subject of the Law and recognizes himself or herself as the "you" of the Other's discourse. See Louis Althusser, "Ideology and Ideological State Apparatuses," in *Lenin and Philosophy*, trans. Ben Brewster (New York: Monthly Review Press, 1971).

16. Film critics discuss the screen as a place in cinema like the mirror in the mirror stage. See, in particular, Kaja Silverman, *The Threshold of the Visible World* (New York: Routledge, 1996), chapter 6. The screen as a physical object is, of course, a stand-in for the psychic screen upon which images are introjected and projected. For me, the speaker as audio component gives us an acoustic screen, which, in turn, is a stand-in for the psychic acoustic screen that registers our introjected and projected voices. I shall argue that there is an imaginary screen that bisects the modern concert hall, with the orchestra on one side and the audience on the other. The modern conductor calls the modern musical text into being precisely at that silent screen.

17. The gaze is a crucial component of Lacanian psychoanalysis. In Lacan, the look is one person making eye contact with another; the gaze is outside the subject, distributed in social spaces. Thus, the famous line "You never look at me from the place at which I see you." See Dylan Evans, *An Introductory Dictionary of Lacanian Psychoanalysis* (New York: Routledge, 1996), 72–73; Laura Mulvey, "Visual Pleasure and the Narrative Cinema," in *Visual and Other Pleasures* (Bloomington: Indiana University Press, 1989); Jacqueline Rose, *Sexuality in the Field of Vision* (London: Verso, 1986). I shall discuss the gaze in greater detail toward the end of this chapter.

18. The appearance of the modern conductor is profoundly paradoxical. On the one hand, he appears as a response to the increasing complexity of music; on the other hand, his presence enables such music to be complex. To try to describe the appearance of the conductor in a single articulation of declarative certainty would be like trying to replace the following two sentences with one: "Music in the eighteenth century became increasingly complex leading to a collapse of orchestral double direction" and "In his dance-like and silent mimicry, the modern conductor enabled a qualitatively new masterwork to come into being."

19. In addition to the orchestra as a whole gradually attaining internal consistency in the late eighteenth and early nineteenth centuries, musical instruments themselves were evolving during the time. The eighteenth-century flute was made of wood or ivory; it had one, four, five, or seven keys (of wood or metal); a very weak sound; and was, according to contemporary accounts, "always out of tune." Not until 1847 was the fifteen-key flute that we know today invented and standardized by Theobald Boehm (Galkin 39). The eighteenth-century oboe, like the flute, was simple and relatively weak. It was made of wood or ivory, with six holes, one key, and smaller reeds than are used today. By 1840, Boehm's inventions for the flute were adapted to the oboe. The modern oboe (the "conservatoire") appeared in 1880

(Galkin 41). The eighteenth-century clarinet also had difficulty producing clean, in-tune pitches. The modern clarinet emerged in the third quarter of the nineteenth century as the Boehm clarinet (Galkin 43–44). The eighteenth-century bassoon had a difficult and unpredictable sound produced by four keys; eight keys were present in bassoons in Beethoven's early period, and by the late nineteenth centuries the two modern bassoons were standardized—the French (lighter and more delicate) and the German "Heckel" instruments (Galkin 44).

The brass instruments included the eighteenth-century natural horn that acquired crooks in 1770 and valves by 1813 (Galkin 45–46). Similarly, the eighteenth century had natural trumpets and trumpets with crooks; the valve trumpet was perfected in the 1830s (Galkin 46–47). The eighteenth-century trombone was very similar to the contemporary trombone with slightly more conical and "hornlike" mouthpieces that produced a sweet, mellow sound (Galkin 47).

Although the eighteenth-century stringed instrument was very much like the contemporary stringed instrument, the bow was not. The modern bow was invented in 1785 by Tourte (Galkin 48). The modern bow enabled a much more powerful sound to emerge from a stringed instrument than earlier, Baroque bows. And it was a sound that could be sustained from tip to frog, producing an instrumental version of a singing tone. The modern bow is an ancestor, as well, of the conductor's baton, since concertmasters "conducted" with their bows (Galkin 48).

20. Modern music history, in many ways, begins in the eighteenth century with the enormous festivals performing Handel's music. Haydn and Mozart joined Handel by the end of the eighteenth century. The birth of modern music history means that a series of reference points are established in the past at which time a great work sprang from the pen of a great composer—at a remove from the time and place of a contemporary performance. The conductor steps into this temporal and spatial displacement as a surrogate for the composer. The birth of modern music history also involves an urge to perform a work perfectly, and it is this urge for perfection that both produces and is produced by the single conductor of the early nineteenth century.

21. Double direction was common in the eighteenth century in England, France, Germany, and Italy.

22. See Galkin for the entire entry quoted in the German original and English translation.

23. I have drawn all of these examples using Adobe Illustrator, being as faithful as possible to the details of the original sketches. The sketches in the original are not unified in terms of design, naming conventions, manner of representing the layout of an orchestra, the relationship between the stage upon which an orchestra plays and the surrounding walls, and the relationship between the performers' space and the audience's space. All graphic elements in the original sketches have been rendered; I have translated the names of instruments into English.

24. Concertgoers will recognize a vestige of this archaic practice with the largely ceremonial tuning up of an orchestra by the concertmaster. Some recordings will even list the "concertmaster" or "leader" of an orchestra on liner notes—a tip of the hat to the lost role of concertmaster as conductor. There are, of course, chamber orchestras that still play with only a concertmaster.

25. Galkin points out that, in addition to the Kapellmeister and the concertmaster, there was often a Musik-director concerned exclusively with extramusical issues.

26. Early instances of crescendo-diminuendo include Terradella's opera *Bellerophon* of 1747 and Jommelli's opera *Artaserse* of 1749.

27. See, for example the following article in the *AMZ*: "Es war eine Freude, zu sehen, wie ein Bogenstrich mit dem anderen auf und niedergieng [sic]; eine Freude zu hören, wie kein Vorschlag im ganzen Orchester von mehr als fünfzig Personen unbemerkt bleib, oder gegen den Sinn des Komponisten unrichtig vorgetragen ward, wie *forte* und *piano* in geschwisterlicher Eintracht vorgetragen wurden, wie das gleichförmige ausgeführete Steigen des *Crescendo* und Fallen des *Diminuendo* dem fühlenden Zuhörer das Herz aufschwellte" (*AMZ* 52 [September 25, 1799]: 882). [(At Mannheim) it was a pleasure to see unified upbows and downbows and a pleasure to hear that no articulation from an orchestra of more than fifty musicians stayed unaccounted for or was not performed as the composer intended, and to hear the uniform rising crescendo and falling diminuendo that matched the rising and falling of the hearts of the emotionally engaged listeners.] See also Schünemann for a discussion of the importance of the concertmasters Stamitz and Cannabich at Mannheim. Such practices at Mannheim were important in giving eighteenth-century listeners a taste of the kind of unified sound from an orchestra that was to become standard in the nineteenth century (209).

28. As Schünemann explains, the omission of the basses in the sketch was a mistake.

29. An early instance of the omission of a keyboard performer in musical performances of the time was a 1772 performance of Grétry's opera *Zémire et Azor* in Brussels (Galkin 316). Although Quantz had written of the urgency of retaining the keyboard, Galkin explains its waning influence as follows: "as more composers began to incorporate the complete harmony and rhythmic pulse into the orchestral parts, the keyboard director, trained as a composer in the choral tradition, steadily lost his usefulness to the group" (318).

30. I suspect that the gradual removal of the conductor from the orchestra was in part a response to an increasingly standardized orchestra that often had complete wind, brass, percussion, and string sections. The new single conductor replaced the pedagogical and interpretive role of the Kapellmeister and took over from the concertmaster the responsibility of beating time. The duty of determining bowings went to the concertmaster and other section leaders. Musically, works required more rehearsal and a greater and more sustained interpretive energy.

31. The original diagram shows that the choir of tenors and basses were elevated a half an "elle" from the floor. An elle is a distance of between 60 and 80 centimeters. Each partial horizontal line in the sketch represents a raised height of one-quarter elle, or 15 to 20 centimeters, over the level beneath. The full horizontal line at the top of the sketch represents an increased height of one elle above the previous level.

32. Apparently, the individual music stand emerged in this period, or shortly thereafter. A writer for the *AMZ* suggests to his readers that sound would project into the audience better if the continuous benches supporting music were broken up into individual stands: "Werfen Sie sie weg, diese Breter, und lassen Sie dafür möglichst schmale Leisten hinnageln! Man denkt gemeiniglich [sic] nicht daran, wie nachtheilig jene Breter dem Klange dadurch werden, daß die den Schall, besonders der Violinen und Violen, zurückwerfen, und folglich theils die Stärke des Klanges für die Zuhörer vermindern, theils, bei großen oder nicht ganz vollen Sälen, einen

falschen Wiederhall und folglich Undeutlichkeit verursachen" (*AMZ* 4 [October 23, 1799]: 60). [Get rid of these planks and nail shorter boards! One never thinks about the effect of the long boards on the sound, that, particularly for the violins and violas, they throw back, diminishing the strength of the sound for the audience. A particularly false echo is thereby created in large and not completely filled concert halls.]

33. Galkin quotes Sir Adrian Boult, who places the date for the standard modern orchestra at 1910 (Galkin 172).

34. In a paragraph of wide-angled insight and synthesis, Schünemann grounds eighteenth-century music in a large-scale arc connecting the affective theories of the ancient Greeks with eighteenth-century rational aesthetics: "Im Verlauf der Arbeit ist häufiger auf die Affektentheorie hingewiesen worden. Sie war der Hintergrund aller Bemerkungen über Musikerziehung, Orchesterspiel und Dynamik. Wie die Betonung der Ausdruckswerte der Musik die bei der Lehre vom griechischen Ethos, bei den Vortragsregeln des gregorianischen Chorals und der a cappella-Kunst erwähnt wurde, im 17. Jahrhundert zu einer neuen, auf Subjektivität gegründeten Literatur und Ausführungspraxis führte, so stehen wir im 18. Jahrhundert vor dem völligen Ausbau dieser praktischen Musikästhetik, vor einem geschlossenen musikalischen System" (Schünemann 230). [Throughout this study, the doctrine of affects has often been mentioned. It has been behind all comments on music education, orchestral playing and dynamics. Just as the emphasis of expression in music in the teaching of Greek ethics, by the performance rules of Gregorian chant and the a cappella singing of the seventeenth century led to a new literature and performance practice based on a new subjectivity, so, too, in the eighteenth century we have arrived at the completed development of this musical aesthetic, an enclosed musical system.]

35. "Die Musik wurde zu meiner größten Verwunderung, wie es doch überall bey solchen fürstlichen Ämtern herkömmlich ist, nicht von dem fürstlichen Hof-Konzertmeister, sondern von dem Rektor Chori der Domkirche, einem Benediktiner-mönche, dirigiert, welcher aber weder einen reinen und festen Violinstrich, noch einige Kenntnisse einer gehörigen Direktion zu besitzen schien. Er stand bey der ersten Violin, kratzte ohne ein angemessenes Tempo genommen zu haben, unbekümmert um das Orchester, auf seiner ohnehin nicht einmal rein gestimmten Violin, ein Stück nach dem andern herunter, schien es nicht eben zu Herzen zu nehmen, ob einer seiner Mitspieler c oder cis griff, usw. Kein Instrument stimmte mit dem anderen, die ganze Produktion war ein immerwährendes Gewühle von Dissonanzen, und da beständige Rückhalten der Trompeten mit den öfters darunter stürmenden, falschen Orgelakkorde, ließ Mozarts Arbeit gar nicht erkennen" (*AMZ* 42 [July 16, 1800]: 730–31). Here is a fragment of a devastating review from the *AMZ* of a performance of a symphony by Haydn in G major. The author writes: "Eine Sinfonie von Haydn aus G dur, hatte ich noch nicht gehört und mag sie auch so nicht wieder hören, denn die Ausführung war kraftlos und unordentlich" (*AMZ* 14 [January 1, 1801]: 237). [(There was) a symphony in G major from Haydn that I had not heard before and hope never to hear again like that; the performance was weak and sloppy.] Also, concerning a performance of Mozart's "Der büssende David": "die Ausführung, besonders der Chöre, war das widerlichste Geschrey und zufällsgste Spektakel, womit die Asche eines rechtschaffenden Komponisten im Grabe beunruhigt werden kann" (*AMZ* 14 [January 1, 1801]: 240). [The performance, particularly the choral numbers, were the most disgusting cries and such a chaotic spectacle that Mozart must have turned in his grave.]

36. Anxiety is, of course, a term that comes into play in a number of contexts. Harold Bloom's influential book *The Anxiety of Influence* (New York: Oxford University Press, 1997) understands the modern era in poetry as based on strong male poets needing to symbolically kill their powerful antecedents, as boys need to symbolically kill their fathers (or surrogates) on emergence from latency. For a discussion of Bloom's ideas applied to music, see Mark Evans Bond, *After Beethoven: Imperatives of Originality in the Symphony* (Cambridge, Mass.: Harvard University Press, 1996).

Anxiety has a rich history in psychoanalysis. For Freud's discussion of "fear, anxiety, shock," see Sigmund Freud, *Beyond the Pleasure Principle* (New York: W. W. Norton, 1961), 11. For an overview of anxiety in Freud and Lacan, see Dylan Evans, *An Introductory Dictionary of Lacanian Psychoanalysis* (London: Routledge, 1996), 10–12. For a discussion of "anxiety hysteria" and "anxiety neurosis" see Jean Laplance and Jean Baptiste Pontalis, *The Language of Psycho-Analysis*, trans. Donald Nicholson-Smith (New York: W. W. Norton, 1973), 37–40.

37. There are several powerful reviews of excellent performances of Haydn in the *AMZ*, particularly his *Creation:* "Es [the *Creation*] ist eigene Schopfung auf eigene Art, und ein eigenes freyes Spiel der Kunst, die sich der hand des Meisters zur Anlehnung eines neuen Gartens, eines neuen Edens bedient" (*AMZ* 17 [January 21, 1801]: 291). [It is a creation in its own right and is its own freedom of art, which lends itself to the creation of a new garden, a new Eden, through the hand of its master.]

38. "Unsre Orchester führen mozartische Sinfonien nicht gern auf. Man kann sich ihren Geist noch immer nicht recht aneignen. Auch jene Ouvertura machte die erwartete hohe Würkung [sic] nicht, und bestätigte das Urtheil, daß Moz. als Instrumentalkomponist, allerdings Haydns Nebenbuhler, aber ein weniger weiser Nebenbuhler sey, und weit mehr Genie als Geschmack beweise"(*AMZ* 33 [May 13, 1801]: 357–58).

39. "Wenn die ältern Komponisten die Blasinstrumente einzeln, sparsam, und fast immer nur als Verstärkung der Saiteninstrumente [sic] gebrauchen, so bringen sie dagegen die neuren Meister auf so verschiedene weise an, daß es beynahe [sic] zu weitläufig ist, die mancherley Arten herzurechnen. Bald füllen sie durch aushaltende Harmonien die Lücken auf, welche der melodische Satz der Saiteninstrumente nicht verhüten konnte; bald bilden sie gleichsam ein zweytes Orchester, welches mit dem Hauptorchester wetteifernd arbeitet: bald ist ihnen ein Gegensatz zu der von den Violinen geführten Melodie anvertraut" (*AMZ* 11 [December 11, 1799]: 193).

40. "Die Blasinstrumente sind, ihrer Natur nach, weit wesentlicher von einander unterschieden, als die mancherley Arten von Saiteninstrumenten. Ihr Ton nähert sich mehr dem göttlichsten aller Instrumente, der Menschenstimme. Sie dringen schneller ans Herz, und erregen, nach ihrer individuellen Beschaffenheit, diese oder jene Gemütsstimmung weit gewisser, als die Saiteninstrumente, welche einen allgemeinern, aber eben deswegen unbestimmtern Charakter haben"(*AMZ* 11 [December 11, 1799]: 196).

41. An otherwise very positive review of a concert by Beethoven criticizes him for overusing the winds: "Endlich bekam doch auch Herr Beethoven das Theater einmal, und dies war wahrlich die interessanteste Akademie seit langer Zeit. Er spielte ein neues Konzert von seiner Komposition, das sehr viel Schönheiten hat— besonders die zwey ersten Sätze. Dann wurde ein Septett vom ihm gegeben, das mit

sehr viel Geschmack und Empfindung geschrieben ist. Er phantasierte dann meis-
terhaft, und am Ende wurde eine Symphonie von seiner Komposition aufgeführt,
worin sehr viel Kunst, Neuheit und Reichtum an Ideen war; nur waren die Blasinstrumente gar zu viel angewendet, so daß mehr Harmonie, als ganze Orchester-
musik war" (*AMZ* 3 [October 15, 1800]: 49). [Finally Beethoven came to the theater,
and it was truly the most interesting academy in a long time. He played a new concerto of his that contained many beautiful moments, particularly in the first two
movements. Then there was a septet of his that was written with much taste and
sensibility. His fantasy was masterful, and finally he played a symphony that contained much art, innovation, and rich ideas. But the winds were used way too heavily, with the result that there was more harmony than unified orchestral music.]

42. "Es sey uns erlaubt, zum Schluß dieses Briefes, noch unsere Meinung über
die malenden Simphonien [sic] zu sagen. Sie scheine seltsam; wir legen sie ab, sobald
sich die Künstler nicht mit ihr aussöhnen können. Dittersdorf in Deutschland und
Rosetti in Italien waren die ersten, die dergleichen Kompositionen versuchten, in
welchen sich der Komponist, nicht nur einen festen, sondern immer auch einen
malerischen Zweck vorsetzt" (*AMZ* 43 [July 23, 1800]: 748).

43. "Die Sitte fast nichts als einzelne Opernscenen und Opernarien in öffentlichen
Volkskonzerten aufzuführen, ist erst seit 12 bis 15 Jahren so allgemein geworden:
vorher gab man lieber zusammenhängende Ganze—nicht gerade immer Oratorien
und andere große Werke, aber besonders kleine oder größere Kantate u.d.gl. Es
giebt mancherley Ursachen der jetzigen Sitte. Die erst Ursache ist wohl der in der
Musik—wie in der Theaterwelt immer mehr überhandnehmende leidige Geschmack
an neuen und nur immer neuen und nichts als neuen Stücken" (*AMZ* 31 [May 1,
1799]: 481).

44. "Die Geschichte, die Situation der Handelnden, die Aktion, die Charaktere
der Singenden—alles das fehlt; gerade das Vorzüglichste wahrer Opernmusik, das
Individuelle, welches mit dem Individuellen der vom Dichter gezeichneten Charaktere zusammenstimmt, fällt ganz weg" (*AMZ* 31 [May 1, 1799]: 483). A writer for the
AMZ also argues against retuning stringed instruments between movements, saying
it destroys a sense of a work's unity: "Auch dulden Sie das so gewöhnliche Nach-
stimmen—wenigstens zwischen den Sätzen eines Ganzen, z. B. einer Symphonie,
eines Konzerts—durchaus nicht. Es wird dadurch das Ganze äußerst unangenehm
zerreisen" (*AMZ* 4 [October 23, 1799]: 59). [Also, do not tolerate the retuning that is
so common, at least between movements of a whole, for example a symphony or
concerto. Thus unity is most uncomfortably torn apart.]

45. "Gewaltsam durchbrechen sie die Schranken, welche die Kunst, von der
Natur angewiesen, ihnen gesezt hat, so dass oft das beste Orchester Mühe hat, ihrem
labyrinthischen Gange zu folgen, diesen öfters nur errathen muss und zuweilen
dadurch in die grösste Verlegenheit gesetzt wird, indem die Begleitung der Stimmen
das Nachgeben durchaus nicht gestattet, und dieses in den meisten Fällen nur durch
Pausieren geschehen kann, welches durch die Unwissenheit nicht selten einem bösen
Willen zugeschrieben wird. Manche treiben ihre Petulanz oft so weit, dass, wenn sie
ihren Unsinn nicht in die vorgeschriebenen Schranken hineinzwängen können, sie
ohne weiters ein, zwey, dritthalb, ja wohl mehr Viertel in einen Takt hineinschus-
tern, ohne Rücksicht zu nehmen, ob diese ihre Verzierungen, die zu barbarischen
Verzerrungen werden, sich mit dem Akkorde vertragen, Mistöne auf Mistöne folgen, Verwirrung im Ganzen daraus entstehe oder nicht: sie massen sich das Ansehen

eines Gesetzgebers an; sie glauben sich zu allem berechtigt, setzen sich über Dichter, Tonsetzer, Kunst, und Künstler hinweg und sehen es als einen schuldigen Tribut an, dass diese ihrem Eigensinne, ihrem verschrobenen Geschmack und ihrer Unwissenheit fröhnen"(*AMZ* 9 [November 24, 1802]: 9).

46. "Auf letzteres kann nur der Instrumentalkomponist mit Zuverlässigkeit rechnen, der den Tonmechanismus—den innern wie den äußern—ganz oder doch größentheils kennt und geschickt anzubringen weiß, der mithin den allgemein gültigen, natürlichen, auf jenes Analogon der Empfindung sich beziehenden Charakter aller Töne, Tonarten, Tonreihen, Harmonien, Rhythmen, Instrumenten-Verbindungen u.s.w., die er gebrauchen will, durch Genie und Studium ausfindig gemacht hat; der endlich auch bey der Anlage und Ausführung seines Werkes nicht blos den ersten besten klingenden oder künstlichen Satz wählte, sondern sich dabey auch selbst bemühte, irgend eine *möglichst bestimmte* [emphasis the author's] Idee oder Empfindung auszudrücken und ihr treu zu bleiben. Einen solchen Komponisten kann nie die Frage treffen: 'Sonate, que me veux-tu?'" (*AMZ* 23 [March 4, 1801]: 397–98). The question "Sonata what do you want of me?" is attributed to Bernard by Jean-Jacques Rousseau, who concludes his "Sonata" entry in his *Dictionnaire de Musique* as follows: "Je n'oublerai jamais la saillie du célebre Fontenelle, qui se trouvant excédé de ces éternelles Symphonies, s'écria tout haut dans un transport d'impatience; *Sonate, que me veux tu?*" ([repr. of the Paris 1768 edition; Hildesheim: Georg Olms Verlagsbuchhandlung, 1969], 452). The English translation, J. J. Rousseau, *A Complete Dictionary of Music*, 2d ed., trans. by William Waring (London: J. Murray, 1779) curiously does not translate the sentence containing the attribution to Bernard.

47. "Man begann mit der Sinfonie von Jos. Haydn, die die dritte ist (D dur) von den sechs in London herausgekommenen. Wer hier jemals ein grosses Instrumentalstück aufführen hörte, wird die Richtigkeit im Ausdrucke, das genaue Zusammentreffen der Instrumente, die gleichsam nur von Einem Bogen geleitet scheinen, besonders aber die reinen Töne der Violin, die Deutlichkeit der Bässe, und das Sanfte der Blasinstrumente bewundert haben. Welchen schönen Eindruck machte nicht auch heute diese Sinfonie! Wie natürlich kamen nicht die so schwierigen Stellen des 1sten Allegro im 6/8 Takt auf einander! Sie wurden von diesem zahlreichen Orchester eben so genau vorgetragen, wie ein Quartet von vier an einander gewönten Spielern. Die sonderbaren Sätze und das Rollen der Bässe im Minore des Adagio, das überraschende abwechselnde, Instrumentenspiel in der Menuet, zeugen von dem Genius des unerschöpflichen Künstlers, der auch in Kleinigkeiten so gross ist. Als aber in dem letzten Allegro, das mit so vielem Feuer ausgeführt wurde, nach dem Minore, eine Stimme nach der andern das Thema in fugirten Nachahmungen und mit Gegensätzen anfing, wurde der Zuhörer, an solche Sätze nicht immer gewöhnt, gleichsam aus sich selbst gerissen. Man sah einander an; es war Einem, als wenn alles nicht mehr in Ordnung ginge; bis endlich nach 50 Takten diese täuschende Spiel sich wieder in grosse kadenzierte Massen ordnete, nach einigen beruhigenden Zwischensätzen schloss, und man so wieder in seinen vorigen Genuss des ruhigen Wohlgefallens zurückgesezt wurde" (*AMZ* 18 [January 26, 1803]: 304–5).

48. The following transcriptions of Haydn's Symphony no. 46 in D Major, "The Miracle," have been made from Joseph Haydn, *Critical Edition of the Complete Symphonies*, vol. 11, ed. H. C. Robbins Landon (Vienna: Universal Editions, 1966). Throughout this book, I refer to music in terms of pitch classes that are always

uppercase (as in the pitch class A-natural); I refer to specific pitches using lowercase with superscripts and subscripts; middle "C" is thus c-natural[1]; the "C" an octave below middle "C" is c-natural, etc. I use roman numerals to refer to harmonies—the standard practice in many music theory texts. In major, the triads are I, ii, iii, IV, V, vi, and vii°; in minor the diatonic triads are i, ii°, III, iv, v/V, VI, and VII.

49. I shall not pursue other textual considerations like this, but the reader should be aware that there are many examples of music being too hard, or quite unclear for contemporary orchestras to play with security. Galkin suggests many such passages in symphonic works. See in particular his discussion of Mozart's *Funeral Ode* (KV 477) (Galkin 83–84), Mozart's *Requiem* (85–86), Cherubini's 1817 *Requiem,* and Beethoven's early symphonies (90–93, 120–23). Galkin discusses at great length the rise of the crescendo-diminuendo in Western music and how it demanded a central agency of articulation separate from a member of the orchestra (70–74); for Galkin, rhythmic complexity also demanded a conductor not constrained by an orchestral part (118–20). For Galkin, increasing use of syncopation destabilized an orchestra's ease in performing together.

50. "Das größte Verdienst des Herrn Schupanzig ist wohl sein kühnes Spiel, das also auch auf seine Art zu dirigiren, vortheilhaften Einfluß hat. Doch können wir, mit aller Anerkennung seines Verdienstes, dem ziemlich verbreteten [sic] Ruf, als sey er das, was man einen großen Direktor nennt, nicht beystimmen. Damit das nicht Tadelsucht scheine, dürfen wir dem Kenner nur anführen: er ist ein sehr geschickter aber doch bloßer Praktiker, ohne alle Kenntnisse der Theorie und der Komposition. Der geschickteste und geübteste Direktor, dem diese Kenntnisse fehlen, kann, unserem Glauben nach, doch nichts weiter, als, seine Stimme richtig und gut abspielen, und wenn Schwanken im Tempo oder andere Fehler des Orchesters eintreten ... in seine Geige hineinreissen, und mit den Füßen stampfen. Zum Verhüten solcher Fehler des Orchesters durch feines Entgegenkommen, von den Zuhörern unbemerktes Zusammennehmen des Orchesters ... zum—von den Zuhörern gleichfalls nicht zu bemerkenden Verbessern und zur Ordnung zurückzubringen, wenn ja so ein Fehler vorgefallen ist—kurz zu allem, was den großen Direktor macht, gehört wahrlich mehr" (*AMZ* 3 [October 15, 1800]: 47).

51. "Die Musik ... wurde mit einer Kraft, Genauigkeit und Delikatesse, unter der feurigen und doch nicht anmaßenden Direktion des Hrn. Schmitt gegeben, daß auch der strengste Kenner hier volles Genüge fand. Keine Sinfonie wurde eher aufgeführt, bis man sich in den sehr kritischen Proben (die immer mit dem vollen Orchester gehalten wurden) bis zu jenen Eigenschaften einer guten Produktion hindurch gearbeitet hatte. Sonderbar ist is, daß je schwieriger eine Sinfonie war, (wie z. B. die Mozartischen in C dur op. 38, und g moll, op. 45) desto feuriger, kraftvoller und tadelloser wurde sie ausgeführt"(*AMZ* 40 [July 1, 1801]: 672).

52. Carl Maria von Weber, *Writings on Music,* trans. by Martin Cooper, ed. and introduction by John Warrack (Cambridge: Cambridge University Press, 1981), 247.

53. "Die Stellung der Instrumente eines Orchesters richtet sich nach dem Bedarf der jeweiligen Oper, und ihr Hauptfordernis ist, dass kein Instrument wirkungslos verstekt stehe, der Direktor Bühne und Orchester gleich gut übersehen, und eben so von allen einzelnen Gliedern wieder gesehen werden könne. Die Wirkung ist auf das ganze Haus berechnet. Die Bänke dicht hinter dem Orchester sind in allen Theatern am übelsten berathen; aber eine Kunstanstalt kann keine so höflichen Rücksichten

wie ein Gesellschaftszirkel beachten" (Carl Maria von Weber, *Dresdner Abend-Zeitung* 22 [January 27, 1818]).

54. "Die Zeiten sind vorbei, wo der Bass einer italienischen Oper so friedlich 8 oder 10 Takte auf die nämliche Note gelagert—und durch unzählige Proben fast auswendig gelernt war, dass er gefahrlos aus der Partitur gespielt werden konnte. Überhaupt der am Clavier Sitzende nur sein Blattumwender war, und das meiste dem Primo Violino überlassen blieb" (ibid.).

55. "Auch konnte man die Ausführung, sowohl von Seiten der Singenden, als des Orchesters, wol [sic] kaum vollendeter wünschen; zunächst eine Folge der das Ganze vollkommen durchdringenden, lebendigen und belebenden, auch ganz einmüthigen Anführung und Leitung der Herren, von Weber und Pollendro" (*AMZ* 7 [February 18, 1818]: 136).

56. Spohr was not always reviewed positively as concertmaster. The following article finds fault with his histrionic gestures as concertmaster: "man könnte ihn in diesem Genre unübertrefflich nennen, wenn er nicht oft durch eine viel zu häufig angebrachte Manier—durch das Herauf- und Herunter- Rutschen mit einem und demselben Finger nach allen möglichen Intervallen—durch das kunstlichen Miau, wie man es nennen möchte, wenn es nicht neckend klänge—uns in diesem Genuss, und zuweilen recht unangenehm, störte"(*AMZ* 20 [February 10, 1808]: 313). [One could call him the very best of conductors were it not for all too frequent mannerisms of sliding his fingers up and down the fingerboard in all kinds of intervals, through his artificial *meow*, as one might call it, and when it is not flattering, it rather disturbs and displeases.]

57. Louis Spohr, *Autobiography*, vol. 2, trans. not given (London: Longman, 1865), 81–82. For the original German, see Louis Spohr, *Lebenserrinerungen*, vol. 2 (Tutzing: Hans Schneider, 1968), 73–74.

58. According to Burney, the harpsichord was omitted from an opera performance in 1772 in a performance of Grétry's opera *Zémire et Azor* (Galkin 316).

59. It is not possible, however, to say that this is the first instance of baton conducting. Carl Maria von Weber had conducted with a baton in 1804 at the age of eighteen: "The boy-conductor seized his baton with all the fire of his eighteen summers; perhaps also with an overweening sense of his new independence, evidenced by this resolve to lead his army to the musical fray wholly according to his own will and fancy" (Baron Max Maria von Weber, *Carl Maria von Weber*, vol. 1 [New York: Greenwood Press, 1969], 58). Weber is also described conducting with a baton in Dresden in 1817 (Galkin 335).

60. "Mir hat von jeher der verfluchte wießbuchne kleine Taktstock Ärgernis gegeben, und wenn ich das Ding dominieren sehen muß, vergeht mir nun einmal alle Musik, es ist als wenn die ganze Oper nur da wäre, damit Takt dazu geschlagen werden könne, und nun gar das geflissentliche Markiren der kleinen Nüancen mit diesem verwünschten Hölzchen, es mag nothwendig sein—wenn ich aber da an Matrimonio segreto denke, wo der Maestro so hübsch ruhig am Keyboard saß, das Recitativo secco accompagnierte, wo alles wie von selbst ging, da bin ich in einer ganz anderen Sphäre, himmelweit von unser gegenwärtigen, die mir auf die crudeste Weise barbarisch, aller Anmuth, ja aller Würde entkleidet vorkommt."

61. Jean-Paul Sartre, *Being and Nothingness*, trans. by Hazel E. Barnes (New York: Washington Square Press, 1956), 346.

62. Lacan, *Four Fundamental Concepts*, 84.

63. Ibid., 95.
64. Ibid., 89.
65. Ibid., 101.

2. Franz Schubert's "Die Stadt" and Sublime (Dis)pleasure

1. My notion of the relationship between metaphor and metonymy is from Roman Jakobsen. For Jakobsen, the metaphoric pole is illustrated by the combination "house" and "hut" in which one substitutes for the other; the metonymic pole is illustrated by the combination "house" and "burns," implying a sequence of events. There are many applications of the metaphor/metonymy binary to music. The metaphoric pole is like harmonic substitution; the metonymic pole is like a dominant-to-tonic progression. See Roman Jakobsen, "The Metaphoric and Metonymic Poles," in *On Language*, ed. Linda R. Waugh and Monique Monville-Burston, 129–33 (Cambridge, Mass.: Harvard University Press, 1990).

2. For a discussion of Kant's debt to *Sturm und Drang* and the "idealists" of the 1790s, see Peter Fenves, "Taking Stock of the Kantian Sublime," *Eighteenth-Century Studies* 28, no. 1 (Fall 1994): 65–82. For a discussion of the sublime focusing on Longinus, Boileau, and Silvain, see Samuel H. Monk, *The Sublime: A Study of Critical Theories in XVIII-Century England* (Ann Arbor: University of Michigan Press, 1960). For a collection of eighteenth-century source readings on the sublime by British authors, see *The Sublime: A Reader in British Eighteenth-Century Aesthetic Theory*, ed. Andrew Ashfield and Peter de Bolla (Cambridge: Cambridge University Press, 1996). For a discussion of the uses of the word *sublime* in seventeenth- and eighteenth-century dictionaries and literature, see Theodore E. B. Wood, *The Word "Sublime" and Its Context, 1650–1760* (Paris: Mouton, 1972).

3. Elaine Sisman, *Mozart: The 'Jupiter' Symphony* (New York: Cambridge University Press, 1993), 13. Sisman points out that rhetoric was a powerful element of the eighteenth-century imagination of Haydn, Mozart, and others, not only in terms of one-to-one correspondences of "figures" in language and music but also the rhetoric of letter writing *(ars dictaminis)*. Sisman points out that the sublime was integrally connected in the eighteenth-century mind with the elevated style of rhetoric (12–13).

4. "The beautiful and the sublime are similar in some respects. We like both for their own sake, and both presuppose that we make a judgment of reflection rather than either a judgment of sense or a logically determinative one." Kant is interested in making a distinction between mere sensory stimulation and perceptions linking sensory data to ideas (Kant, *Critique of Judgment*, trans. Werner S. Pluhar [Indianapolis: Hackett Publishing Company, 1987], 97). For a discussion of Kant that brings the beautiful and the sublime into a wide area of commonality, see Kirk Pillow, *Sublime Understanding* (Cambridge, Mass.: MIT Press, 2000).

5. "*Emotion* [Kant's emphasis], a sensation where agreeableness is brought about only by means of a momentary inhibition of the vital force followed by a stronger outpouring of it, does not belong to beauty at all" (72).

6. Jean-François Lyotard describes the emotion of the sublime as follows: "compared to the pleasure of the beautiful, the pleasure of the sublime is (so to speak) negative. . . . It involves a recoil, as if thinking came up against what precisely attracts

it" (*Lessons on the Analytic of the Sublime,* trans. Elizabeth Rottenberg [Stanford, Calif.: Stanford University Press, 1994], 68).

7. For the mathematical sublime see Kant 103–18; for the dynamical sublime, see 119–40. Edmund Burke anticipates Kant's categories: "greatness of dimension is a powerful cause of the sublime"; and "infinity has a tendency to fill the mind with that sort of delightful horror, which is the most genuine effect and truest test of the sublime." See Edmund Burke, *A Philosophical Enquiry into the Origin of Our Ideas of the Sublime and the Beautiful* (Menston, UK: The Scholar Press, 1970), 127–29; a facsimile of Burke's 1759 edition).

8. Paul Guyer points out that Kant was not interested in defining either the beautiful or the sublime, showing that the German word *Erklärung* means "explanation" as much as "definition" and that Kant was interested in the former not the latter. For Guyer, Kant is interested in establishing "a complex set of relations among feelings of aesthetic response, explanations of such responses, and the status of the judgments which give expression to these responses." See Guyer, "Kant's Distinction between the Beautiful and the Sublime," *Review of Metaphysics* 35, no. 4 (June 1982): 753–84.

9. Kant views most music as free beauty: "What we call fantasies in music (namely, music without a topic [Thema], indeed all music not set to words, may also be included in the same class [free beauty])" (Kant 77). Robert Wicks suggests that, although Kant does not develop a theory of the artistic sublime in the *Critique of Judgment,* he does point in that direction with respect to genius. For Wicks, Kant views artistic genius as the human equivalent of the chaos of nature evoking a sublime response in the subject. See Robert Wicks, "Kant on Fine Art: Artistic Sublimity Shaped by Beauty," *The Journal of Aesthetics and Art Criticism* 53, no. 2 (Spring 1995), 189–93.

10. Burke's notion of astonishment is closely related to my sense of the "catch" of reiteration in music: "the passion caused by the great and sublime in nature . . . is Astonishment; and Astonishment is that state of the soul, in which all its motions are suspended, with some degree of horror" (see Burke 95–96). Lyotard describes such a "catch" in the sublime as a "spasmodic state": "when thinking reaches the absolute, the relation reaches the without-relation. . . . How can the without-relation be 'present' to relation? It can only be present as disavowed (as metaphysical entity), forbidden (as illusion). This disavowal, which is constitutive of critical thinking, is the avowal of its own fury. It forbids itself the absolute, much as it still wants it. The consequence for thought is a kind of spasm. And the *Analytic of the Sublime* is a hint of this spasm" (Lyotard 56).

11. James Webster, "The Creation, Haydn's Late Vocal Music, and the Musical Sublime" in Elaine Sisman, *Haydn and His World* (Princeton, N.J.: Princeton University Press, 1997), 57.

12. Sisman, *Haydn and His World,* 16.

13. Gustav Schilling, "The Sublime," in *Music and Aesthetics in the Eighteenth and Early Nineteenth Centuries,* ed. Peter le Huray and James Day (New York: Cambridge University Press, 1981), 474.

14. Schilling 473.

15. Johann Georg Sulzer, "The Sublime," in *Music and Aesthetics in the Eighteenth and Early Nineteenth Centuries,* ed. Peter le Huray and James Day (New York: Cambridge University Press, 1981), 139. For an overview of eighteenth-century theories of

the sublime in French, English, and German, see Johann Georg Sulzer, *Allgemeine Theorie der Schönen Künste nach alphabetischer Ordnung*, vol. 2 (Hildesheim: Georg Olms, 1967), 108–14. Sulzer also reviews a few writings on the sublime and painting in the eighteenth century. He also references a work on the sublime by Moses Mendelssohn (grandfather of Felix Mendelssohn). According to Sulzer, the elder Mendelssohn held that there were two forms of the sublime—the sublime in itself and the sublime evoked by art: "Bekannter Maßen nimmt Mendelssohn zweyerley [sic] Gattungen des Erhabenen an, ein, an und für sich selbst erhabenes, und ein, durch die Darstellung des Künstlers erhaben ausgebildetes Objects" (Sulzer, *Schönen Künste*, 111.)

16. Michaelis, quoted in le Huray and Day (287–88); see *Allgemeine Musikalische Zeitung [AMZ]* 9, no. 43, 676.

17. Michaelis, quoted in le Huray and Day (290); see *Berlinische Musikalische Zeitung*, no. 46 (1805), 179.

18. "Erstens ist die bekannteste Art des Erhabenen in der Musik diejenige, welche ich das Männlich- oder Odenmäßig-Erhabene nennen möchte, weil es, nach der Analogie des menschlichen Charackters beurtheilt, ein Sinnbild der raschen, muth- und kraftvollen äußeren Thätigkeit des Mannes darbietet.... Zweitens giebt es ein Erhabenes, welches man das Elegisch-Erhabene nennen und mit der stillen Größe und edlen Zurückgezogenheit weiblicher Charaktere vergleichen könnte. Die Bewegung der Modulation ist in dieser Gattung Ernst...sanft und gemäßigt; die Einfachheit ist hier größer; die Fortschreitung weniger kühn, weniger rasch, als in jener Art. Schwermütige Resignation scheint ihre Stimmung auszumachen" (Christian Friedrich Michaelis, "Über das Erhabene in der Musik," in *Monatschrift für Deutsche*, Erster Band (Leipzig: n.p., 1801), 48–49. My thanks to Ludwig Holtmeier for making this German original available to me.

19. Franz Liszt, *Frederic Chopin*, trans. by Edward N. Waters (London: Collier-Macmillan, 1963), 77. My notion of a delicate dimension of the sublime owes an intellectual debt to current writings in musicology that explore various forms and aesthetic implications of "smallness" in early nineteenth-century music. See, in particular, Jeffrey Kallberg's study of delicacy in Chopin's piano music, "Small Fairy Voices: Sex, History, and Meaning in Chopin," in *Chopin at the Boundaries: Sex, History, and Musical Genre* (Cambridge, Mass.: Harvard University Press, 1996). For a discussion of Chopin's Prelude in A minor, Op. 28, no. 2, that theorizes musical ambiguity, see Lawrence Kramer, "Impossible Objects: Apparitions, Reclining Nudes, and Chopin's Prelude in A minor," in *Music as Cultural Practice: 1800–1900* (Berkeley and Los Angeles: University of California Press, 1990). For a related discussion of homoeroticism in a Schubert song, see Lawrence Kramer, "The Ganymede Complex: Schubert's Songs and the Homoerotic Imagination," in *Franz Schubert: Sexuality, Subjectivity, Song* (New York: Cambridge University Press, 1998). For a discussion of the fragment in music of the period, see Charles Rosen, *The Romantic Generation* (Cambridge, Mass.: Harvard University Press, 1995).

20. Issues of cyclical integrity concern all three of Schubert's song cycles: *Die schöne Müllerin* (1823–24), *Winterreise* (1827), and *Schwanengesang* (1828).

For an interpretation of the cyclical structure of *Die schöne Müllerin* as a large-scale tritone connecting the first song "Das Wandern" in B-flat major with the last song "Des Baches Wiegenlied" in E major, see Patrick McCreless, "Schenker and Chromatic Tonicization: A Reappraisal," in *Schenker Studies*, ed. Hedi Siegel (New

York: Cambridge University Press, 1990). John Daverio argues that the cycle is held together by characteristic accompaniment figures in songs centered on the brook. See John Daverio, "The Song Cycle: Journeys through a Romantic Landscape," in *German Lieder in the Nineteenth Century*, ed. Rufus Hallmark (London: Prentice Hall, 1996), 287. For a study of *Die schöne Müllerin* that explores images of sexuality and mortality in the texts and their resonance in Schubert, see Susan Youens, *Schubert, Müller, and Die schöne Müllerin* (New York: Cambridge University Press, 1997), 159–203.

Daverio considers *Winterreise* a "double cycle" since the first part (songs 1–12) were written before Schubert discovered additional poems by Müller and wrote the second part (songs 13–24) (Daverio 286). For an extended discussion of *Winterreise* based on this binary division, see Richard Kramer, *Distant Cycles* (Chicago: University of Chicago Press, 1994). For an interpretation of *Winterreise* based on an ironic use of mode, see my *Listening Subjects: Music, Psychoanalysis, Culture* (Durham, N.C.: Duke University Press, 1997). For a study of *Winterreise* based on a close reading of Müller's poetry cycle and Schubert's settings, see Peter Gülke, *Franz Schubert und Seine Zeit* (Regensburg: Laaber-Verlag, 1991), 235–65.

Schwanengesang is a miscellaneous collection of songs of widely differing character. People have speculated for some time about the cyclical nature of the six Heine settings. Much of the speculation has to do with the ordering of the songs. According to the order in which the poems appeared in Heine's *Die Heimkehr*, the songs would be ordered: "Das Fischermädchen," "Am Meer," "Die Stadt," "Der Doppelgänger," "Ihr Bild," and "Der Atlas." For a study of Schubert's Heine settings that argue cyclical coherence in poetry and music based on the order of Heine's publications in *Die Heimkehr*, see Richard Kramer, "Schubert's Heine," *19th-Century Music* 8, no. 3 (Spring 1985), 213–25. Kramer suggests long-range voice-leading across six songs from "Das Fischermädchen" to "Am Meer" to "Die Stadt" to "Der Doppelgänger" to "Ihr Bild" to "Der Atlas." Martin Chusid argues for a large-scale descending chromatic motion across the Heine settings. See Martin Chusid, "The Sequence of the Heine Songs and Cyclicism in *Schwanengesang*," in *A Companion to Schubert's Schwanengesang* (New Haven, Conn.: Yale University Press, 2000), 150–60.

21. Makkreel discusses the role of temporality in relation to the sublime. For Makkreel, the imagination under normal conditions apprehends a series of sensations and creates out of them a whole. In the case of the sublime, the imagination fails to achieve this whole out of a series and a "regress of the imagination" occurs. For me, this is precisely what happens in the works at hand when materials are re-iterated. See Rudolf Makkreel, "Imagination and Temporality in Kant's Theory of the Sublime," in *The Journal of Aesthetics and Art Criticism* 42, no. 3 (Spring 1984) 303–15: "Thus instead of the linearly ordered time required for the progressive apprehension and mathematical determination of nature, we have an instant or moment in time which allows for aesthetic comprehension and reflection" (308).

22. For more on this distinction, see my *Listening Subjects: Music, Psychoanalysis, Culture*, 168, n. 19. Most forms of repetition do operate in symbolic space: the shot/reverse in classic Hollywood cinema ties the viewer to the narrative through displaced identification; the repetition of phrases in classical melody balance phrases that modulate to a new key. Such repetitions are not really repetitions at all, since what happens a second time is different from what happened initially. For a discussion of the repetition of phrases in classical music, see Charles Rosen, *The Classical*

Style (New York: Viking Press, 1971). Exact repetitions are perhaps more interesting. Some deepen meaning, as a second statement is meant to make an initial one "sink in." Some exact repetitions erase meaning, as in the game that children play repeating a word over and over till it looses its meaning.

23. From *The Fischer-Dieskau Book of Lieder,* English trans. George Bird and Richard Stokes (New York: Alfred A. Knopf, 1977), 176–77.

24. The following musical examples are interpretive sketches or transcriptions of the songs found in Franz Schubert, *Complete Works,* volumes 16 and 17, in the Dover edition. The main note of the melody is f-sharp². The vocal line touches on the note in measure 8 supported by a dominant harmony; the vocal line reaches the note in measure 11, supported by a first-inversion tonic major chord; in measure 16 the note begins its descent, supported not by a tonic sonority but by a D-major chord—the diatonic mediant of B minor. I hear this work as a study for the later "Der Doppelgänger." "Der Doppelgänger," also in B minor, has an obsessive F-sharp and a structure that moves back and forth from tonic B minor to the diatonic mediant D major. For the appearance of the double, the music bursts through the diatonic mediant to the chromatic mediant D-sharp minor. The pitch class F-sharp, of course, is a common tone to both the diatonic and chromatic mediant.

25. Fischer-Dieskau 188.

26. See *Schubert Handbook,* ed. Walther Dürr and Andreas Krause (Kassel: Bärenreiter Verlag, 1997), 252.

27. Schubert chose to set poems of Heine in *Die Heimkehr* that had subtle, implicit issues of psychic split (with the possible exception of "Der Atlas," which is direct and melodramatic). Schubert did not set poems that involve direct aggression toward the beloved that is the pervasive object of desire in Heine. For example, in poem no. 19 (directly before no. 20 that became "Der Doppelgänger") Heine writes, "I stood in the hall where she swore / To be faithful, weeping and kissing: / Where her tears once fell on the floor, / Serpents were crawling and hissing" (*The Complete Poems of Heinrich Heine,* trans. Hal Draper [Boston: Suhrkamp/Insel, 1982], 84). Schubert also avoided all the poems with proper names and explicit literary references in favor of poems not rooted in time and place.

28. Fischer-Dieskau 334.

29. See Heinrich Schenker, "Ihr Bild," trans. Robert Snarrenberg, in *Der Tonwille,* vol. 1 (New York: Oxford University Press, 2004), 41–43. Michaelis points to a connection between simplicity and the sublime in song: "So, too, the unison in music... and simple songs seem to us sublime" ["So wirkt auch das Unisono in der Musik... und den einfachen Gesängen, erhaben auf uns"] (Michaelis, *Monatschrift,* 46).

30. "Am Meer" also has an ambiguous opener similar to the B-flats that open "Ihr Bild." "Am Meer" begins with a famous and enigmatic progression heard in measure 1 and again in measure 2. It can be heard as a single C-major chord with several dissonant nonchord tones sounded on the beat that resolve into the chord. It can also be heard as a German augmented-sixth chord that resolves, not to the dominant but directly to tonic C major. In either case, there are three half-step motions from dissonances to consonant pitches in the C-major tonic triad: D-sharp goes to E-natural (the third of the triad); F-sharp goes to G-natural (the fifth of the triad) and A-flat goes to G-natural as well; the tonic C-natural is held throughout. The tonal ambiguity of this opening progression is well known. See Joseph Kerman, "A Romantic Detail in Schubert's *Schwanengesang,*" in *Schubert: Critical*

and Analytical Studies, ed. Walter Frisch (Lincoln: University of Nebraska Press, 1986). Richard Kramer hears the sonority as part of a family of chords and key relations shared among "Das Fischermädchen," "Die Stadt," and "Am Meer." See Richard Kramer, *Distant Cycles* (Chicago: University of Chicago Press, 1994), 128–29.

31. Heinrich Heine, *Historisch-kritische Gesamtausgabe der Werke,* vol. 1, no. 1, ed. Manfred Windfuhr (Hamburg: Hoffman and Campe, 1975).

32. Fischer-Dieskau 335.

33. Susan Youens connects Heine's "Die Stadt" to the Romantic tradition of associating nature and the sublime: "[in] Heine's 'Am fernen Horizonte' ('On the distant horizon' which Schubert set to music as 'Die Stadt'), the personae are adrift on an ocean whose depths are symbolic of passion and whose liquid substance bespeaks that which is female, changeable, without firm footing." See Susan Youens, *Schubert's Late Lieder: Beyond the Song Cycles* (New York: Cambridge University Press, 2002), 14.

34. Lawrence Kramer hears the form differently: "Die Stadt, from *Schwanengesang,* offers a skeletal, almost schematic example of Romantic presentation in Schubert. The song follows an *a b a' b' a* design. In the *a* sections, the piano creates an impressionistic haze by obsessively arpeggiating a functionless diminished-seventh chord. A nominally tonic pedal point pulses along underneath, but its effect is to cloud the sonority, not to clarify the harmony." See Lawrence Kramer, "The Schubert Lied," in *Schubert: Critical and Analytical Studies,* ed. Walter Frisch (Lincoln: Nebraska University Press, 1986), 207.

35. It is tempting to hear "Am Meer" as a continuation of "Die Stadt." "Die Stadt" closes with a single C-natural held by a fermata; "Am Meer" opens with held C-naturals in three octaves with two iterations of a German augmented sixth chord. Robert Morgan suggests that the fully diminished seventh chord left hanging at the end of "Die Stadt" resolves in the opening progression of "Am Meer." See Robert P. Morgan, "Dissonant Prolongations: Theoretical and Compositional Precedents," *Journal of Music Theory* 20, no. 1 (Spring 1976), 58.

Schubert is very sensitive to the differences between fermatas and notated silences. See, in particular, "Die Post" from *Winterreise* for a wonderful example of one measure of notated silence (repeated once) that signifies the ongoing pulse of time and the narrator's heart in the time of recognition in which he realizes that he will not get a letter from his fantasy-beloved.

36. In reference to the B section of the work, Joseph Kerman suggests that "the grisly arpeggio is revealed as illustration of the chill wind rocking the poet's boat, and it rustles away with almost expressionistic fixity during the entire center stanza of the song" (53).

37. Gernot Gruber points out that it is precisely the B section's working out of the fully diminished seventh chord that undermines the music's tonal organicism: "Unterminiert hat Schubert...die tonale und damit auch formale Faßlichkeit des Stückes durch seinen Akzent auf das Material des B-Teiles" [Schubert undermines the tonal and with it the formal cohesion of the work through his accent on the material of the B section] ("Romantische Ironie in den Heine-Liedern?" in *Schubert-Kongreß Wien,* [1978; repr., Graz: Akademische Druck-u.Verlagsanstalt, 1979], 326).

38. The Neapolitan is an altered subdominant. Instead of a chord spelled F-natural/A-flat/C-natural (the subdominant in C minor), Schubert writes F-natural/A-flat/*D-flat.*

39. The German musicologist Heinrich Werle discusses the appearance of "jene Stelle" as a thought lingering just beneath the consciousness of the narrator: "Zwischen Verschwimmendes der Umrisse schiebt sich rhythmisch gestraffte Bewußtheit innerlichen Schauens. Doch über, mitten, unter all dem zuckt Errinern auf an 'jene Stelle, wo ich das Liebste verlor'" [Between shifting boundaries of the outlines, a pattern of rhythmic consciousness moves in internal terror. Memory of "that place where I lost my dearest" emerges from it] (*Franz Schubert: Der Mensch und Sein Werk* [Bayreuth: Gauverlag Bayerische Ostmark, 1941], 356).

40. Lawrence Kramer asserts that the Neapolitan harmony expands the harmonic language of the work at precisely the moment of the narrator's psychic disintegration. ("The Schubert Lied," 208).

41. Leonard Meyer, *Emotion and Meaning in Music* (Chicago: University of Chicago Press, 1956).

42. My thanks to the Pierpont Morgan Library in New York City for their help in providing me with a photocopy of this page.

43. My thanks to Patrick McCreless, Timothy L. Jackson, Stephen Slottow, and Walt Everett for their critical assistance in the generation of this graph.

44. I initially discussed hearing "Die Stadt" as a big $\hat{5}$ piece with Jenny Kallick; my thanks to her for this idea.

45. A "cover tone" is a technical term specific to Schenkerian voice-leading analysis. Voice-leading analysis locates and notates essential elements in music. The analytical technique makes careful distinctions between content that is latent and content that is manifest—to apply to music terms familiar to most readers from Freudian psychoanalysis. A cover tone is a hidden note that, at a crucial moment of a work, rises to the surface and appears, "covering up" another note to which our attention might otherwise have been transparently drawn.

46. Fischer-Dieskau 335.

3. Music and the Birth of Psychoanalysis

1. There are, of course, famous instances of the idée fixe in French music, perhaps most notably, in the *Sinfonie fantastique* by Hector Berlioz.

2. For an overview of theories of trauma from the mid-nineteenth century to the posttraumatic stress disorder of the Vietnam era, see Ruth Leys, *Trauma: a Genealogy* (Chicago: University of Chicago Press, 2000). Leys locates one of the beginnings of modern theories of trauma with the writings of John Ericson, "who during the 1860s identified the trauma syndrome in victims suffering from the fright of railway accidents and attributed the distress to shock or concussion of the spine" (3). An undercurrent in theories of trauma from the mid-nineteenth century through the great shell shock debates following World Wars I and II and into the posttraumatic stress disorder of the Vietnam years is the question whether trauma is mimetic or antimimetic. Mimetic theories of trauma hold that the etiology of trauma runs parallel to the psychic apparatus; mimetic theories hold that traumatic wounds can be healed through hypnosis and suggestion. Antimimetic theory holds that trauma is unlike anything inherent to psychic formations; antimimetic theory holds that trauma occurs as an invasion from without—a breach of the subject's boundaries, a wound for which the psyche is unprepared. Throughout the period explored here

(the mid-nineteenth century to 1895, roughly) hypnosis was an established technique; only gradually did the "talking cure" of modern psychoanalysis and symbolic theories of transference replace hypnosis in the early twentieth century. The discussion of traumatic hysteria that follows will show that writers of the second half of the nineteenth century spoke of predispositions toward hysteria on the one hand (early versions of the mimetic approach) and acquired hysteria on the other (early versions of the antimimetic approach).

3. Of course the concerns of doctors cross the boundaries: French *and* German writers are concerned with traumatic accidents, certainly. But it was particularly in England that studies of the traumatic dimension of accidents caused by industrialization and modernization emerged.

4. See Pierre Janet, *The Major Symptoms of Hysteria* (New York: Macmillan, 1907), 14.

5. Quoted in Gilles de la Tourette, *Die Hysterie nach den Lehren der Salpêtriére,* ed. Karl Grube (Leipzig und Wien: Franz Deuticke, 1894), 1.

6. Writings on hysteria occasionally discuss hysteria in men. Lepois asserted that hysteria in men and children did occur. For some writers, hysteria in men required that the theory of an infected uterus be expanded to include infected male sexual organs. For an extended discussion of hysteria in men written in German, see Johannes Zippel, *Über männliche Hysterie* (Halle: Hofbuchdrunkerei von C. A. Kaemmerer, 1895); Zippel bases this document (his doctoral dissertation) on the French tradition of hysteria theory, with particular attention to the role of puberty in symptom formation in cases of hysteria among young men. Louyer-Villermay in 1816 writes that hysteria proper belongs to pathologies affecting women; for him, so-called male hysteria is something else. See Jean-Baptiste Louyer-Villermay, *Traité des maladies nerveuses ou vapeurs et particulièrement de l'hysterie et de l'hypochondrie* (quoted in Tourette 12). Writing in 1838, Hufeland also believed that true hysteria was found in women only; so-called male hysteria, according to him, was hypochondria (quoted in Tourette 15). Landouzy (1846), Schutzemberger (1846), Négrier (1858), and Chairon (1870) concur (Tourette 15–16).

7. No first names provided (Tourette 11). Other eighteenth-century writers on hysteria include Sauvages (1760), Astoni (1761), and Pommel (1760–1782) (Tourette 12).

8. At the end of the seventeenth century there were around three thousand women at the Salpêtrière; by the end of the nineteenth century, there were more than four thousand. See Georges Didi-Huberman, *The Invention of Hysteria,* trans. Alsia Hertz (Cambridge, Mass.: MIT Press, 2003), 13.

9. See *De la physiologie du système nerveux et specialment du cerveau* (Paris: n.p., 1821), quoted in Tourette 13. Possession and somnambulism have been associated with women for centuries. Modern psychoanalysis grows out of a systematic attempt to theorize the connections among the wide variety of altered states associated with hysteria in the nineteenth century. If Tourette is right that Georget is the first or one of the first to name the "état second" in hysterics, then this is one among many points of "origin" for modern psychoanalysis.

10. Charcot published a book on connections between deformity and art, arguing that the latter represented the deformities of nature with uncanny thoroughness and accuracy. See J.-M. Charcot. *Les difformes et les malades dans l'art* (Paris: Lecrosnier et Babé 1889).

11. Charcot, "Hysterie und Entartung beim Manne," *Poliklinische Vorträge,* 1887–1889 (n.p.; the date for this lecture is given as 1895).

12. See G. Guinon, *Les agents provocateurs de l'hystérie* (Paris: n.p., 1889 ["1898" is printed in the text, but the text was published in 1894; I suspect a transposition of numbers resulted in the impossible date]), quoted in Tourette 41.

13. Tourette discusses both male and female hysterics. For Tourette, hysteria is common among young women and older men; men are supposedly susceptible to hysteria in maturity through a traumatic shock (Tourette 34).

14. See Mosso, *La peur* (Paris: n.p., 1886), quoted in Tourette 42. Mosso discusses the fears of children at night and the fears of soldiers in battle—a forerunner of the enormous literature on shell shock in the years during and after World War I.

15. For an early discussion of the traumatic dimensions of railway accidents, see Erichsen, *On Railway and Other Injuries of the Nervous System* (London: n.p., 1866). Erichsen discusses symptoms of the brain, symptoms of the spinal cord, and symptoms of the extremities in railroad accidents (quoted in Tourette 47). See also Page, *Injuries of the Spine and Spinal Cord without Apparent Mechanical Lesions and Nervous Shock* (London: n.p., 1885), quoted in Tourette 48.

16. Janet acknowledges Charcot as the one who first mentioned the importance of the idée fixe; see Janet, "The Mental State of Hystericals," in *Significant Contributions to the History of Psychology,* series C, vol. 2, ed. Daniel N. Robinson (Washington, D. C.: University Publications of America, 1977), 487.

17. Hypnosis in various forms has been a common element of Western culture since the ancients. See, in particular, Brugsch-Pasha [no first name provided], "Die Hypnose in Alterthume," *Zeitschrift für Hypnotismus, Suggestionstherapie, Suggestionslehre und verwandte psychologische Forschungen* 2 (1894): 215–21.

18. A more recent writer on trauma, Bessel A. van der Kolk, sees in Janet a precursor of modern notions of the unique status of traumatic memory. For van der Kolk, traumatic memory involves both an exaggerated intensity of memory that for years vividly repeats traumatic events and, at the same time, a kind of amnesia that prevents the memories from being incorporated. Van der Kolk speculates that traumatic memory may exist in a different logical class from other memories (clearly divided between "declarative" memories of explicit, conscious awareness, and "non-declarative" memories of reflexive skills, habits, emotional responses). Van der Kolk combines psychological, sociological, and biological approaches to trauma theory. See Bessel A. van der Kolk, "Trauma and Memory" in *Traumatic Stress,* ed. Bessel A. van der Kolk, Alexander C. McFarlane, and Lars Weisaeth (New York: The Guilford Press, 1996), 279–302.

19. "Things take place as if the system of the psychological phenomena, which forms the personal perception with all men, were with these individuals [patients suffering form hysteria] disintegrated and giving birth to two or more simultaneous or successive groups, mostly incomplete, and robbing each other of sensations, images, and consequently movements which should be normally reunited in one and the same consciousness" (Janet 505). For Janet, a wide variety of weaknesses can lead to hysterical degeneration, including alcoholism (519) and hereditary disposition (522). In general, French writers consider weakness as central to hysteria; German writers do not. There are exceptions to this binary, perhaps most notably the work of H. Oppenheim, who in 1890 argued that hysteria was caused by weakness of

body and mind that blocks proper motor responses. According to Oppenheim, the doctor can reinstate health by reaching the patient with a pleasurable or unpleasurable "shock" that will counteract the symptom. See H. [only initial given] Oppenheim, "Thatsächliches und Hypothetisches über das Wesen der Hysterie," *Berliner Klinische Wochenschrift*, no. 25, (June 23, 1890): 553–56.

20. Alfred Binet, "On Double Consciousness," in *Significant Contributions to the History of Psychology*, series C, vol. 5, ed. Daniel N. Robinson (Washington, D. C.: University Publications of America, 1977), 70.

21. Alfred Binet, "The Mechanism of Thought," in *Significant Contributions to the History of Psychology*, series B, vol. 4, ed. Daniel Robinson (Washington, D.C.: University Publications of America, 1977), 795. First published in the *Fortnightly Review*, 1894.

22. P. J. Moebius, "Über den Begriff der Hysterie," *Zentralblatt für Nervenheilkunde, Psychiatrie und gerichtliche Psychopathologie* 11 (1888), 66.

23. P. J. Moebius, "Über die gegenwärtige Auffasung der Hysterie," *Monatsschrift für Geburtshilfe und Gynäkologie* 1, no. 12 (1895), 18.

24. For Moebius, "one often finds that . . . hysterical daughters have hysterical mothers" (ibid, 17). Moebius understands the inheritance of pathology in biological terms, not representational terms. Psychoanalysis will emerge with this crucial shift from biology and inherited degeneracy to a structural interaction between somatic and psychosomatic representations.

25. August Forel, "Was ist Hysterie," *Zeitschrift für Hypnotismus, Psychotherapie sowie andere psychophysiologische und psychopathologische Forschung* 5 (1897), 92.

26. Sigmund Freud, "Die Abwehr-Neuropsychosen. Versuch einer psychologischen Theorie der acquirirten Hysterie," *Neurologisches Centralblatt* 13 (1894), 363–64.

27. Sigmund Freud and Josef Breuer, *Studies on Hysteria*, vol. 2 of *The Standard Edition of the Complete Psychological Works*, trans. and ed. James Strachey (London: The Hogarth Press, 1955), 12.

28. Sigmund Exner published a book in Vienna only a year before Freud and Breuer's *Studies on Hysteria* that contains language that prefigures Freud's notion of the unconscious and its workings in dream: "Then in sleep are great containers [grosse Fasergebiete] with greatly reduced affective energy [in ihrer Erregbarkeit bedeutend herabgesetzt], there are rows of associations, which can pass easily into consciousness through association [die sonst associativ leicht ins Bewusstsein treten], as if they were not there" (Sigmund Exner, *Entwurf zu einer Physiologischen Erklärung von Psychischen Erscheinungen* [Leipzig und Wien: Franz Deuticke, 1894], 323).

29. According to the editor, this is the first use of the term "repressed" in Freud's writings.

30. Freiherr von Schrenk-Notzing, a contemporary of Freud and Breuer working in Vienna, writes of an "Ober- und ein Unterbewusstsein"; Schrenk-Notzing mentions many writers on hysteria, but neither Freud nor Breuer are noted. He is interested in a fluid relationship of mutual dependence between the two realms of the psyche, and his discussion of the "Unterbewusstsein" relies on a theory of reflexes and partially voluntary reflexes, such as the conscious motions and learned reflexes used in performing a musical instrument ("Über Spaltung der Persönlichkeit," *Wiener klinische Rundschau* 10, no. 11 [March 15, 1896]: 182).

Eduard von Hartmann discusses the unconscious and conscious parts of the mind in a philosophical treatise. For him, "the unconscious divides into the relative unconscious and the absolute unconscious" (*Philosophie des Unbewussten,* part 1, *Phänomenologie des Unbewussten* [Leipzig: Hermann Haacke, 1904], xxxvi). Hartmann goes on to assert that "all consciousness is passive, purely receptive and incapable of action; all unconsciousness is active and productive" (ibid.).

31. Breuer is aware of the contradictory dimension of the phrase "unconscious idea": "the objections that are raised against 'unconscious ideas' existing and being operative seem for the most part to be juggling with words. No doubt 'idea' is a word belonging to the terminology of conscious thinking, and 'unconscious idea' is therefore a self-contradictory expression. But the physical process which underlies an idea is the same in content and form (though not in quantity) whether the idea rises above the threshold of consciousness or remains beneath it" (Freud and Breuer, *Studies on Hysteria,* 223).

32. Oskar Vogt acknowledges Freud and Breuer's work and argues that in severe cases of traumatic neurosis, when all else fails, self-observation can lead to a cure of hysteria if (1) the person wants to observe him-/herself, (2) if the patient has the energy to realize this wish, and (3) if there is sufficient emotional intensity [Bewusstseinselemente eine genügende Erregbarkeit zeigen] for the observation to work ("Zur Methodik der aetiologischen Erforschung der Hysterie," *Zeitschrift für Hypnotismus* 8 [1898], 72).

33. See Frederic W. H. Myers, "The Subliminal Consciousness" in *Proceedings of the Society for Psychical Research,* volume 8, 1892.

34. Morton Prince, "A Contribution to the Study of Hysteria," *Proceedings of the Society for Psychical Research* 14, pt. 34 (1898). Although published in 1898, Prince notes in his article that the paper was actually written in 1891. Even though we can certainly not assume that all the authors discussed here read each others' work as it was published, it might be useful to know that Prince's article was written well before Freud and Breuer's 1895 publication of *Studies on Hysteria.* Prince's notion that hysteria can be linked to specific parts of the brain was common in nineteenth-century writing; see, for example, C. L. Dana, "The Study of a Case of Amnesia of 'Double-Consciousness,'" *Psychological Review* 1 (1894). Dana's article is a purely medical treatise arguing that amnesia is produced by a traumatic event that puts out of function the brain's ability to associate memories with one another. For a purely medical treatise on traumatic hysteria in German, see Paul Seiffert, "Über vollständige kutane und sensorielle Anästhesie in einem Falle von traumatischer Hysterie," *Deutsche Zeitschrift für Nervenheilkunde* 27 (1905).

35. Pearce Bailey, "The Prognosis of Traumatic Hysteria Based on the Subsequent Histories of a Number of Litigated Cases," *Medical Record* 60, no. 8 (August 1901), 272.

36. Predisposing factors include gender, age, physical health, and "race": "[H. B. aged twenty-two] was a Hebrew, and consequently somewhat predisposed to the development of nervous disorders by reason of his race" (282).

37. For an article in German on the traumatic effects of repeatedly falling from a horse, see L. (first initial only provided) Wick, "Über einen Fall von traumatischer Hyserie" *Wiener medizinische Wochenschrift* 60, no. 5 (1901). The case under discussion occurs in a man in military service and emphasizes the traumatic dimension of repeated accidents and their associations.

38. There are many sources in the literature of semiotics and psychoanalysis for split subjectivity. Particularly clear and useful discussions include Kaja Silverman's *The Subject of Semiotics* (New York: Oxford University Press, 1983), 126–93, and

Bruce Fink's *The Lacanian Subject: Between Language and Jouissance* (Princeton, N.J.: Princeton University Press, 1995).

39. By "structural," I mean an approach to a text (whether a dream, a poem, a symptom, or something else) informed by a binary opposition between manifest and latent content. The text comes into being as rules of transformation operate on basic materials "beneath" a threshold of perceptibility. See Jonathan Culler, *Ferdinand de Saussure* (Ithaca, N.Y.: Cornell University Press, 1986).

40. The *Sechs Orchesterstücke*, Opus 6 (original version), are scored for four flutes, two piccolos, alto flute, two oboes, two English horns, three clarinets in B-flat, one clarinet in E-flat, two bass clarinets in B-flat, two bassoons, one contrabassoon, six horns in F, six trumpets in B-flat, four trombones, bass tuba, two harps, celeste, three timpani, triangle, glockenspiel, Rute (a birch brush used for playing the bass drum), cymbals, tam-tam, snare drum, bass drum, low orchestra bells, and strings. The re-orchestrated version of Opus 6, no. 4, is scored for flutes, piccolo, alto flute, English horns, clarinets in B-flat, clarinet in E-flat, bass clarinets in B-flat, horns in F, trumpets in B-flat, trombone, bass tuba, timpani, cymbals, tam-tam, snare drum, bass drum, and low bells. I discuss the original orchestration of the work in the following pages; for an analysis of the 1928 re-orchestration, see James M. Baker, "Coherence in Webern's *Six Pieces for Orchestra*, Op. 6," *Music Theory Spectrum* 4 (1982): 1–28. Baker's analysis uses atonal pitch-class set theory to find unifying features across the six pieces of the Opus 6; Baker finds a referential pitch-class set based on the vowels of "Schoenberg." Baker calls this a motto that suggests a dual program to the work: to Webern's mother and to his teacher Arnold Schoenberg (26–27); it is set 6-Z44, or (012569).

41. For example, Berg's *Lyric Suite* for String Quartet "represents" a relationship between Alban Berg and Hanna Fuchs, indexed into the work through a movitic elaboration of their initials that become pitches: [A]lban [B-flat]erg [H]anna [F]uchs; the Violin Concerto enacts the death of a young girl, Manon Gropius. Such programs, whether "hidden" or on the surface of the music, derive from the tradition of program music of the nineteenth century in the programmatic works of Berlioz, Liszt, and Strauss.

42. Webern was born in 1883 and studied musicology at the University of Vienna; he began studying composition with Schoenberg in 1904, completing the *Orchesterstücke*, Opus 6, in 1909. Webern's atonal works are mostly quite short, minimal, and severe in affect. Webern wanted his pieces to be condensed and highly concentrated works combining extensions of the chromatic harmony and voice leading of Wagner with the wit and brevity of medieval music. In his atonal works, Webern felt that pieces too easily gravitated to tonal hierarchies and he shut his pieces down sooner and sooner upon hearing such a tonal orientation emerge in the music. As a result, some of his pieces last only seconds. This urge to miniaturization and compression culminates in 1910 with the *Four Pieces for Violin and Piano*, Opus 7.

43. The work was first performed in the infamous "Skandalkonzert" of March 31, 1913, with Schoenberg conducting. Disturbances in the audience caused the concert to be cancelled before the performances could be concluded (Walter Kolneder, *Anton Webern* [Rodenkirchenj/Rhein: P. J. Tonger, 1961], 52).

44. Quoted in Hans and Rosaleen Moldenhauer, *Anton Webern: A Chronicle of His Life and Work* (New York: Knopf, 1979), 126.

45. The following musical examples are either interpretive sketches or approximate transcriptions of passages based on the score. See Anton Webern, *6 Stücke für Orchester,* Ursprüngliche Fassung (Vienna: Philharmonia Partituren, n.d.). Andreas Krause hears the beginning, end, and pauses in this work as follows: "In op. 6/IV a ground-noise [Grundgeräusch] is created through bass drum (later also snare drum), tam-tam, and low bells placed in the distance; across this spatial soundscape [vorausahnenden Raumklang] almost electronic noises [fast elektronische Klänge] are placed" (*Anton Webern und Seine Zeit* [Laaber: Laaber Verlag, 2001], 148).

46. For a discussion of pitch-centricity in an early work of Alban Berg (also D-natural, curiously), see Christopher Lewis, "Tonal Focus in Atonal Music: Berg's op. 5/3," *Music Theory Spectrum* 3 (1981): 84–97. Lewis discusses the way Berg "surrounds" D-natural with half-steps and whole steps in both directions (95); this "surrounding" idea occurs precisely around a missing D-natural as well, as shall be shown below in flute cluster II. Webern's *Sechs Bagatellen für Streichquartett,* Opus 9, no. 5, also expands outward from d-natural[1]; see György Ligeti, "Aspekte der Webernschen Kompositionstechnik," *Musik-Konzepte Sonderband. Anton Webern II,* edited Heinz-Klaus Metzger and Rainer Riehn, November 1984, 72–74. See Webern's *Sechs Bagatellen für Streichquartett,* Opus 9, no. 4, for another piece that suggests a tonal referent (I am indebted to Patrick McCreless for pointing this out to me). The work ends with the first violin outlining in artificial harmonics an augmented dominant of A. For a discussion of atonal "phrasing" in a twelve-tone work by Webern, see Graham H. Phipps, "Harmony as a Determinant of Structure in Webern's Variations for Orchestra," in *Music Theory and the Exploration of the Past,* ed. Christopher Hatch and David W. Bernstein, 473–504 (Chicago: The University of Chicago Press, 1993).

47. For the reader familiar with atonal pitch-class set theory, this is a {0134} pitch-class set—a symmetrical pitch-class set around a missing D-natural, pitch-class 2. The pitch-class set belongs to set class (0134) and is, as Richard Taruskin says, "octatonic-specific." The collection has pervaded much tonal, chromatic, and atonal music. See Richard Taruskin, "The Traditions Revisited: Stravinsky's *Requiem Canticles* as Russian Music," in *Music Theory and the Exploration of the Past,* ed. Christopher Hatch and David W. Bernstein, 525–50 (Chicago: The University of Chicago Press, 1993), 525.

48. This is an example of *Klangfarbenmelodie*—a technique of using color as a structural device in atonal music. The very first piece of the Opus 6 works contains a famous example of *Klangfarbenmelodie* in which a single strand of melody is played by the flutes, muted trumpet in B-flat, and finally muted horn in F. The term was used by Arnold Schoenberg for the first time in his *Harmonielehre,* published in 1911. Walter Kolneder hears a direct relationship between the flute/horn/trumpet sonorities in the Opus 6, no. 4, given above and Schoenberg's "Farben" (Kolneder 49–50).

49. A scream is a cry, an utterance, a singular gesture that can neither be taken back nor repeated, an articulation of a limit. There are many examples of screams in the classical literature, particularly the death screams of both of Berg's central female characters of both of his operas— *Wozzeck* and *Lulu.* Screams are style clichés in blues and soul, and much recent popular music contains spectacular screams. For me, screams are poised at the threshold between signification and nonsignification.

For that reason, human screams are always different from animal "screams." Human screams often contain embedded affirmation or denial.

50. I am arguing that the "augmented sixth" motion is an audible but barebones evocation of traditional procedures. It is a linear gesture only. Just as Kandinsky's paintings of the period contain taglike signifiers of representation, so, too, this bass line evokes a tonal procedure as a container for the workings out of atonal pitch structures. For a discussion of tonal implications in another of Webern's twelve-tone works, see Graham H. Phipps, "Tonality in Webern's Cantata I," *Music Analysis* 3, no. 2 (July 1984): 125–58. Phipps hears "tonic"/"dominant" implications in transpositions of rows, and entries of voices in a polyphonic setting. For example, Phipps suggests that beginning on B-flat at the start of the third movement of the Cantata ("dux") is answered as would be expected in a fugue by a row beginning on E-flat ("comes"), (152). Phipps discusses a BACH idea in the Cantata at length.

51. Forte mentioned this idea in a public lecture in spring 2005 at the College of Music, University of North Texas. The pitch-class C-sharp can be associated with the cross because the name of the pitch in German is "cis"—assonant with "Kreuz."

52. Martin Zenck understands the Opus 6, no. 4, "Marcia funebre" as an expression of traumatic shock in many of the ways under discussion here. Zenck also discusses a traumatic dimension of other, more compressed works of Webern. See Martin Zenck "Weberns Wiener Espressivo," *Musik-Konzepte Sonderband. Anton Webern I,* ed. Heinz-Klaus Metzger and Rainer Riehn, November 1983, 193.

53. In contemporary theories of trauma, writers speak of the contradictory roles of memory and forgetfulness in the experience of patients suffering from trauma: on the one hand they need to remember traumatic experiences in order to work through them, to attach words and repressed emotions to them so they can be purged, or abreacted; on the other hand, they need to forget traumatic memories so they can move on and not be fixed in the past. See Ruth Leys, *Trauma: A Geneology* (Chicago: The University of Chicago Press, 2000), 10.

54. Webern withdrew the marking "Marcia funebre" for his reorchestrated version of the piece of 1928.

55. Shell shock suffered by World War I soldiers revived psychoanalytic theories of trauma in the late 1910s and early 1920s. Hypnosis and the cathartic cure were the focus of the debates; see Leys, chapter 3, "Traumatic Cures: Shell Shock, Janet, and the Question of Memory."

56. Sigmund Freud, *Beyond the Pleasure Principle,* trans. and ed. James Strachey (New York: Norton, 1961), 11.

57. Cathy Caruth discusses trauma as the desire for a wounded voice to be heard (*Unclaimed Experience* [Baltimore: The Johns Hopkins University Press, 1996], 8–9). In Webern's piece, the muted brass throughout suggests a contained, even constrained voice.

58. Jacques Lacan, *The Four Fundamental Concepts of Psycho-Analysis,* ed. Jacques-Alain Miller, trans. Alan Sheridan (New York: Norton, 1981), 55. The Real is a concept that Lacan developed late in his career. It is a crucial component of his theories and it underwrites much of this book. Lacan's topography suggests that psychic activity as it represents itself to us can be located within the triad Imaginary—Symbolic—Real. The Imaginary is the register of mutually exclusive binary oppositions: self/other, presence/absence, plenitude/lack. It is typified by the mirror phase described by Lacan in *Écrits* (aee chapter 1, note 13). The Imaginary is a world of

blacks and whites. The Symbolic is a world of greys; it is the register of linguistic deferral that is neither empty nor full. The Real is the inscrutable "thingness" of life that supports both the Imaginary and the Symbolic. The Real is both a necessary support of signification and something that can never be grasped. The Real appears in moments of personal and collective crisis. The eighteenth-century sublime is edged with the Real; the Real appears in the hysteric's symptom, in the fixed gaze, in the too-much-ness of traumatic breach. For an introduction to the Real, see Dylan Evans, *An Introductory Dictionary of Lacanian Psychoanalysis* (London: Routledge, 1996), 159–60; David Schwarz, *Listening Subjects: Music, Psychoanalysis, Culture* (Durham, N.C.: Duke University Press, 1997), 34–37; Slavoj Žižek, *Looking Awry* (Cambridge, Mass.: MIT Press, 1991), 31–32; Slavoj Žižek, *The Plague of Fantasies* (London: Verso, 1997), 95; Jacques Lacan, *The Four Fundamental Concepts of Psycho-Analysis*, 279–80.

59. This splitting of subjectivity recalls the language of French and German doctors writing on dual consciousness in the mid- to late nineteenth century concerning traumatic hysteria. Also, for Sandor Ferenczi, "splitting was imagined as producing the separation of the ego from the object; it was the very process which constituted the subject as a subject by the splitting apart of the ego from the objective world" (Leys 125).

60. It is striking to *see* a percussion player play a trill on a bass drum, no matter how quietly.

61. The discourse of psychoanalysis under discussion in this chapter is based upon the phallus and the fantasy formations that result from castration anxiety. Recent writers, however, are exploring possibilities of other psychoanalytic discourses. For example, Elisabeth Bronfen outlines a psychoanalysis of the *omphalos* not *phallus*, based on the metaphor of the navel as that representation of "naught" upon which subjectivity is based. For Bronfen, a psychoanalysis of *omphalos* means seeing the cutting of the umbilical cord as a representation of separation from the body of the mother and a subjectivity based on living in a vulnerable body. For her, "shifting critical attention from phallus to omphalos implies confronting the way the subject emerges as a knot shielding itself from its originary wound by avoiding . . . traumatic knowledge of mortality. In other words, the initial incision produces a split in the subject from which sexual desire, cultural images of potency and immortality (as well as neurotic symptoms) may emerge as secondary screen phantasies. At the same time, this traumatic incision is also what knots the subject *together* at the navel of its being" (*The Knotted Subject* [Princeton, N.J.: Princeton University Press, 1998], 17; Bronfen's emphasis). Bronfen's model of subjectivity based on the separation from the body of the mother adds particular poignancy to Webern's "Marcia funebre," which thus embodies in its muted anguish and ending of stuck noise at once a traumatic return to maternal separation—death-separation as inverted birth-separation; the umbilical cord cut for a second time—and, more precisely, the very *impossibility* of such a return.

4. Left! Right! Left! Right!

1. Klaus Theweleit, *Male Fantasies*, vol. 1, trans. Stephen Conway (Minneapolis: University of Minnesota Press, 1987). This study evokes the subject positions of the national socialist SS officer based upon analyses of diary entries, letters, and government documents.

2. The dimension of drive is the psychic apparatus moving again and again, reiteratively toward a point impossible to reach. It is often described by Žižek as a motion around a broken circle with energy constantly moving over the breach. For me, it is productive to distinguish between desire that moves toward its object in an infinite series of signifiers that always slip just past and out of reach and the dimension of drive in which the psychic apparatus is stuck and starts to enjoy its own stuckness (Lacanian *jouissance*). See Dylan Evans, *An Introductory Dictionary of Lacanian Psychoanalysis* (London: Routledge, 1996); see "death instincts" and "life instincts" in Laplanche and Pontalis, *The Language of Psycho-Analysis*, trans. Donald Nicholson-Smith (New York: Norton, 1973); Sigmund Freud, *Beyond the Pleasure Principle*, trans. and ed. James Strachey (New York: Norton, 1961); David Schwarz, *Listening Subjects: Music, Psychoanalysis, Culture* (Durham: Duke University Press, 1997), 69; Slavoj Žižek, *For They Know Not What They Do* (London: Verso, 1991), 272; and Jacques Lacan, *The Four Fundamental Concepts of Psycho-Analysis*, trans. Alan Sheridan (New York: Norton, 1978), chapter 13.

3. David Schwarz, "Oi: Music, Politics, and Violence," in *Listening Subjects*. For a German translation of an early draft of this chapter, see "Oi! Musik, Politik, und Gewalt," *PopScriptum* 5 (1995): 16–45. I focus in these works on right-wing skinhead music. The reader should know, however, that Oi encompasses a very broad semantic field including leftist Oi-Musik.

4. See in particular Fred K. Prieberg, "Säuberung noch und noch," in *Musik im NS-Staat* (Frankfurt: Fischer Verlag, 1982).

5. The national socialists were particularly skilled at refiguring the nature of the German folk song. See Monika Tibbe and Manfred Bonson, *Folk—Folklore—Volkslied* (Stuttgart: J. B. Metzlersche Verlagsbuchhandlung, 1981), 14–48. Tibbe points out that folk songs were expressions of agricultural rhythms until the industrial revolution split workers from their rural living conditions and a one-to-one correspondence between work and product. She points out that folk songs became split with the industrial revolution into (a) a rediscovery of old folk songs, and (b) folk songs of farmers, craftsmen, and workers. She points out that the very term "folk song" originated in the late eighteenth century with Johann Gottfried Herder at the very moment of this cultural split (14–15).

6. Prieberg refers to this cleansing as "Korrektur," or as "Säuberung." The national socialist urge to cleanse German culture of the music of the other was intensive and thorough. It reached into the academy as well. Prieberg points out that in 1935 the "Staatliche Institut für Musikforschung" was founded in Berlin. There were three divisions: music history, the folk song, and the archives for musical instruments (Prieberg 364–65).

7. A very clear example of national socialist appropriation of the music and ideology of the communist-socialist tradition can be seen in a musical guidebook to holidays published in 1938, in which there is a large section on what songs to sing to celebrate May 1—refigured in the book to refer unequivocally to the national socialist worker. See Wilhelm Ehmann, ed., *Musikalische Feiergestaltung* (Hamburg: Hanseatische Verlagsanstalt Hamburg, 1938), 53–61.

8. In 1933 and 1934, Horst Büttner argued with national socialist urgency for a new kind of radio programming that would go well beyond the classical masterworks in appealing to a mass audience. He coins the phrase "Funkpotpourri" for this new form made possible by the technology of the microphone and recording

studio. See Horst Büttner, "Musikalische Dramaturgie des Rundfunks," *Neue Zeitschrift für Musik* 100, pt. 2, vol. 12 (December 1933), and Hortst Büttner, "Die Instrumentale Verwendung von Volksweisen im Rundfunk" *Neue Zeitschrift für Musik* 101, vol. 3 (March 1934). Hermann Roth wrote in 1938 of the power of radio to appeal to the ears, of film to appeal to the eyes, and the printing press to appealto the mind. Roth is aware as well that sounds can be registered on both a conscious and an unconscious level: "Wen er [das Hörens durch den Rundfunk] trifft, der nimmt ihn bewußt—oder aber auch unbewußt auf. [whoever meets it (the power of sound through the radio) takes it in consciously, or indeed unconsciously] ("Die musikalische Aufgabe des Rundfunks," in *Musik im Volk,* ed. Wolfgang Stumme [Berlin: Chr. Friedrich Vieweg, 1944], 275). See also Heinz Pohle, *Der Rundfunk als Instrument der Politik* (Hamburg: Verlag Hans Bredow-Institut, 1955).

9. See Joseph Wulf, *Musik im Dritten Reich: Eine Dokumentation* (Reinbeck: Rowohlt, 1966), 9. Johannes Hodek suggests: "Thought structures, patterns of behavior, and musical ideas appeared, in addition to organizational, institutional, and personal structures, that at first sight seemed to have nothing to do with politics and dominance but which, in fact, were bound up with fascism and its power" ["Es tauchten Denkstrukturen, Verhaltensweisen, Kategorien, Begriffe im Zusammenhang mit Musik auf, organisatorische, institutionelle Strukturen und persönliche Verstrikungen, die auf den ersten Blick mit Politik, Macht, und Herrschaft überhaupt nichts zu tun zu haben schienen, die aber doch mit dem Faschismus und seiner Gewalt verbunden waren"] ("Sie wissen, wen man Heroin nimmt," in *Musik und Musikpolitik im faschistischen Deutschland,* ed. Hanns-Werner Heister and Hans-Günter Klein [Frankfurt: Fischer, 1984], 22).

10. The first major postwar study of music and fascism came out in 1963. German musicology students made an unofficial attempt to bring the topic of music and fascism into the open at the 1974 meeting in Berlin of the Gesellschaft für Musikforschung. In 1981, a group of postwar German musicologists began an open and systematic exploration of the role of music and fascism at a four-day conference in Bayreuth. The study of music and national socialism became well established with the 1982 publication of Prieberg's *Musik im NS-Staat.*

11. For an account of national socialist projects to bring the folk song to a wide population of German youth, see Prieberg 242–59.

12. "[Diese Musik soll dienen] dem Marschsingen, dem Volkssingen, dem Heimabend, dem Kameradschaftsabend, dem Schulungsabend, der Lagerfeier, der Werkfeier, dem Appell, der Kundgebung, dem Volksfest" (Ehmann 3–4).

13. "Von 'Erfüllung' ist die Rede. Das heißt, es müssen mit dem Musikmachen und Singen eigene Gefühle, Stimmungen und Sehnsüchte bewegt worden sein, die dann zu einer wie von oben angestrebten Organisierung und Mobilisierung der Sinnlichkeit führten" (Hodek, "Sie wissen, wenn man Heroin nimmt," 22–23).

14. "Die Maßstab für die Sammler als 'echte' Volkslieder bezeichnen, wirkten sich als Zensur aus. Herder und Goethe bemühten sich allerdings noch um eine unverfälschte Wiedergabe der Texte, während die von außen kommenden Normen fast alle Sammlungen des 19. Jahrhunderts immer stärker beherrschten. Texte, die zu grob, zu sinnlich oder gar politisch sind, werden nicht abgedruckt oder einfach verändert. Das deutsche Volkslied wird so immer mehr zum harmlosen Liedchen, welches die Natur, die Liebe in naiver, traulicher Form besingt" (Tibbe 16).

15. "Kaum in einem anderen Volke als dem deutschen ist der Begriff des 'Volksliedes' so klar und allgemein gültig herausgewachsen. Von Anfang an ist das Volkslied der umfassende Zeuge für das Wachsen und Werden deutscher Volkskultur" (Gerhard Nowottny and Carl Hanneman, "Volksmusikalishe Arbeit in der NS.-Gemeinschaft 'Kraft durch Freude,' in *Musik im Volk,* ed. Wolfgang Summe [Berlin: Chr. Friedrich Vieweg, 1944], 177).

16. All translations of German war song lyrics are mine.

17. "Die drohende Gefahr einer nur archaischen Haltung ist überwunden. Auch die Gefahr der Artistik ist überwunden durch die Erkenntnis des Wesens und der Aufgabe der Laienmusik: wir haben zur Einfachheit der Mittel und zur Klarheit der Form zurückgefunden. So haben neuströmende musikantische Kräfte, geformt von einem geistig gebundenen Gestaltungswillen, uns zur Vertiefung des Kunstwerks geführt: zum Kunstwerk, das nicht mehr scheint, als es ist, sondern das mehr ist, als es scheint" (Carl Hannemann, preface to *Lobeda-Singebuch,* quoted in Wulf Konold, "Kantaten, Fest- und Feiermusiken," in *Musik und Musikpolitik im faschistischen Deutschland,* ed. Hanns-Werner Heister and Hans-Günter Klein, 163–71 [Frankfurt: Fischer, 1984], 164.

18. Prieberg quotes writers, for example, who find Gregorian chant a music that connects the ancient Greeks with the modern German subject; another writer asserts that the finale of Beethoven's *Fidelio* prefigures the national socialist project of giving birth to a new nation (355, 362–63).

19. For an excellent account of such issues, see Hanns-Werner Heister and Jochem Wolff, "Macht und Schicksal: Klassik, Fanfaren, höhere Durchaltemusik" in *Musik und Musikpolitik im faschistischen Deutschland,* ed. Hanns-Werner Heister and Hans-Günter Klein, 115–25 [Frankfurt: Fischer, 1984]. See also Robert Schlesinger, *Gott sei mit Unserem Führer: Der Opernbetrieb im deutschen Faschismus* (Vienna: Löcker Verlag, 1997), and Oliver Rathkolb, *Führertreu und gottbegnadet: Künstlereliten im Dritten Reich* (Vienna: ÖBV-Publikumsverlag, 1991).

20. However, one of the main features of the fascists' control of the musical lives of its subjects was the blurring of boundaries of conventional musical signification. Hanns-Werner Heister and Jochem Wolf point out that the Nazis created a new kind of "classic" out of the works of Beethoven and Wagner in particular: "Sie unterstützte zweitens die psychologische Kriegsvorbereitung, wurde dann...maßgeblich als höhere Durchaltemusik eingesetzt und ergab...Grundtypen für zahllose, dem NS-Geist verpflichtete musikalische Nachahmungen in Sinfonien, Opern, Film-, und Wochenschaumusik, Sondermeldungen und sogar Kampflieder" [Secondly, they support the psychological preparations for war and were then decisively used as a higher form of music that resulted in prototypes for countless musical imitations of symphonies, operas, movie scores, weekly show music, special announcements, and even war songs that pledge themselves to the Nazi spirit] (Hanns-Werner Heister and Jochem Wulf, "Macht und Schicksal," in *Musik und Musikpolitik,* 115–16). For me, this use of classics to create *Durchhaltemusik* is a crucial step in the formation of what I call the West's first ambient music.

21. For a discussion of the relationship between musicians and the political climate in which they worked in the national socialist era, see Michael H. Kater, *The Twisted Muse* (New York: Oxford University Press, 1997).

22. "Auf diese Weise bewegt, wirken die Lieder zugleich steif. Sie wurden in ganz bestimmten Steh- und Sitzhaltungen gesungen und organisierten den Mangel an

eigener Körpererfahrung. Der Singende aber erlebte sein fehlendes Körpergefühl gar nicht oder nur so vermittelt, als sei der Mangel natürlich" (Hodek 25–26).

23. "Mein Bruder und ich mußten . . . tatsächlich morgens, zum Frühstück und als Gute-Nacht-Gruß auch mit Händen und Füßen den deutschen Gruß leisten als letzte Zärtlichkeit zwischen Eltern und Söhnen. In meinem Fall . . . inkarnierte sich der Nazistaat in meinem eigenen Körper meines Erzeugers und Ernährers, dem Körper des strafenden Kleinbürgers des schwachen fehlerhaften, verängstigt um seine Ideale gebrachten, leicht komischen und doch gefürchteten, unberechenbaren Fanatikers" (Hans Werner Henze "Es tut gut, sich zu erinnern zu müssen," in *Musik und Musikpolitik im faschistischen Deutschland,* ed. Hanns-Werner Heister and Hans-Günter Klein, 13–18 [Frankfurt: Fischer, 1984]).

24. See Marie-Luise Gättens, *Women Writers and Fascism* (Gainesville: University of Florida Press, 1995). Gättens discusses women's complicity in the national socialist project and how the structures of the family contributed to it in selected women writers.

25. See Louis Althusser, "Ideology and Ideological State Apparatuses (Notes towards an Investigation)," in *Mapping Ideology,* ed. Slavoj Žižek, 100–140 (London: Verso, 1994); Slavoj Žižek, *Metastases of Enjoyment* (London: Verso, 1994). 57–62; and David Schwarz, *Listening Subjects,* 196 n80.

26. See Jacques Lacan, "The Mirror Stage," in *Écrits,* trans. Alan Sheridan, 1–7 (New York: Norton, 1977). See also Kaja Silverman, *The Subject of Semiotics* (London: Oxford University Press, 1983). There are imaginary mirrors throughout the present book; the first chapter, on the rise of the conductor, explores the mirror as metaphor in the modern concert hall; the second chapter, on Schubert, discusses "Ihr Bild" as a musical mirror fantasy; the third, on the history of psychoanalysis and Webern, discusses psychic split and self-(mis)representation in nineteenth-century discourse of the hysteric; and the final chapter on *Parsifal* contains mirror fantasy as well—there are twin Parsifals in Syberberg's film.

27. Friedrich Trautwein writes in 1936, for example: "Die Technik ist kein Dämon, sondern auch sie wird getragen von verantwortungsbewußten Volksgenossen, mit denen der Künstler in bester Kameradschaft zusammenarbeiten kann und soll für das neue Deutschland" [Technology is no demon, but it is run by responsible Germans with whom artists can and should collaborate in the most collegial fashion for a new Germany] ("Wesen und Ziele der Elektromusik," *Zeitung für Musik* 102, no. 6 [June 1936], 699; quoted in Prieberg 371). Cesar Bresgen, writing in 1944, urges caution concerning the radio, arguing that it can dilute the act of listening: "Hier fordern wir, daß beim Ertönen von Musik im Konzertsaal, im Haus und anderwärts zugehört werde, d.h. daß beim Anhören von Musik, und dies gilt gerade für den Rundfunkempfang, geschwiegen werde" [Here we demand that while hearing music in the concert hall, at home, and other places that is while listening to music, especially broadcasts, that there be silence] ("Zur Frage der 'neuen Unterhaltungsmusik,'" in *Musik im Volk,* ed. Wolfgang Stumme [Berlin: Chr. Friedrich Vieweg, 1944], 290).

28. See Émile Benveniste, *Problems in General Linguistics,* trans. Mary Elizabeth Meek (Coral Gables, Fla.: University of Miami Press, 1971), chapter 18.

29. I will be arguing throughout this chapter that we interpellate prior to mirror identification and all of its registers of (mis)recognitions. Previsual interpellation is acoustic, and it is carried by the voice, by music, by song. Volker Kühn discusses "the hit" and its appeal to disenfranchised members of social space. He says "where the irrational celebrates its victory, where appeals are made to the emotions, and

where the recipient of the music (after Adorno), is disenfranchised, then all is made possible" ["Wo das Irrationale Triumphe feiert, wo ans Emotionale appelliert wird und der Adressat, laut Adorno, der Unmündige ist, wird denn auch fast alles möglich"] ("Man muß das Leben nehmen, wie es eben ist...," in *Musik und Musikpolitik*, 213). The German word *Unmündig* condenses my sense of acoustic interpellation prior to the visual regimes of the mirror stage. *Mundig* suggests empowerment and *un-* negates it. Power resides in the ability to speak; the way the German language denotes disenfranchisement is to suggest a mute subject—someone who can perhaps hear but who cannot speak.

30. The motto of the "Wehrmachtwunschkonzert" condenses the dynamic of Althusserian interpellation precisely: "Die Front reicht ihrer Heimat jetzt die Hände,— die Heimat aber reicht der Front die Hand" [While the front reaches out to the homeland with its hands, the homeland reaches out to the front with its hand]. The plural hands of the soldiers on the front are clasped in the singular hand of the homeland. The medium of this interpellation is the radio (Prieberg 379).

31. "Wurd'ich so ein bißchen nach unten, dann hab' ich immer automatisch Nazilieder gesungen, dann ist das sofort wieder alles stramm, geradeaus.... Das ist mir eine gute Medizin gewesen. Weil diese Lieder in mich eingespritzt worden sind wie eine Droge. Sie wissen, wenn man unter den Nazis aufgebracht worden ist, dann bleiben diese Nazilieder noch für zwanzig, dreißig Jahre im Hirn" (Prieberg 242; quoted in Hodek 23).

32. In the early 1930s, a prominent national socialist working on the radio as an instrument of propaganda expressed the power of the radio as the vehicle for what we now think of as ideological interpellation: "out of the 40 million people who voted 'yes,' the radio has to forge a single people who at its most inner core is national socialist" ["Der Rundfunk muß aus vierzig Millionen, die zu einer politischen Aktion 'Ja' gesagt haben, ein Volk machen, das in seinem tiefsten Denken and Handeln nationalsozialistisch ist"] (Eugen Hadamowsky, "Der Rundfunk im Dienste der Volksführung," quoted in Heinz Pohle, *Der Rundfunk als Instrument der Politik* [Hamburg: Verlag Hans Bredow-Institut, 1955], 235). The predominantly pedagogical use of the radio in the Weimar Republic was thus turned into an instrument of interpellation with a powerfully coercive edge.

33. See Žižek's rereading of Althusser's "little theater" of ideological interpellation in *Metastases of Enjoyment*, 57–61.

34. "Machen Sie es gut, dann werden wir das Volk gewinnen, und machen Sie es schlecht, dann wird das Volk am Ende von uns weglaufen" (Joseph Goebbels, quoted in Pohle 228).

35. "Die ungeheure Bedeutung des Marschliedes im Leben des Soldaten dürfte heute wohl allgemein bekannt sein. Hundemüde von einem Marsch, der endlos erschien, strafft sich die Haltung jedes Mannes, sobald ein frisches Lied angestimmt wird. Aber nicht nur Marschlieder braucht der Soldat, auch andere Lieder sind ihm lebensnotwendig, bildet doch das Lied gelegentlich gewissermassen das Ventil, durch das der Soldat seinem Unmut, seinem 'inneren Schweinehund,' seiner Sehnsucht, aber auch seiner Ausgelassenheit Luft verschaffen muss" (W. E. Häfner, "Soldaten und ihre Lieder," *Neue Zeitschrift für Musik* 107, vol. 1 [June 1940]: 334).

36. The author locates the singing of good war songs with German culture. He was a prisoner of war during World War I, imprisoned near a British camp. He claims to have heard during his months in prison not a single Englishman sing a war song.

This binary is very clear in Friedrich Högner's "Das Lied der Soldaten" (*Neue Zeitschrift für Musik* 107, vol. 3 [March 1940]: 129–34).

37. Häfner 334–36. The journal *Neue Zeitschrift für Musik* stopped publication from 1943 through 1949. The journal had a subheading "Monatschrift für eine geistige Erneurung der deutschen Musik" beginning in 1925, volume 92, part I. The heading changed to "Monatschrift für eine stete geistige Erneuerung der Musik" beginning in 1950, volume 111.

38. Earlier songs are always included in German war song anthologies of both World War I and World War II. Including such songs gave each anthology a sense of historical depth to its implied listeners.

39. *Empor mein Volk! Kreigslieder aus unseren Tagen mit neuen Weisen*, vol. 1; *Ein Hänlein woll'n wir rupfen: Neue Kriegslieder nach alten Texten und Weisen*, vol. 2; *Wohlauf Kameraden: Soldatenlieder zum 'heiligen Krieg,'* vol. 3; *Deutsches Herz, verzage nicht: Vaterlandslieder aus grosser Zeit*, vol. 4; *Jeder Schuss, ein Russ! Neue Kriegslieder*, vol. 5; *Jeder Stoss, ein Franzos! Neue Kriegslieder*, vol. 6 (Jena: Eugen Diedrichs, 1914). *Musketier seins lust'ge Brüder: Alte liebe Soldatenlieder*, vol. 7; *Jungs, holt fasst! Oole un neeie Krigs- un Suldatenleeider*, vol. 8; *Ich weiss einen Lindenbaum stehen: neue Kriegslieder*, vol. 9; *Heil Kaiser dir! Kriegslieder aus unseren Tagen*, vol. 10; *Nun lasst die Rosse traben! Neue Kriegslieder*, vol. 11 (Jena: Eugen Diedrichs, 1915).

40. Here are the keys and meters of the songs from the first volume, *Empor mein volk*: Nr. 1 "Kriegslied," D major, 4/4; Nr. 2, "Furor tuetonicus," F major, 2/2; Nr. 3, "Deutschlands Fahnenlied," A major, 6/8; Nr. 4, "Deutsches Soldatenlied," G major, 2/2; Nr. 5, "Berliner Landturm," F major, 2/4; Nr. 6, "Deutsches Matrosenlied," F major, 4/4; Nr. 7, "Sturmlied 1914," A major, 4/4; Nr. 8, "Gebet ans Volk," E-flat major, 3/4; Nr. 9, "Der heilige Reiter," F major, 6/8; Nr. 10, "Ein Erntewagen," C major, 4/4; Nr. 11, "Flotten-Sturm!" B-flat major, 12/8; Nr. 12, "Marsch! Marsch!" F major, 4/4; Nr. 13, "General Emmich," C major, 6/8; Nr. 14, "Das Marienburger Lied," F major, 3/4; Nr. 15, "Garde-marsch!" C major, 4/4; Nr. 16, "Lied an Alle," D major, 4/4; Nr. 17, "Deutschlands Siegesdank," A major, 6/8.

41. The e-natural^{2}s can be heard as upper neighbor notes decorating d-natural^2 in measures 7 and 13.

42. This is a common strategy in these songs. Ending on the mediant, third scale degree in a strophic song makes returning to the top sound like a melodic resolution of an ongoing structure and not just a static starting over again.

43. Nr. 1, "Aufforderung an alle Deutsche," F major, 4/4; Nr. 2, "Ein frommes Pilgrimslied der Deutschen," B-flat major, 4/4; Nr. 3, "Soldatenlied," G major, 4/4; Nr. 4, "Zwei andächtige Lieder von der Schlacht," F major, 4/4; Nr. 5, F major, 4/4; Nr. 6, "Das Preussenlied von der Lütticher Schlacht," G major, 4/4; Nr. 7, "Dankgebet nach Schlacht und Sieg," B-flat major, 4/4; Nr. 8, "Husarenabschied," G major, 4/4; Nr. 9, "Der Jäger," G major, 4/4; Nr. 10, "Soldatenabschied," A major, 4/4; Nr. 11, "Soldatentod," A major, 4/4; Nr. 12, "Die Lütticher Parole," A-flat major, 4/4; Nr. 13, "Soldatenlobung," A major, 4/4; Nr. 14, "Siegeslied," G major, 4/4; Nr. 15, "Preussenausmarsch," A major, 2/4; Nr. 16, "Kanonenlied," G major, 2/4; Nr. 17, "Ruf zum Kampf!" G major, 4/4; Nr. 18, "Truss Russland," F major, 3/4; Nr. 18, "Nun danket all Gott," A major, 4/4.

44. "Nun danket all Gott," "Melodie von Joh. Cueger 1649, bearbeitet fon J. S. Bach, Satz von H[ermann] W[irth]. [Text von] Martin Rinckart (1586–1649)."

45. "Nun danket all Gott," BWV 386, *Neue Ausgabe Sämtlicher Werke*, Serie III: *Motetten, Choräle, Lieder*; Band 2, Teil 1 (Basel: Bärenreiter, 1991), 101.

46. Nr. 1, "Wohlauf Kameraden, aufs Pferd," B-flat major, 4/4; Nr. 2, "Die neue deutsche Wacht," B-flat major, 4/4; Nr. 3, "Die deutsche Faust," text only; Nr. 4, "Deutschland," text only; Nr. 5, "Vorwärts," text only; Nr. 6, "Fridericus Rer," E major, 4/4; Nr. 7, "Prinz Eugen," F major, 5/4; Nr. 8, "Lille, du wunderschöne Stadt," text only; Nr. 9, "Zu Strassburg auf der Schanz," E-flat major, 4/4; Nr. 10, "Es geht," D major, 4/4; Nr. 11, "Frisch auf, Soldatenblut," A major, 2/4; Nr. 12, "Ich habe Luft im weiten Feld," G major, 4/4; Nr. 13, "O Deutschland hoch in Ehren," B-flat major, 4/4; Nr. 14, "Sesst zusammen die Gewehre," D major, 2/4; Nr. 15, "Des Morgens," D major, 4/4; Nr. 16, "Lippe-Detmold, eine wunderschöne Stadt," C major, 4/4; Nr. 17, "Der König von Sachsen", D major, 3/4; Nr. 18, "Brüder, uns ist alles gleich," A major, 4/4; Nr. 19, "Radetsky-Lied," F major, 4/4; Nr. 20, "Jungster Lüttich," text only; Nr. 21, "Der neue Kutsche," F major, 2/4; Nr. 22, "Das Treue Ross," text only; Nr. 23, "Hinter Metz, vor Paris und Chalons," D major, 4/4.

47. I shall return to this point in the discussion of national socialist war songs; unison singing has, I shall argue, a pointed ideological structure in national socialism.

48. Arnold Mendlessohn (1885–1933) was a descendant of Felix Mendlessohn. Arnold was a musician active in church music. He became a professor of music in 1899 and had among his students Paul Hindemith (*Lexikon der Musik* [Frankfurt and Vienna: Humboldt-Verlag, 1955]).

49. From volume 5, *Jeder Schuss, ein Russ*, "Des Königs Artolleren" by Arnold Mendlessohn is in F minor; from volume 6, *Jeder Stoss, ein Franzos!* "Spielmans Tod" by Arnold Mendelssohn is in D minor; from volume 9, *Ich weiss einen Lindenbaum stehen*, "Der sterbende Soldat" by Arnold Mendelssohn, discussed above, begins in F minor and shifts to F major; from volume 11, *Nun lasst die Rosse traben!* "Nun grünt es schon und blühet" by W. Eigenbrot is in E minor.

50. From volume 4, *Deutsches Herz, verzage nicht!* "Der deutsche Rhein" by Robert Schumann, 1840, and "Schwertlied" by Carl Maria von Weber, 1814.

51. The following songs in the series are by women: from volume 6, "Soldatenlied" by Emma Vivie is a bright 2/4 march in E major; from volume 9, "Gebet" by Louise Mendelssohn; from volume 10, *Heil Kaiser dir!* "Antwerpen" in D minor by Elizabeth Nelson-Schemmann (it has pop symbols above the pitches suggesting harmonic accompaniment); also from volume 10, "Soldatenleben" by Gräfin Gertrud von Dennwitz; from volume 11, *Nun lasst die Rosse traben*, "Kanonierliedlein" by Elizabeth Nelson-Schemmann (it also has pop symbols above the pitches suggesting harmonic accompaniment); and also from volume 11, "Deutsche Helden" by Marianne Lüdecke.

52. "Im Auftrag des Nationalsozialistichen deutschen Studentenbundes, der Reichsschaft der Studierenden der deutschen Hoch- und Fachschulen, der deutschen Fachschulschaft, der deutschen Studentenschaft und in Verbindung mit dem Reichsbund Volkstum und Heimat herausgegeben von Gerhard Pallman. Bärenreiter Verlag zu Kassel, 1934." I am grateful to Professor Hans-Günther Klein at the Preussische Staatsbibliothek in Berlin for granting me access to the music archives in which I found *Wohlauf Kameraden* and many other volumes of music. Bärenreiter was actively involved in national socialist propaganda. On the back cover of *Wohlauf Kameraden*, a statement urges Germans to use music both as professionals and amateurs to rekindle the German spirit. The company offered free monthly publications: *Lied und Volk, Musik und Volk, Zeitschrift für Hausmusik*, and *Der Rhythmus*.

53. That the national socialists pulled the "worker" resolutely toward the right is well known and documented. The national socialist party, after all, focused on the worker in its very name. Work songs began in Germany in the nineteenth century as expressions of the working classes against the interests of ruling- and middle-class exploitation. The lyrics were very powerful and often landed people who sung them in jail. The work song "Das Weberlied," sung during the Weberaufstand or Weavers' Revolt of 1844, is one of the most famous examples. Work songs of the nineteenth century were not isolated, aesthetic objects. Often their texts were grafted onto older melodies (Tibbe 26–28).

54. "So wird die Musik mit aufgerufen, das Volk als Natur und Geschichte zur wesentlichen Gestalt zu bringen.... Die uns aus der letzten Geschichtsspanne über-nommene Waffe der Musik kennt solche Ordnung und Bindung nicht" [Thus music will also be called upon to give substantial form to the people as nature and his-tory.... The weapon of music that we have taken over from recent history does not, however, know such order and heritage] (Wilhelm Ehman, Introduction to *Musika-lische Feiergestaltung* [Hamburg: Hanseatische Verlagsanstalt Hamburg, 1938], 3).

55. Hodek condenses this rewriting of German music history in the anthology: "Die Sammlung reicht von Johann Walthers *Wach auf, wach auf, du deutsches Land*, über Luthers Choral *Ein feste Burg*, über zahlreiche Landsknechts-, Soldaten- und Bauernlieder, bis hin zu *Die Knechtschaft hat ein Ende* und *Die Gedanken sind frei* aus den Freiheitsbewegungen um 1800. Man findet Lieder aus den Zeiten der Stände, solche, in denen Städte und Landschaften besungen werden, und nicht zuletzt ver-schiedene textliche Versionen des bis heute traditionellen Gewerkschaftsliedes *Brüder, zur Sonne zur Freiheit*" [The collection ranges from Johann Walthers's "Wach auf, wach auf, du deutsches Land" to Luther's chorale "Ein feste Burg" to numerous pro-letarian, soldier, and farmer songs, to "Die Knechtschaft hat ein Ende" to "Die Gedanken sind frei" from the liberty movement of 1800. One finds, as well, songs from the class system which sing of cities and landscapes and of union songs such as "Brüder zur Sonne zur Freiheit"] (Hodek 28). The Nazis were also adept at adopt-ing high art works for propaganda purposes. Hanns-Werner Heister and Jochem Wolff argue that the Nazis used, manipulated, and adapted a wide range of "Wag-nerian" musics, citing the opening of Riefenstahl's *Triumph of the Will* as an exam-ple ("Macht und Schicksal: Klassik, Fanfaren, höhere Durchhaltemusik," *Musik und Musikpolitik*, 118–20).

56. "Wenn diese Waffe in den eigenen Reihen erprobt, um sie dereinst in die Hände des deutschen Arbeiters zu legen, so trägt die wesentlich zur Sicherung und inneren Vollendung der nationalsozialistischen Revolution in Deutschland bei. 'Wohlauf Kameraden' soll daher ein Kampfruf sein, unter dem die Kameradschaften der jungen Mannschaft auf den deutschen Hoch- und Fachschulen zu einer neuen großen Aufgabe antreten mit dem Willen zu einer neuen inneren Einigung der Na-tion auf der Grundlage ihres tausendjährigen kulturellen Erbes" (*Wohlauf Kamer-daden*, ed. Gerhard Pullman [Kassel: Bärenreiter, 1934], 3).

57. For an article that compares war songs from 1870–71, World War I, and World War II, see Friedrich Hoegner, "Das Lied der Soldaten," *Neue Zeitschrift für Musik*, 107, vol. 3 (March 1940), 129–34. Hoegner sees a unifying factor among German war songs that become absorbed in later anthologies: the star as a metaphor of the beloved left behind, defense of the homeland, and love of weaponry.

58. The phrase "mündlich überliefert" is a cover for textual revision in the case of the song "Brüder, formiert die Kolonnen," a rewritten version of "Brüder zur Sonne zur Freiheit" to be discussed below. As a source, the editor provides "Dichtung und Weise mündlich in die SA überliefert" [poetry and music transmitted orally to the SA].

59. "Er gräbt und schaufelt, solang er lebt, und gräbt, bis er endlich sein Grab sich gräbt."

60. There are very few borrowings between these two volumes. "Es geht" from *Wohlauf Kameraden* (1914) becomes "Der Soldat" in *Wohlauf Kameraden* (1934)—transposed from D major to C major. "Der Soldat" has been arranged as a duet. "Lippe-Demold, eine wunderschöne Stadt" from *Wohlauf Kameraden* (1914) is reproduced with minor variants in *Wohlauf Kamerden* (1934).

61. Notes were organized from the ancient Greeks to the early eighteenth century in *modes* patterns of whole steps and half steps in myriad combinations. If you play D-natural to D-natural on a piano you get the *dorian* mode. It sounds like a minor scale with a lowered leading tone.

62. It is possible to hear the third phrase of the song moving to F. Then the c-natural^2 is the fifth of F, as a-natural^1 is the fifth of D. I hear the song exploring the entire range of D dorian within one octave.

63. One of the more spectacular revisions cited by Prieberg is the rewritten stanza of "Silent Night" published by Gerhard Pallman in 1940: "Stille Nacht, heilige Nacht / Deutschlands Söhne halten Wacht. / In dem Schützengraben verschneit / liegen wir Mann für Mann bereit, / lauern bei Tag und bei Nacht." In English: "Silent Night, holy Night / Germany's sons are on watch. / In the snowy trenches / we lie man by man at the ready / alert by day and by night." The word *lauern* suggests a hostile intent difficult to translate into English. Pallman's rhetorical shift transforms a third-person contemplation of a winter landscape and its sacred connotations into a first-person plural pronoun with a sneer of threat aimed at the other.

64. The melody comes from a Hessian soldier's song (Tibbe 45).

65. I argue elsewhere that the Oi song "Mann für Mann" of 1984 relies on text and music in a heavy metal context setting up a condition of impotence that a homophobic homoerotic fantasy of erection masters. The dynamic here of the archaic D dorian and awkward 5/2 meter of "Gelöbnis" set up and motive the modern B-flat major and luxuriant 4/4 of "Die Fahne hoch" in a similar textual and musical ploy (*Listening Subjects,* chapter 6).

66. For an articulate and mildly racist version of a national socialist musicology based upon "Bodenständigkeit," see Walter Wiora, "Die deutsche Volksliedweise und der Osten" (Berlin: Georg Kallmeyer Verlag, 1940).

67. "Überhaupt ersingt sich der Mensch im Liede am sinnfälligsten wieder das vielfach verlorengegangene Bewußtsein seiner Einbettung in ewige Ordnungen. Tageslauf, Jahreslauf, Lebenslauf, diese unverrückbaren Grundfesten eines naturnahen Lebens" [Generally, man sings the songs that come back to him again, of the commonly lost consciousness of his place in the eternal order of days, of years— the unchanging groundedness of natural life] (Richard Eichenauer, "Musik im Bauerntum," in *Musik im Volk,* ed. Wolfgang Summe [Berlin: Chr. Friedrich Vieweg, 1944], 302).

68. See Wilhelm Ehmann, ed., *Musikalische Feiergestaltung* (Hamburg: Hanseatische Verlagsanstalt Hamburg, 1938). The book ends with a section on music to be

sung at a celebration of German war dead. November 9 and November 11 are provided as specific dates upon which national socialists mourn their dead.

69. The documentation says that the poem is by Ernst Leibl; the setting is by
Walther Henkel. A note goes on to locate the song at a precise moment of German
history, relying on the people's collective rage at post–World War I reparations:
"Das Lied, entstanden aus der Not der Deutsch-Böhmen im Grenzlande, erklang
zum ersten Male am Pfingstsonntag 1919 in der Stadt-Kirche zu Waltsch bei Karls-
bad" [The song, a product of the need felt by the Germans in Bohemia at the bor-
der, sounded for the first time on Sunday, Pfingsten 1919 in the city's main church at
Waltsch near Karlsbad].

70. In the original, there is a repeat sign at the end of measure 4, enabling a repetition of the opening melody to new text.

71. Tibbe claims that the third stanza has been changed (Tibbe 39–40). *Wohlauf
Kameraden* reveals that both the second and the third stanzas have been changed.

72. See Ludwig van Beethoven, *Complete Edition of All His Works,* vol. 29 (New
York: Kalmus Publishers, n.d.), (197) 22. In Beethoven's "Abbe Stadler," the first voice
sings the first half of a fourteen-measure phrase alone; in measure 8, the second
voice begins. In measure 15, voice one has sung the entire melody and the second
voice is halfway through. Then Beethoven adds a new seven-measure phrase for
voice one. After this, there are three iterations of (a) the first half of the melody, (b)
the second half of the melody, and (c) the new seven-measure phrase. Beethoven
transforms a simple canon into triple counterpoint. The text: "Signor, Abate, io
sono, io sono, io sono, ammalato" (the first half of the phrase), "Santo Padre! Vieni
e date mi las benedizione, la benedizione" (the second half of the phrase), "Hol' Sie
der Teufel wenn Sie nicht kommen, hol' Sie der Teufel wenn Sie nicht kommen,
Hol' Sie der Teufel!" "Arbeiter, tretet ein" is a straight canon. The highest note in
"Abbe Stadtler is a g-natural^2—a very high note for a male voice; it was probably
bought down to f-natural^2 within the key of F minor for practical reasons.

73. In measure 8 in the original there is a half note followed by an eighth rest; I
have reproduced this rhythmic mistake in the example.

74. I find it very difficult to translate the line "du lustiges Hitlerblut." "Hitlerblut"
suggest the blood of Hitler, and perhaps also a flower, a blossom. "Lustig" suggests
funny, amusing, true, loyal, entertaining.

75. My thanks to Cindy McTee for suggesting that this song is a reworking of the
Polish song "The Trumpeter of Krakow," who is struck by an arrow while playing
the trumpet.

76. Disavowal and repression are very different. Repression is a part of normal
psychic growth. We repress hidden wishes and they come out in symbolic form in
slips of the tongue, jokes, and dreams. Disavowal, on the other hand, is far more
dangerous. Disavowal suggests putting something aside that cannot be incorporated
into one's psychic universe. It can lead to psychotic formations (see Laplance and
Pontalis 118–19).

77. My sense of this self-pitying nostalgia is indebted to Žižek's notion of nostalgia in which a fantasy is produced of a subject watching a projection of himself at
one remove (Slavoj Žižek, *Looking Awry* [Cambridge, Mass.: MIT Press, 1991], 107–22).

78. One way of understanding this difference concerns mode as it functions in
each of the iterations of *Wohlauf Kameraden.* In 1914, the vast majority of the songs
were in major; in 1934 complex transformations of modality and tonality occur,

with the minor mode as frequent as the major. The clarity of the major/minor duality in 1914 suggests a clearer subject position than the more fluid modal transformations that pervade the 1934 volume.

79. Evans 167.

80. Freud proposes that the more primary impulse to gain pleasure by mastering the body of the other and inflicting various levels of psychic and physical pain can become transformed into a turning against the self of the same sadistic urges. This is similar, perhaps, to Freud's notion of the double object of suicide. Primal aggression outward is (re)directed inward, out of guilt and/or fear. For Freud's discussion of sadism and masochism, see "Three Essays on the Theory of Sexuality" in *The Freud Reader,* edited by Peter Gay, 239–93 (New York: Norton, 1989). For the text in German, see *Sexualleben. Drei Abhandlungen zur Sexualtheorie (1905). Studienausgabe,* Band V (Frankfurt: Fischer Verlag, 1982), 67–69.

81. Lacan, *The Four Fundamental Concepts,* 170.

82. Ibid., 182–83.

83. Ibid., 183.

84. I mean to suggest both an everyday sense of the imaginary here as well as the Lacanian term. Lacan suggests that the Imaginary Order is a phase of development from six to eighteen months in which the child identifies with the mother (or her surrogate) through a series of mutually exclusive binary oppositions (plenitude/lack, for example). The Imaginary Order in Lacan is primarily visual and forms the basis of a complex series of identifications, and, crucially, (mis)identifications. (Mis)identifications arise with the child's mastery of his or her body and he or she gradually realizes that what he or she had thought was a reflection of his or her ideal self in the mirror (or mother's face, or the face of her surrogate) was in fact flat, two-dimensional, and illusory. The child partially frees him- or herself from this imaginary conflict through language that turns the black-and-white experiences of the Imaginary Order into the infinite gradations of grey of the Symbolic Order.

85. "Keiner, der die ersten Monate der nationalsozialistischen Herrschaft 1933 in Berlin beobachte, konnte das Moment tödliche Traurigkeit, des halbwissend einem Unheilvollen sich Anvertrauens übersehen, das den angedrehten Rausch, die Fackelzüge und Trommeleien begleitete. Wie hoffnungslos klang das deutsche Lieblingsleid jener Monate, 'Volk ans Gewehr,' in der Passage Unter den Linden" [No one who had experienced those first months of Nazi power of 1933 could help notice the moment of deathly sadness, the semiconscious urgings accompanied by torches and drums. How sad must the German's favorite song "Volk ans Gewehr" have sounded along Unter den Linden] (Adorno, quoted in Hodek 33).

86. The song was arranged and published for three women's voices (two sopranos and an alto), mandolins and choir, men's choir, and band—all published by the Verlag für deutsche Musik. There are no printed dates on the scores; handwritten remarks suggest 1934 for the above publications. In addition, Arno Pardun wrote marches entitled "Für Freiheit und Recht," "Brigade 25," "Heil Führer Dir," and "Wir sind nun mal Soldaten."

87. The binary between pure, German music and music of the other is blurred on occasion, as well. For example, soon after Richard Strauss was appointed president of the Reichsmusikkammer in 1933, Hitler made an exception to the national socialist policy of forbidding Jewish influences in opera. Over objections from

Goebbels and several national socialist functionaries, Hitler gave Strauss permission to perform his opera "Die schweigsame Frau" with its text from the Jewish Stefan Zweig (Prieberg 200–206).

88. Otto Rathke published a version of the song with an assertive march played by the piano in D major. This dramatic gesture brings out the darkness with which the song proper begins (Otto Rathke, "'Volk ans Gewehr' über das Lied von Arno Pardun" [Berlin: Verlag für deutsche Musik, n.d.]). A version for band entitled "Paraphrase über das Lied Volk ans Gewehr" by Bernhard Kutsch was published by the Verlag für deutsche Musik, no date given. Pardun also published "3 Kampflieder: 'Marschiert, marschiert,' 'Nicht Geld, nicht gut,' and 'Deutschland, du mein Deutschland'" by the Verlag für deutsche Musik, no date given.

89. The strain of the voice at this moment of the song is like a scream, a tearing apart of the voice, a separation of linguistic signifiers from the Real of the voice. The sadistic violence of such a male scream lies at the heart of such separation.

90. The reader might recall Hodek's notion that the 4/4–4/5 meter of "Mich brennts in meinen Reiseschuhen" has a musical, corporeal, and ideological function. In "Volk ans Gewehr," as well, the sadness of D dorian and the shrill minor seventh in the melody function as musical elements to be mastered and purged.

91. For an account of the urge of the male, fascist subject to purify himself, see Theweleit.

92. A manuscript in the Deutsche Staatsbibliothek in Berlin shows that Pardun wrote a version of "Volk ans Gewehr" in 1931. This version is written for piano with the text written over the top of the right hand part; the voice clearly is meant to double the top voice of the accompaniment. The simple harmonization evokes a religious sonority with a plagal cadence at the ends of the first two phrases. This version has the music move to the submediant B-flat major for the third phrase with F major to the first phrase "Volk ans Gewehr," followed by a dominant-tonic cadence back in D minor for the second "Volk ans Gewehr" phrase (Prieberg 130).

93. I use the term "repetition" to suggest a sign whose reappearance is connected to an earlier appearance. Repetition creates meanings of subordination or coordination. I use "reiteration" to suggest a sign whose reappearance is not connected to an earlier appearance. Reiteration is a function of several dimensions: the Real, the traumatic, the oceanic, the sublime, information. See the chapter 2 on Schubert for more on this binary opposition.

94. I am grateful to Eric L. Santner of the University of Chicago, Department of Germanic Languages for first suggesting to me that fantasies of dismemberment might be specific to German art and literature of the modern era.

95. The national socialists clearly knew how to allow for exceptions. It is remarkable that Leni Riefenstahl was able to convince the national socialists to let her not only make a film of the Nurnberg rally but to get very close to Hitler in filming *Triumph des Willens*.

96. One way in which *Wohlauf Kameraden* (1914) entertains a greater degree of difference than *Wohlauf Kameraden* (1934) is in its language and dialect. *Wohlauf Kameraden* (1914) has one volume entirely in "Niederdeutsch" or Plattdeutsch; no gesture of including dialects of German occurs in *Wohlauf Kameraden* (1934) or in later national socialist songbooks. National socialists were interested in interpellating their subjects into the singular state along the trajectory suggested by the chant "Ein Volk, ein Reich, ein Führer"; when the soldiers in *Triumph des Willens* call out

their home regions, they do so with the implicit understanding that these are regions that are part of the larger whole. Having an entire volume of war songs in a specific dialect would detract from the unifying imperative of national socialist ideology. There are gentler gestures of daily speech that inflect many of the songs of *Wohlauf Kameraden* (1934), but they suggest the daily routine of workers not specific to regions. A common example is "nit" instead of "nicht."

5. Closing the Wound

1. Eschenbach's epic was printed in Germany in 1477 by Johann Mentelin; an edition was published in 1833 by Karl Lachmann, in 1836 and 1841 by San Marte, and in 1841 by Karl Simrock (Ulrich Müller, "Wolfram, Wagner, and the Germans," in *A Companion to Wolfram's Parzival*, ed. Will Hasty [Columbia, S.C.: Camden Press, 1999], 247).

2. Peter Wapnewski, "Der Parzival des Wolfram von Eschenbach," in *Zum Raum wird hier die Zeit*, ed. Sabine Borris, publication of the Berlin Philharmonic Orchestra, October 2001, 15. The account of Eschenbach that follows is from Wapnewski.

3. William Kindermann, "Die Entstehung der *Parsifal* Musik," *Archiv für Musikwissenschaft* 52, no. 1 (1995): 70 (hereafter Kinderman, "Entstehung 1").

4. Dietmar Holland, "'Parzival' und 'Parsifal': Von Wolfram von Eschenbach zu Richard Wagner," in *Zum Raum wird hier die Zeit*, ed. Sabine Borris, publication of the Berlin Philharmonic Orchestra, October 2001, 26.

5. Linda and Michael Hutcheon point out that Wagner moves the location of Amfortas's wound from the genitals to his side to strengthen the latent association between Amfortas and Christ in *Parsifal*. They also suggest that the nature of the wound strongly suggests symptoms of syphilis—a painful and common venereal disease of the time. See Linda Hutcheon and Michael Hutcheon, "Syphilis, Sin, and the Social Order: Richard Wagner's *Parsifal*," *Cambridge Opera Journal* 7, no. 3 (November 1995).

6. Holland 27.

7. The flower maidens in act 2 refer to the fact that Parsifal has slain many of their playmates. For Kindermann, however, "A crucial aspect of this dramatic progression [from an interest in Amfortas to Parsifal] would be the treatment of Parsifal's response to Kundry's seduction attempt in Act II such that it project not utter passivity on the part of Parsifal, but self-possession, shown through his identification with and compassion for Amfortas and his conscious realization of the nature of his mission" (William Kindermann, "Wagner's *Parsifal*: Musical Form and the Drama of Redemption," *Journal of Musicology* 4, no. 4 [Fall 1985–86]: 438).

8. I will argue at the end of this chapter however, that the relationship between Parsifal and Amfortas, his wound and his office, involve more complex motives grounded in the imperative-as-question of Amfortas's father Titurel: "Mein Sohn, bist du am Amt?"

9. See Arthur Schopenhauer, *The World as Will and Representation*, vol. 1, trans. E. F. J. Payne (New York: Dover Publications, 1969), 285, 329, 334, 379, 380, 383, 386–87.

10. Schopenhauer 382; see also 284–85, 329, 334.

11. Kindermann discusses in great detail Wagner's compositional process. There are compositional materials written in pencil and orchestral materials written in

ink. The *Parsifal* materials are particularly fragmented (Kindermann, "Entstehung 1," 70–71).

12. Kindermann points out that the musical beginnings of *Parsifal* have an American source. Wagner was commissioned to write a march for the Philadelphia World's Fair at the Centennial celebration. Upon a sketch from February 9, 1876, for the flower maidens' music, Wagner wrote "Amerikanish sein wollend!" (Kindermann, "Entstehung 1," 84).

13. The libretto was published in 1877 in Mainz; the vocal score was published in Mainz in 1882; the full score was published in Mainz in 1883 (*The New Grove Dictionary of Music and Musicians*, 2d. ed., vol. 26, ed. Stanley Sadie [New York: Macmillan, 2001], 960).

14. Eduard Hanslick describes the scene vividly: "six years have passed since the Festival Theatre was first opened to cast the spell of Wagner's four-day wonder, *Der Ring des Nibelungen*. Since then, the odd theatre in the mountains has been closed, the hot, dusty road leading up to it deserted." See Hanslick, "Parsifal," in *Music Criticisms*, trans. and ed. Henry Pleasants (Baltimore, Md.: Penguin Books, 1950), 187. Hanslick has perceptive things to say about the premiere, particularly about the libretto and large-scale interpretive comments on characterization (not without humor); he says very little about the music, however, except that he very much liked the Transformation Music in act 1 and the flower maidens' music in act 2.

15. Kindermann, "Entstehung 1," 144–45. Cosima's diary entry reads as follows: "Gestern am Nachmittag, wie ich noch im Saal war, freute sich R. einer großen Terz von fis, ais, zu f, a, welche ihm eben eingefallen" (Cosima Wagner, *Die Tagebücher*, Band II. 1878–1883, ed. Martin Gregor-Dellin and Dietrich Mack (Munich: Piper Verlag, 1977), 1100.

16. There are a plethora of sources that introduce readers to large-grain aspects of the work from dramaturgical and musical points of view. I would recommend Lucy Beckett, *Richard Wagner: "Parsifal"* (Cambridge: Cambridge University Press, 1981). There are two highly detailed, musical-theoretical articles to be recommended as well.

Patrick McCreless, in "Motive and Magic: A Referential Dyad in *Parsifal*" (*Music Analysis* 9, no. 3 [October 1990]: 227–65), argues that a single dyad E–F plays itself out across the entire work. McCreless shows how the dyad is present at many dramatically charged moments and that it is a kind of "nexus" that expands, for example to E–F–G-flat, or F–E–D-sharp, and so on. So many of the work's "deceptive cadences" take the bass line of the music, for example from E-flat (dominant of A-flat) to F-flat (in particular the harmonic motion connecting the *Vorspiel* to act 1 and act 1 proper and the end of the Transformation Music in act I to the Grail music).

David Lewin's argument, in "Amfortas's Prayer to Titurel and the Role of D in *Parsifal*: The Tonal Spaces of the Drama and the Enharmonic C-flat/B" (in *19th Century Music* 7, no. 3 [April 3, 1984]: 336–49), about large-scale harmonic substitution in the opera focuses on musical and musical-theoretical discrepancies between "Stufen space" and "Riemann space" in the work. Lewin discusses at length the kiss between Kundry and Parsifal in act 2, showing that, at the moments their lips touch, the music of the vocal line and the orchestra pull in different directions across the "seam" of the enharmonic C-flat/B.

17. The following musical examples are based upon the score of *Parsifal* from Richard Wagner, *Sämtliche Werke*, vol. 14, pts. 1–3, ed. Egon Voss and Martin Geck

(Mainz: B. Schott's Söhne, 1972). I have taken care to represent the musical and dramatic content of the original score. However, I have also had to combine parts and omit some details for readability. "Mit Dämpfer" appears on these parts in the first published score of the work; the marking is not, however, present on the autograph, nor on the score used for the premiere of the work (note on page 1 of the authoritative edition).

18. "The harmonic tension created by this striking inflection casts a shadow of ambiguity over the tonic key of A-flat major, which sounds, momentarily, like the flat sixth of C minor" (Kindermann, "Wagner's *Parsifal,*" 433). Elsewhere Kindermann cites Cosima Wagner, who wrote in her diary on August 11, 1877, that the Grail music (an elaborated version of the opening) was for Richard Wagner the "Kern des Ganzen" [the root of the matter] ("Entstehung 1," 88). Kindermann argues that Wagner wrote the Grail music before writing the opening and that knowing that is crucial to an appreciation of Wagner's compositional strategy: "Bevor Wagner begann, ein solches Vorspiel im Kompositionsentwurf zu gestalten, musste er die damit zusammenhängenden Passagen durcharbeiten. Dieser Arbeitsprozess ist durch die Skizzen und Entwürfe zu *Parsifal* deutlich dokumentiert" [Before Wagner began to give form to the *Vorspiel* in the composition sketches, he needed first to have fully worked through the interrelated passages. This work process is clearly documented through sketches and drafts of *Parsifal* (Kinderman, "Entstehung 1," 89). This procedure of outlining a tonal pairing in an initial statement of musical materials is also highly reminiscent of *Tristan und Isolde,* which opens with a series of progressions pointing to A major/minor, then C major/minor, then E major/minor. See Robert Bailey, "Analytical Study." in *Prelude and Transfiguration from "Tristan and Isolde,"* 113–46 (New York: Norton, 1985).

19. "'Die schmerzen Amfortas' werden im dritten Takt in der Wendung zur C moll Harmonie angedeutet-, eine Geste, die durch das Crescendo und den rhythmischen Kontext untermauert wird" (William Kinderman, "Die Entstehung der *Parsifal*-Musik," *Archiv für Musikwissenschaft* 52, no. 2: 156; hereafter given as "Entstehung 2").

20. "[Dieser Schlussakkord] steht an Stelle des dissonanten absteigenden Halbtons, der von allem Anfang an eine wesentliche Quelle der musikalischen Spannung gewesen war" (Kindermann, "Entstehung 2," 161).

21. The Peters Edition, piano-vocal score to *Parsifal* has the D-flat minor music notated in C-sharp minor. D-flat minor opens the association between the poignancy of the Transformation Music and (Parsifal witnessing) Amfortas's failed crisis of investiture.

22. In reference to the pitch-class dyad E/F, McCreless says that "it constitutes a motive of the most far-reaching dramatic and musical significance in *Parsifal;* it occurs, often with considerable rhetorical emphasis, in climactic moments throughout the drama, and through it the opera works out its principal philosophical theme—that of sin, suffering, and redemption" (McCreless, "Motive and Magic," 227).

23. The transposition up a half step suggests Bailey's theory of expressive tonality in Wagner in which transposed repetition represents an increase in affective intensity. See Patrick McCreless, *Wagner's "Siegfried": Its Drama, History, and Music* (Ann Arbor, Mich.: UMI Research Press, 1982).

24. See Lewin 341.

25. See Slavoj Žižek and Mladen Dolar, *Opera's Second Death* (New York: Routledge, 2002), 173.

26. The fragment of processional music in the first tympanum in measures 1135–36 stands for Titurel; Wagner writes a similar passage in measures 455–56 as Gurnemanz refers to Titurel's majesty.

27. Recall that the relationship between questions and silent answers is crucial in Eschenbach's *Parzival,* too. In Eschenbach, Parzival must not ask questions; in Wagner, Parsifal first cannot then does not answer them. Rather he acts to undo what has already occurred.

28. Michel Poizat discusses the role of women in opera in similar terms: "The neurotic avatar of masculine desire described by courtly literature is especially apt to underpin the quest for the Voice as opera structures it. The Woman may be a stand-in for 'Nothingness,' for that which, like Euridice, immediately disappears when exposed to the human gaze or to the light of day; or her Absolute Beauty... may make her a stand-in for the divine. In either case, The Woman, thus fantasized, incarnates the 'lack of lack,' the emblematic figure that is supposed to bridge the gap that causes desire" (*The Angel's Cry,* trans. Arthur Denner [Ithaca, N.Y.: Cornell University Press, 1992], 150).

29. See Lewin 349. In his postwar stagings of *Parsifal* at Bayreuth, Wieland Wagner constructed the stage according to a "cross" that intersects at the point of the kiss between Kundry and Parsifal. The horizontal axis goes from "Kundry" on the left to "Amfortas" on the right; the vertical axis goes from "Parsifal" the redeemer at the top to "Parsifal" at the bottom, held down by the eternal feminine: "Der ewig weibliche Urgrund." See Hans-Joachim Bauer, *Richard Wagner Lexikon* (Bergisch Gladbach: Gustav Lübbe Verlag, 1988), 348–49.

30. There are two passages in act 3 with major thirds that descend by half steps: measures 369–70 and 776–77.

31. It was assumed for centuries that the tritone (diminished fifth or augmented fourth) was the "devil in music." Avoiding the tritone in church music was a powerful force in melodic writing and in counterpoint for much of the second millennium of Western music.

32. See Jacob Katz, *The Darker Side of Genius: Richard Wagner's Anti-Semitism* (Hanover, N.H.: The University Press of New England, 1986), 8.

33. Friedrich Schlegel, "Aus der Schrift: Über die Sprache und Weisheit der Indier," in *Kritische Schriften,* ed. Wolfdietrich Rasch (München: Carl Hanser Verlag, 1964), 587–91. For Schlegel, only great languages support great literature and expression. According to Bernard Lewis, these "Indo-Germanic" or "Indo-European" languages were "Aryan": "Its transformation [the term Aryan] from a linguistic to an ethnic and ultimately even racial designation was an error of scholarship that was to have profound social, political and moral consequences" (*Semites and Anti-Semites* [New York: Norton, 1986], 44).

34. "In einer traurigen Gegend der Welt aber, in dunklen, ungeheuren Wäldern, oder in öden von der Sonne versengten Erdstrichen, wo der Mensch, sich gleichsam verlierend, ins Unermessliche ausschweift, kann die Mythologie keine andre als die abendteurliche Gestalt und das Gepräge der überspanntesten oder erhitzesten Einbildungskraft erhalten [In a desolate part of the earth, however, in dark and scary forests, or in the wilderness where the sun has singed the land, where Man, loosing himself, drifts among the infinite, mythology can only take on the form of adventure

and forms of the most exaggerated imagination]. (Friedrich Wilhelm Joseph von Schelling, *Schellings Werke*, vol. 1, ed. Manfred Schröter [München: Beck'sche Verlagsbuchhandlung, 1965], 38).

35. "Ihnen Bürgerrechte zu geben, dazu sehe ich wenigstens kein Mittel, als das, in einer Nacht ihnen die Köpfe abzuschneiden und andere anzusetzen, in denen auch nicht eine jüdische Idee sey. Um uns vor ihnen zu schützen, dazu sehe ich wieder kein anderes Mittel, als ihnen ihr gelobtes Land zu erobern, und sie all dahin zu schicken" (Johann Gottlieb Fichte, *Sämmtliche [sic] Werke*, pt. 3, vol. 1, ed. von J. H. Fichte: *Zur Politik und Moral* [Berlin: Verlag von Veit und Comp., 1845], 150).

36. Bruno Bauer, *The Jewish Problem*, trans. Helen Lederer (Cincinatti, Ohio: Hebrew College–Jewish Institute of Religion, 1958), 22. The German original was published in Brauenschweig in 1843.

37. Bauer argues that Jews cannot be subjects of enlightened reason: "The individual as well as the nation which in its thought and deeds follows universal laws will progress with history; for universal laws have their base in reason and liberty, they develop with the progress of Reason. This progress is to be expected and it is effected with certainty and easily, because Reason in its laws has to do with its own products, and does not have to ask permission from a foreign, supernatural power. In the Orient [associated with Jews in the material right before this quote] man does not yet know that he is free and gifted with reason" (Bauer 14).

38. "The Political emancipation of the Jew, the Christian, and religious man in general implies the emancipation of the state from Judaism, Christianity, and religion in general" (Karl Marx, *Selected Writings*, ed. David McLellan [Oxford: Oxford University Press, 2000], 51).

39. "Das Nichtemancipiren belässt sie fortwährend in einem Zustande der Belagerung, und der Belagerte bleibt Feind und verteidigt sich instinktmässig mit allen möglichen Waffen, also auch in diesem Falle besonders mit den ihm natürlichsten einer uns wildfremden Nationalität. So erhalten wir gerade das lebendig in den Juden, was uns gründlich zuwider ist; alle die innerlichsten Lebensmaximen, die uns hundertfach und schreiend widerstreben, werden durch unsre halbe Abwehr aufrecht erhalten im Charakter der Juden. Entweder wir müssen Barbaren sein und die Juden bis auf den lezten Mann austreiben, oder wir müssen sie uns einverleiben" (Heinrich Laube, "Einleitung" to *Struensee* [Leipzig: J. J. Weber, 1847], 22).

40. Dieter Borchmeyer, "The Question of Anti-Semitism," in *Wagner Handbook*, ed. Ulrich Müller and Peter Wapnewski, trans. John Deathridge (Cambridge, Mass.: Harvard University Press, 1992), 168.

41. According to Peter Viereck, Wagner's tendency to projection is grounded in his own anxiety concerning the possibility that his biological father Geyer was Jewish. See Peter Viereck, "Hitler and Richard Wagner," in *Musik-Konzepte 5*, ed. Heinz-Klaus Metzger and Rainer Riehn (München: Johannesdruck Hans Pribil, n.d.), 18–19.

42. Wagner revised the essay and published it under his name in 1869, with an appendix. See *Richard Wagner's Prose Works*, vol. 3, trans. William Ashton Ellis (London: Kegan, Paul, Trench, Trübner, 1894), 76. The article appears in volume 5 of the *Gesammelten Schriften*. In the quotes that follow, there may be small discrepancies between German and English. The German is from Wagner's essays as originally published in *Die neue Zeitschrift für Musik*; the English is from Ellis's translation of Wagner's 1869 revisions. For an introduction to the history of Jews in music in Ger-

many, see Nachum T. Gidal, *Jews in Germany from Roman Times to the Weimar Republic* (Cologne: Könemann, 1998), 218–19.

43. The famous fact of the Jewish conductor Hermann Levi conducting the premiere of *Parsifal* in Bayreuth is not a sign of Wagner's friendly attitude toward Jews. In deep financial trouble after the *Ring* productions, Wagner had turned to Ludwig II, who helped him on condition that his Kapellmeister Hermann Levi would conduct the work. Wagner had no choice but to agree. See Robert W. Gutman, *Richard Wagner: The Man, His Mind, and His Music* (New York: Harcourt Brace Jovanovich, 1968), 410–11.

44. "Der Jude ist, nach dem gegenwärtigen Stande der Weltdinge, wirklich bereits mehr als emancipiert: er herrscht, und wird so lange herrschen als das Geld die Macht bleibt, vor der all unser Thun und Treiben seine Kraft verliert" (K. Freigedank [Richard Wagner], "Das Judentum in der Musik," *Neue Zeitschrift für Musik,* no. 19 [September 3, 1850]: 102).

45. "Als durchaus fremdartig und unangenehm fällt unserem Ohr zunächst ein zischender, schrillender, summsender und mucksender Lautausdruck der jüdischen Sprechwiese auf: eine unserer nationalen Sprache gänzlich uneigenthümliche Verwendung und willkürliche Verdrehung der Worte und Construcktionen, giebt diesem Lautausdrucke vollends noch den Character einers unerträglich verwirrten Geplappers, bei dessen Anhören unsere Aufmerksamkeit unwillkürlich mehr bei desem widerlichen Wie, als be deim enthaltenden Was der jüdischen Rede verweilt" (ibid., 103).

46. "So lange die musikalsiche Sonderkunst ein wirkliches organisches Lebensbedürfnis in sich hatte, bis auf die Zeiten Mozarts und Beethovens, fand ich nirgends ein jüdischer Componist [sic]: unmöglich konnte ein, diesem Lebensorganismus gänzlich fremdes Element an den Bildungen dieses Lebens Theil nehmen. Erst wenn der innere Tod eines Körpers offenbar ist, gewinnen die ausserhalb liegenden Elemente die Kraft, sich seiner zu bemächtigen, aber nur um ihn zu zerfetzen. Dann loest sich wohl das Fleisch dieses Körpers in wimmelnde Viellebigkiet von Würmer auf" (K. Freigedank [Wagner], "Das Judentum in der Musik," *Neue Zeitschrift für Musik,* no. 20 [September 6, 1850]: 111).

47. "Kritikern von Fach, die hierüber zu gleichem Bewusstein mit uns gelangt sein sollten, möge es überlassen sein, diese zweifellos gewisse Erscheinung aus den Einzelheiten der Mendelssohn'schen Kunstproduktionen nachweislich zu bestätigen, uns genüge es hier, zur Verdeutlichung unserer allgemeine Empfindung uns zu vergegenwärtigen, dass bei Anhörung eines Tonstückes dieses Komponisten wir uns nur dann gefesselt fühlen konnten, wenn nichts anderes als unsre, mehr oder weniger nur unterhaltungssüchtige, Phantasie durch Vorführung, Reihung und Verschlingung der glättesten, feinsten und kunstfertigsten Figuren, wie im wechselnden Farbenspiel des Kaleidoskopes, angeregt blieb, wogegen unsere höhere Empfänglichkeit stets da nicht befriedigt wurde, wo diese Figuren Gestalt tiefer, markiger menschlicher Herzensempfindungen anzunehmen bestimmt waren" (K. Freigedank [Wagner], "Das Judentum in der Musik" *Neue Zeitschrift für Musik,* no. 20 [September 3, 1850]: 107).

48. "Nemmt rückhaltslos an diesem selbstvernichtenden, blutigen Kampfe Theil, so sind wir einig und untrennbar! Aber bedenkt, dass nur Eines Eure Erlösung von dem auf Euch lastenden Fluche sein kann, die Erlösung? Uhasver's: Der Untergang!" (Freigedank, "Das Judentum in der Musik" [September 6, 1850]: 111–12).

49. Klaus P. Fischer, *The History of an Obsession: German Judeophobia and the Holocaust* (New York: Continuum Books, 1998), 30.

50. For a reading of "Das Judentum in der Musik" that is very different from Borchmeyer's, see Hartmut Zelinksy, "Rettung ins Ungenaue," in *Richard Wagner "Parsifal*," ed. Heinz-Klaus Metzger and Rainer Riehn, Musik-Konzepte 25, 74–115 (München: Hans Pribil, 1982). Zelinsky argues that Wagner's writings, especially "Das Judentum in der Musik," and works, especially *Parsifal*, embody Wagner's messianic fantasy of a Germany fully purged of the other. See also Zelinsky's, "Die 'feuerkur' das Richard Wagners oder die 'neue religion' der 'Erlösung' durch 'Vernichtung,'" in *Richard Wagner: Wie antisemitisch darf ein Künstler sein?* ed. Heinz-Klaus Metzger and Rainer Riehn, Musik-Konzepte 5, 79–112 (München: Hans Pribil, 1978). For a reading of "Das Judentum in der Musik" that analyzes the work in terms of a mixture of the rhetorical forms of Juvenalian satire and lampoon, see Lawrence Kramer, *Opera and Modern Culture: Wagner and Strauss* (Berkeley and Los Angeles: University of California Press, 2004), 58.

51. "Erkenne Dich" was published in the *Bayreuther Blätter* in February–March 1881; "Heldenthum und Christenthum" was published in the *Bayreuther Blätter* in September 1881. "Erkenne Dich" is a more mature version of "Das Judentum in der Musik," and its anti-Semitic content is intensified by the founding of the German nation-state and unprecedented incorporation of Jews into German social space.

52. "Dass ich die jüdische Rasse für den geborenen Feind der reinen Menschheit und alles Edlen in ihr halte: dass namentlich wir Deutschen an ihnen zu Grunde gehen werden, ist gewiss, und vielleicht bin ich der letzte Deutsche, der sich gegen den bereits alles beherrschenden Judaismus als künstlerischer Mensch aufrecht zu erhalten wusste" (letter to Ludwig II, November 22, 1881, in *König Ludwig II und Richard Wagner Briefwechsel*, ed. Mittelsbacher Ausgleich-Fonds and Winifred Wagner [Karlsruhe: G. Brauen Verlag, 1936], 230).

53. Cosima Wagner's *Diaries*, vol. 2: *1878–1883*, ed. and annotated by Martin Gregor-Dellin and Dietrich Mack, trans. Geoffrey Skelton (New York: Harcourt, Brace, 1978), 378. "Ich lese eine sehr gute Rede des Pfarrers Stoecker über das Judentum. R. ist für völlige Ausweisung. Wir lachen darüber, daß wirklich, wie es scheint, sein Aufsatz über die Juden den Anfang dieses Kampfes gemacht hat" (Cosima Wagner, *Tagebücher*, 2:424).

54. Hans Rudolf Vaget, "Wieviel 'Hitler' ist in Wagner," in *Richard Wagner und die Juden*, ed. Dieter Borchmeyer, Ami Maayani, and Susanne Vill (Stuttgart and Weimar: J. B. Metzler, 2000), 200.

55. Hans-Jürgen Syberberg, *Confessions of Frau Wagner*, 1975.

56. Vaget points out that the name is a pseudonym for the author's real name, Josef Engel Janosi. Josef Engel de Sinoja, *Das Antisemitentum in der Musik* (Zürich, Leipzig, Wien: n.p., 1933), quoted in Vaget 189.

57. According to Vaget, Chamberlain's work was written in 1899. Chamberlain also wrote a letter on October 7, 1923, that Hitler acknowledged as a powerful influence on his ideas on race; according to Vaget, Chamberlain sees Hitler as a new Parsifal for Germany (Vaget 200–201). For more on the relations between *Parsifal* and Hitler, see Hartmut Zelinsky, "Zu schönen Klängen eine brutale Ideologie," *Der Spiegel*, no. 29 (July 19, 1982). According to Zelinsky, Wagner referred to the "Vernichtungsklang der Pauke" [the annihilating sound of the tympanum] in *Parsifal*

(Zelinsky 135). In terms of the general effect of his music, Wagner wrote to Mathilde Wesendonk in August of 1859: "Nun denken Sie, meine Musik, die mit ihren feinen, feinen, geheimnisvoll-flüssigen Säften durch die subtilsten Poren der Empfindung eindringt, um dort alles zu überwältigen, was irgend wie Klugheit und selbstbesorgte Erhaltungskraft sich ausnimmt, alles hinwegschwemmt, was zum Wahn der Persönlichkeit gehört und nur den wunderbar erhabenen Seufzer des Ohnmachtsbekenntnisses übriglässt" (quoted in Zelinsky 135) [Just think about my music with its fine, secretly flowing juices that penetrate the subtlest pores of sensation, dismantling defenses; everything disappears that had to do with the insanity of personality, leaving behind in its wake only the sublime sigh of surrender]. See also Zelinsky, "Rettung ins Ungenaue" and "Die 'feuerkur' des Richard Wagner."

58. Josef Arthur Graf Gobineau, *Essai sur l'inégalité des races humain* (1853; repr., Paris: P. Belfond, 1967). According to Hermann Danuser, Wagner read the work two years before his death in 1883. In 1881 Wagner was finishing *Parsifal*; see Hermann Danuser, "Universalität oder Partikularität?" in *Richard Wagner und die Juden*, ed. Dieter Borchmeyer, Ami Maayani, and Susanne Vill (Stuttgart and Weimar: J. B. Metzler, 2000), 92 n25. For more on the influence of Gobineau on Hitler, see Robert W. Gutman, *Richard Wagner: The Man, His Mind, and His Music* (New York: Harcourt Brace, 1968), 431 n6.

I am indebted to Gottfried Wagner for telling me during a personal conversation that Winifred Wagner had a blue, metal box that contained correspondence between Hitler and the Wagner family. According to Gottfried Wagner, that box has disappeared.

59. Herman Rauschning, *The Voice of Destruction* (New York: Putnam, 1940), 230. Rauschning writes this book as a kind of diary and ongoing informal interview with Hitler. The quoted passage above is Rauschning's transcription of a conversation with Hitler in 1934.

60. "They [Wagner's operas] are also pillars of bourgeois self-affirmation, in that they glorify capitalism as a spectacle of supernatural, archaic, elemental forces" (Thomas Elsaesser, "Myth as the Phantasmagoria of History: H. J. Syberberg, Cinema, and Representation," *New German Critique*, no. 24/25 [Autumn 1981/Winter 1982], 177). Klingsor is the character that connects *Parsifal* to bourgeois capitalism.

61. For a reading of *Parsifal* that explores both the anti-Semitic and misogynist elements of Kundry's protrayal, see Jean-Jacques Nattiez, *Wagner Androgyne*, trans. Steward Spenser (Princeton, N.J.: Princeton University Press, 1993), 166–69.

62. "R. von einigen Tagen sagte, die Kundry sei seine originellste Frauengestalt; wie er erkannt habe: die Gralsbotin ist dieselbe wie Amfortas' Verführerin, da habe er alles gehabt, nun hätten Jahre vergehen können, er habe gewußt, wie es würde" (Cosima Wagner, *Tagebücher*, 2:351).

63. Slavoj Žižek, *The Plague of Fantasies* (London: Verso, 1997), 76.

64. Eric L. Santner, *On the Psychotheology of Everyday Life* (Chicago: University of Chicago Press, 2001), 5.

65. The idea that is more in us than ourselves assumes that what we mean by "I" includes all the positive attributes that obtain to us. It also includes unconscious forces, twitches, gestures, and involuntary habits of speech and pronunciation. In some sense, these attributes are "more than I" in the sense that I am not conscious of them and they are not included in standard databases that name me in public.

And of course, there is always an exterior edge to all of these attributes; we share them with others, otherwise they would not be coherent or endearing. Thus all attributes in their shared heritage are excessive, outside, of the other.

66. Žižek and Dolar, *Opera's Second Death*, 164.

67. Theodor Adorno offers a particularly dark reading of the Knights of the Grail: "the glorified blood-brotherhood of *Parsifal* is the prototype of the sworn confraternities [sic] of the secret societies and *Führer*-orders of later years, which had so much in common with the Wahfried circle—that clique held together by a sinister eroticism and its fear of the tyrant, with a hypersensitivity that bordered on terrorism towards that which did not belong" (*In Search of Wagner*, trans. Rodney Livingstone [London: NLB, 1981], 140).

68. One of Wagner's most effective ways to get the "validity" of meaning under our skin before we can encode the messages that validity will occupy in drama is through the orchestral Preludes that precede each act of *Parsifal*, and Wagner's other operas as well. In the diegetic space of the Knights of the Grail, the Knights are interpellated "before" they hear the content of Titurel's imperative-as-question. It is the sound of his voice that "validates" the act of his speech.

69. John Sandford, "Hans-Jürgen Syberberg: Films from Germany" in *Syberberg, a Filmaker from Germany*, ed. Heather Stewart (London: Hill and Garwood, 1992), 6. His films include *Fritz Kortner (Rehearsing Schiller)* (1965), *Romy, Anatomy of an Actress* (1965), *Kortner Monologue (Shylock)* (1966), *Wilhelm von Kobell* (1966), *The Counts Pocci* (1967), *Scarabea—How Much Land Does a Person Need?* (1968), *Sex-Business Made in Pasing* (1969), *San Domingo* (1970), *Brecht Film—After My Last Move* (1971), *Requiem for a Virgin King* (1972), *Ludwig's Cook* (1974), *Karl May—In Search of Paradise Lost* (1974), *The Confessions of Winifred Wagner* (1975), *Hitler—A Film from Germany* (1977), *Parsifal* (1982), *The Night* (1985), *Fräulein Else* (1986), *Molly Bloom's Monologue* (1986), *Penthesilea* (1987), *Die Marquise von O...* (1989) (Sandford 5–11, 44–56).

70. *The Confessions of Winifred Wagner* is typical of this kind of Syberberg film. In this film (of which there are many versions), Syberberg asks an occasional question off-camera. He reads very spare captions throughout the film, and for the vast majority of the footage, Winifred Wagner simply talks to Syberberg on camera in her rooms at Wahnfried, without make-up, in ordinary dress.

71. *Hitler—ein Film aus Deutschland* is a typical example of this kind of Syberberg film. For a discussion of Syberberg's treatment of Hitler as an attempt to de-reify Hitler from German consciousness, see Fredric Jameson, "'In the Destructive Element Immerse': Hans-Jürgen Syberberg and Cultural Revolution" *October* 17 (Summer 1981): 99–118. For a discussion of Syberberg's *Trauerarbeit*, its relationship to Freud, Mitscherlich and postwar German culture, see Eric L. Santner, *Stranded Objects: Mourning, Memory, and Film in Postwar Germany* (Ithaca, N.Y.: Cornell University Press, 1990).

72. In animating an object (or, more properly, an attribute of an object), Syberberg's wound belongs to the category of animation of spirits and magical symbols, not people and animals. See Frank Proschan, "The Semiotic Study of Puppets, Masks, and Performing Objects," *Semiotica* 47, no. 1–4 (1983): 14–17.

73. "Oh! Oh! Deepest night! Insanity! O rage! O misery! Sleep...sleep...deep sleep...death!"

74. The Easter bells in the opera sound two perfect fourths (evocative of the powerful role of perfect fourths in the opera, first heard in the *Vorspiel* to act 1 from measure 44 to measure 45) C-natural/G-natural, A-natural/E-natural. The bells in the opening moments of the film are struck very hard, blurring their fundamentals with the overtones.

75. Proschan is arguing against the idea that splitting voice and actor in *bunraku* puppet practices produces a Brechtian alienation effect. Proschan points to many French theater practices in which word and action are split producing not alienation but rather a disjunction that binds audience to theater (Proschan 20).

76. Kay F. Turner, "The Cultural Semiotics of Religious Icons: La Virgen de San Juan de los Lagos," *Semiotica* 47, no. 1–4 (1983): 317.

77. It may seem odd that very serious images exist side by side with comic ones such as these. Jiři Veltruský points out that the emotional responses of comedy and the uncanny are not necessarily mutually exclusive as the products of puppets in theater: "the comic and the uncanny are intertwined. In many cultures and the most varied forms of art, the two are inseparable, although the dividing line between them keeps shifting from culture to culture and from one period to the next" ("Puppetry and Acting," *Semiotica* 47, no. 1–4 (1983): 109.

78. See John Bell, ed., *Puppets, Masks, and Performing Objects* (Cambridge, Mass.: MIT Press, 2001).

79. For a study of animated objects in puppetry and the theater, see Veltruský 85–88.

80. This interiority is a spatial correlate for Parsifal's experience of taking into himself the knowledge of his guilt at killing the swam, his empathetic identification with Amfortas's wound, and finally, his role as redeemer of the Knights of the Grail. The German "er" encapsulates this sense of interiority, a taking-in.

81. "Nachdem all ihre Stelle eingenommen und ein allgemeiner Stillstand eingetreten war, vernimmt man, vom tiefsten Hintergründe her, aus einer gewölbten Nische hinter dem Ruhebette des Amfortas, die Stimme des alten Titurel, wie aus einem Grabe heraufdringend" [After all have taken their places and a general silence has settled over all, one hears the voice of the aged Titurel from the great depths, rising from a crevice behind Amfortas's bed, as if from a grave].

82. The scene in act 1 when Kundry bathes Parsifal's face prefigures the scene in act 3 when Kundry, humbled to the point of near evacuation of subjectivity, bathes Parsifal's feet and dries them with her hair.

83. Syberberg casts Parsifal I and Parsifal II in such a way that the binary opposition male/female is not so much complicated and made as complementary as possible. Parsifal I, ostensibly male, has delicate features and a full head of hair. Parsifal II, ostensibly female has her hair pulled back and flattened to suggest an air of stern discipline.

84. "Nun ist dies Kind in diesem Film kein Kind mehr, sondern als Figuration des Glaubens und endlicher Vereinigung von alten, entgegenstehenden Welten ein durchscheinendes und reflektierendes Wesen der Unschuld geworden, wie es dieses Alter zwischen den Epochen der menschlichen Existenz nach der Kindheit und vor der Teilung in seine bewusste Zweigeschlechtlichkeit gerade noch zu sein möglich macht" (Syberberg, *Parsifal: Ein Filmessay* [München: Wilhelm Heyne Verlag, 1982], 243).

85. A nineteenth-century precursor of "kitsch" is "decadence." For Nietzsche,

"for every style of *décadence:* always anarchy of the atoms. . . . Everywhere paralysis, distress, and torpor, or hostility and chaos, always becoming more striking, as one ascends to ever higher forms of organization. The whole has ceased to live altogether; it is composite, summed up, artificial, an unnatural product" (Friedrich Nietzsche, "The Case of Wagner," in *The Works of Friedrich Nietzsche,* vol. 11, ed. Alexander Tille, trans. Thomas Common [New York: Macmillan, 1908], 25).

86. See "Man will mich töten" (André Müller spricht mit Regisseur Hans-Jürgen Syberberg), *Die Zeit,* September 30, 1988. See also a review of Syberberg's *Die freudlose Gesellschaft,* "Syberberg's Kampf," *Die Zeit,* July 31, 1981.

87. Syberberg self-consciously comments on his work as cinema and on German culture as cinema in *Hitler—Ein Film aus Deutschland,* in which, for example, Edison's Black Maria (a primal embodiment of the cinema) is an important prop.

88. Syberberg filmed *Hitler—Ein Film aus Deutschland* in twenty days. "Ohne Irrationalismus ist Deutschland nichts," *Der Spiegel* 44 (October 30, 1978): 266–68.

89. Susan Sontag, "Syberberg's Hitler," in *Under the Sign of Saturn* (New York: The Noonday Press, 1972), 158.

90. It seems true that Syberberg does not embrace chance in his films, but Jameson is right to point out that there is something of the home movie in his work (Jameson 100). Particularly in *The Confessions of Winifred Wagner,* there are many imperfect moments that were not edited out (changing reels of film are often visible), audio levels are suddenly adjusted throughout the film, and so on.

91. Syberberg expresses outright contempt for the classic Hollywood editing practice of shot/reverse and other techniques. See Syberberg, *Parsifal: Ein Filmessay* (27, 48, 78, and 123), for material critical of "manic" techniques of classic Hollywood editing.

92. If there is one word in his Parsifal essay that stands out for me, it is "Ruhe"—calm, peace, with connotations of death. Syberberg's own voice that can be heard sparingly in *The Confessions of Winifred Wagner* is quiet and clear, articulating every syllable of every word.

93. See Heinrich von Kleist, "Über das Marionettentheater," in *Sämtliche Werke* (München: Droemersche Verlagsanstalt, n.d.), 825–31.

94. Syberberg's reactionary attitudes toward postwar German and Western culture are well documented in critiques of his films and in his own words. In addition to "Man will mich töten" and *Parsifal: Ein Filmessay,* see his *Die freudlose Gesellschaft* (Frankfurt: Ullstein, 1983); see also Gabriele Förg, "Der Schlaf der Vernunft gebiert Monstren: Eine Collage zu Hans-Jürgen Syberberg," in *Unsere Wagner: Joseph Beuys, Heiner Müller, Karlheinz Stockhausen, Hans-Jürgen Syberberg,* ed. Gabriele Förg (Frankfurt: Fischer, 1984).

95. Jameson's argument concerning *Hitler—Ein Film aus Deutschland* focuses on de-reification: "Such a 'method' may be characterized as a forcible short-circuiting of all the wires in the political unconscious, as an attempt to purge the sedimented contents of collective fantasy and ideological representation by reconnecting its symbolic counters so outrageously that they de-reify themselves" (Jameson 111). I do not believe that Syberberg de-reifies either Hitler or Wagner in this work; rather he is stuck between an apocalyptic representation of the end of Western culture and the way in which such an apocalyptic vision (not unlike the death drive) keeps his imagination alive.

96. The singularity of the gesture of turning pockets inside out suggests for me the logic of Nietzsche's remark on Wagner as the great composer of miniatures: "Once more let it be said that Wagner is only worthy of admiration and love in the invention of minutiae, in the elaboration of details; here we have every right to proclaim him as a master of the first rank, as our greatest *miniaturist* in music, who compresses into the smallest space an infinitude of meaning and sweetness" (26; Nietzsche's emphasis). The miniature is the spatial correlate of a moment, the logical other pole of monumental myth.

Index

David Schwarz is assistant professor of music theory at the University of North Texas. He is author of *Listening Subjects: Music, Psychoanalysis, Culture.*